The Ards
in the
Seventies

*Written and Compiled
by Terence Bowman
and Tim Johnston*

BALLYHAY BOOKS

Published by Ballyhay Books,
an imprint of Laurel Cottage Ltd.,
Donaghadee, Northern Ireland.
Copyrights reserved.
© Terence Bowman 2015.
Contributed texts are copyright of individual contributors.
Photographs are reproduced by permission.
All rights reserved.
No part of this book may be reproduced or stored on any media without the
express written permission of the publishers.
Printed by Gutenberg Press, Malta.
ISBN 978 1 910657 03 4

The Ards in the Seventies is dedicated to the late
William Norman (Billy) Graham, 1945-2014
A true son of Newtownards

Contents

The Ards in the Seventies

Introduction

Disconnected memories of a boy from Drumawhey ...

When Terence asked me to write an introduction to this book my first reaction – which would probably be mirrored by all my contemporaries – was "don't be daft, I'm far too young to be doing that". But, as Terence pointed out, the Seventies were my teenage years, a time in everyone's life when, because you're rapidly changing from child to adult and everything is new, all the memories seem to be painted in vivid technicolour – so maybe it's not such a daft idea after all ...

I suppose being born in the very last month of the Fifties meant I was a child of the Sixties but to be honest free love, drugs and rock 'n' roll were never a big part of life in Drumawhey where, looking back, my sister Irene and I spent our teenage years safely cocooned from the turmoil going on in the wider world as Northern Ireland descended into the poisonous grip of 'The Troubles.'

We'd moved to Drumawhey in the late 1960s after my father and mother purchased the smallholding where Daddy had grown up. The family had deep roots in the adjoining townlands of Ballyhay and Drumawhey, as did many of our neighbours, engendering a strong sense of belonging and community which I was happy to buy into. While it's roughly 3,794.7 miles between Muskogee and Drumawhey, in many respects Merle Haggard could have

Born in and reared in The Ards, Tim attended the Cottown Primary School and Regent House.

A lifelong love of all things mechanical took him to Imperial College in London to study mechanical engineering before joining Short Brothers in Belfast where, to his regret, career advancement moved him away from pure engineering.

As such, when the opportunity arose in 1990 to set up Cottage Publications in partnership with his wife Alison, they opted to seize the chance. Despite the considerable risks involved, the attraction of being self-employed outweighed the concern that they knew nothing about publishing – a situation which he readily admits has only marginally changed in the intervening 25 years.

been writing about me when he penned his famous song – although it's probably lucky for him he didn't, as "Culchie from Drumawhey" doesn't rhyme nearly as well as "Okie from Muskogee."

Having attended the Cottown Primary School with a total enrolment of some 50 or so pupils, it was quite a culture shock to move to Regent House with its

Regent House and the canal which contributed to the distinctive fragrant bouquet of the mud at the Comber Road rugby pitches!

1,200 students and I immediately established my credentials as an innocent abroad by addressing prefects as 'Sir' until the more streetwise of my new friends advised this wasn't the done thing! In truth I wasn't the only awestruck country boy in First Form as the school drew its intake from the villages and countryside the length and breadth of the peninsula on one side of the Lough and as far as Killinchy on the other, as well as from the larger urban settlements of Newtownards and Dundonald. This, allied to the nature of the 11+ at the time (a verbal reasoning test for which coaching did not seem to improve your chances), meant the pupils at Regent were an eclectic bunch from all walks of life and social classes.

The teachers were an equally varied bunch – from the gently spoken such as Miss Camlin – who on one memorable occasion ran in horror from her room, having been confronted by a large clear plastic bag full of cows' eyes sourced by a friend and me from the local abattoir for dissection in a later biology class – to the less dulcet tones of head of games 'DA' McMaster, whose love of rugby was only matched by his anger when any pupil (especially of 'his rugby lads') failed to live up to the standards he sought, not only on the pitch but also in general behaviour.

One big difference I noticed between my school friends from 'the town' and others like myself from the country, was the variation in out-of-school activities. If you lived in the town other friends were usually within easy reach, whereas in the country people were a bit thinner on the ground. In truth though, I can't say I ever noticed not having a bunch of friends right on my doorstep as any sort of disadvantage, as the days were hardly long enough to explore all the entertainment opportunities that surrounded me. Besides, as anyone reared in the country by hard-working parents will know, looking bored was never a good option as there were always loads of jobs needing done by a 'volunteer' at a loose end!

If Irene or I wanted to go out we relied on our parents for lifts, whether for outings to the newly-opened Ards swimming pool, the BB, Young Farmers' Club events, or the Table Tennis Club at 1st Donaghadee on a Saturday evening where, as an additional treat, we could nip down to Kennedys to spend our few pence of pocket money on sweets, having pushed past the small gang of men patiently waiting for the roar of the 'Tele' Transit van arriving at speed to deliver the Ireland's Saturday Night with all the day's sports results.

Other things friends from the town did off their own bat, such as visits to the cinema, were only done as family outings due to the transport issue, although as my father would very often be working late, such outings more often than not saw us arriving midway through the first showing and then sitting on through the second up to the point we had come in. Neither the Regent nor the Ritz in Newtownards seemed particularly concerned about this practice, although they would have been quite strict in other respects, such as the under-age viewing of X-rated films. This caused some embarrassment when, at the age of around 13, I convinced my parents to take me to see 'The Godfather' not long after it came out. I was big for my age and could have passed for 18, but Daddy somewhat blew the gaff when he walked up to the box office and asked for two adults and a child; only some very fast improvisation by my mother got me in past a very suspicious attendant!

Evenings when we weren't out and the number of outstanding jobs at home had been deemed by my parents to be at an acceptably low level (it never got to zero) would have been spent watching TV, playing cards or reading. To select something to watch on TV you had to get up and walk right across the room although, with only three channels choice was a bit limited compared to today (there again if you removed all the Seventies programmes from today's schedules it would take a lot less time to flick through the on-screen TV guide), and it can't be denied there were some real gems. I'm not sure that any cop show has ever equalled The Sweeney, while Monty Python's Flying Circus and Fawlty Towers were comedic landmarks, and for college students late in the decade the compulsory Saturday morning viewing – Tiswas – brought a level of anarchy and fun not seen before or since.

My mother was an avid reader and to encourage Irene and me to follow her example there was always an ample supply of books and comics. My favourite was The Rover, which I eagerly looked forward to every week and which was mostly written stories. Unlike the comic strip-filled comics, which could be skipped through in 10 minutes, The Rover provided a good evening's worth of entertainment, although it may have had some negative effect on my moral compass as I could never quite see why there was so much fuss about drugs in sport during the 1980s after reading for years about the Amazing Wilson who had been using a potion – given to him by a Welsh Druid – to help him smash world records when he was over 100 years old!

Although today I get great pleasure from a wide and eclectic range of music, I'd have to admit I wasn't a big fan of pop music, preferring in my teenage years the mellow tones of the Big T Country Show on the recently launched Downtown Radio to the raucous cacophony of punk music. That said, the Sunday evening chart countdown on Radio One was crucial listening, if only so I wouldn't appear totally square in the inevitable discussions of 'what was going up and what was going down' in school the following morning. However, I'd have to admit this limited study of popular music left something to be desired and it was only in later years that I found out the Tartan Gangs which sprang up in the early Seventies were not in fact fans of the Bay City Rollers but something considerably more sinister that had emerged from the ongoing Troubles in the Province.

Looking back, and with the benefit of hindsight, the Tartan Gangs were not the only thing I was naïve about regarding the Troubles, insofar as we were lucky enough that none of my family or close friends were hurt or worse in any of the dreadful atrocities going on around us. Although we would have been well aware of events from reports in the media and seeing the aftermath of terrorist bombs in local towns etc., sheltered by our parents in Drumawhey, life for Irene and me very much continued as normal – although, having said that, I was forced to re-evaluate my definition of 'normal' towards the end of the decade when I visited Harrods in London with an English friend. Walking through their entrance foyer there were, ahead of us, a couple of uniformed door attendants on duty. Without breaking conversation with my friend I automatically stepped up to one of the attendants, raising my arms and spreading my legs for the expected body search.

His alarmed expression alerted me to my mistake and I offered an embarrassed apology, but it certainly made me think how different life was at home compared to England – body searches in every major store, town centres barricaded off and turned into ghost towns at night, armed police and soldiers patrolling the streets, the flash of concern if you saw an unattended car in the town centre, people checking under their cars for bombs before they drove off, innocents murdered for no better reason than what particular branch of the church they were perceived to belong to or their choice to serve their community – yet as teenagers we didn't see it as especially abnormal if we even thought about it at all. Maybe I was just particularly lucky but I don't think my take on things was radically different from that of the majority of my friends living in the Ards area, who, like me, were fortunate enough to be untouched directly by tragedy and were just getting on with being an awkward teenager.

As I said earlier, being a bit more isolated out in the country, getting together with friends outside of organised activities wasn't so easy. I suppose I was very lucky that I shared many interests with my

My father, Sam Johnston, demonstrating a Taarup forage harvester

father, who had served his time as a mechanic but whose day job was now selling farm machinery rather than repairing it. In particular we both had a fascination for anything mechanical – especially if there was an element of speed involved – and at every opportunity I would tag along with him, whether it was working at some hare-brained project in the workshop we had in one of the barns at home, or demonstrating some new piece of farm machinery in his job.

Farming in the Seventies was undergoing rapid changes as increased mechanisation impacted all aspects of the industry; indeed there seemed to be a de facto arms war going on between the tractor manufacturers and the makers of the machinery farmers attached to them. This was particularly the case in the production of winter fodder, with hay being replaced at the end of the Sixties by silage as the bulk fodder of choice. In the early Seventies silage would be cut by single chop harvesters driven by 40-50hp tractors, but then the manufacturers introduced double chop harvesters which would have a 50hp tractor 'on its knees'. Tractor makers responded with bigger tractors that had so much power they would wreck the gearboxes on the harvester, necessitating a bigger machine, and so on…

By the end of the decade Ford's turbo-charged 7000 (which was one of the tractors

Cooke Brothers self-propelled forage harvester

my father sold), 'screwed in' for even more power by farmers in a hurry to get their crops in, were blowing black smoke and gearboxes all over the countryside, opening the way for dedicated self-propelled forage harvesters. Obviously these were generally supplied by the large manufacturers, but many from the farming community will recall one with origins closer to home. Designed and built with limited resources by the Cooke Brothers, it was a remarkable feat of engineering ingenuity which always attracted fascinated onlookers wherever it was working. Even if they were midgets compared to the behemoths of today, for a machinery-mad teenager these machines were a mighty impressive sight in their day.

To satisfy our interest in speed Daddy and me didn't have to travel too far in the Ards: for traditional motor racing there was Kirkistown which, as Richard Young recounts elsewhere in this book, was the scene of epic battles between the likes of the McGarritys and future Formula 1 team owner Eddie Jordan, while for motor-cycling fans there was the Carrowdore 100.

For me there is absolutely no doubt that lying in a field near the end of the Upper Gransha Road, with your head stuck out through a hole in the hedge to see a pack of riders hurtle past, barely in control as they hit the bumps just before the row of cottages at easily 150mph, only a few feet away, is one of the most exciting spectating experiences you could ever have. Likewise, walking up through the centre of Carrowdore eating chips from their soggy newspaper wrapping as the bikes were accelerating out of New

Riders flagged away by Carrowdore farmer and lifelong Carrowdore 100 supporter Joe Boyle

Road and up the Main Street, the noise bouncing off the houses, with the metallic scream of the two-strokes interspersed with the bass rumble of Sam McClements' Norton or Ray McCullough's QUB rising to a howl as they raced away towards Ballyboley, is something I'll never forget.

And to show that every cloud does have a silver lining, as Frank Weir explains later on, during festival week in Newtownards there was kart racing round its empty streets, which were sealed off at night to prevent terrorists from driving their bombs into the town. As with Carrowdore, a big part of the excitement was the close proximity of the action, with the safety barriers for much of the course consisting of just a few bales or a piece of string – all a far cry from the recent Circuit of Ireland stage in the town when, thanks to 'health and safety', the spectators were cocooned behind barriers that wouldn't have looked out of place at the edge of the 'Green Zone' in Baghdad.

Of course no look back at motorsport in the Ards in the 1970s would be complete without a mention of stock car racing. Clandeboye Park in Bangor was the earliest home of the sport in the Ards / North Down area, back in the late Sixties, but by the early Seventies the regular Saturday evening meetings had moved to the Cooke Brothers' quarry just outside Newtownards. The quarry provided a natural amphitheatre for the crowds who flocked there; indeed at times it seemed like half the population of Newtownards had made the trek up the Tullynagardy Road to witness the likes of Robin Kerr and George McGivern doing battle with Davy Muckle from Carrowdore and Tom Houston from Killinchy, who were the men to beat round the figure of 8 track. For a couple of years in the mid-Seventies racing moved to a new home at Carrowdore Quarry, before returning to Tullynagardy in the latter half of the decade. However, by then interest had waned and staging the events was no longer financially viable. Sadly the sport wilted and died in the Ards area, though it still thrives in other parts of the Province.

Talking of old bangers reminds me of my mother's kingfisher blue Morris Minor – Minors were still common in the early Seventies although not in the particular hue of my mother's, which was the result of a bodywork refurbishment programme carried out by my father and me one weekend on a very limited budget using the exterior gloss left over from when we'd repainted the woodwork on the house, prompting my mother to refer to it thereafter as 'the Noddy Car'. She needed a car at Drumawhey in the early Seventies as my father used his for meeting his customers and there was only an extremely limited bus service to Newtownards. So between transporting Irene and me about, shopping, etc., life would have been impossible without the trusty 'Noddy Car'.

Another use the car was put to was transporting soda bread my mother baked in 'the bake house' Daddy had built for her in an out-house. I can still recall those cold, dark winter mornings going down the yard to the bake house where Mummy would have been working hard since 5am, with only the radio and our pet dog Lassie for company. Looking in over the open half-door I'd be met by the welcoming warmth from the big griddle and the mouth-watering smell of cakes of soda at various stages of cooking, Mummy up to her elbows in flour

My mother, Margaret Johnston – champion baker

which came in one hundredweight bags and buttermilk from a 10 gallon metal churn.

She worked at a bench covered in cheap green Formica and stood on some planks to keep her feet off the cold concrete floor – a nod towards health and safety which Daddy and I had taken to extreme lengths by also whitewashing the crumbling plaster walls. The freshly-cooked sodas would be neatly stacked in bakers' trays at one end of the bench ready to put in the car to be taken to Jacky Hillis's shop in Newtownards where, on a Saturday morning, you could find a queue stretching round the shop and on to the street waiting for the warm sodas to arrive. I'm sure those people weren't aware how rudimentary the conditions were in the bake house where their soda had been crafted and maybe it wasn't a huge crowd – but to a 10-year-old boy it seemed the whole world had come to pay homage to the best baker in the country!

Jacky's shop in Greenwell Street was probably a bit ahead of its time in the early 1970s as the layout would have been broadly similar to a small convenience store today, with the groceries laid out on shelves for the customers to 'self service'. Most small shops of the time, such as Burns's in South Street, would still have provided an over-the-counter service, as indeed would many of the larger grocers in the town, with one of the last of the type, Morrison's beside the Northern Bank in High Street, only pulling down the shutters in the latter part of the decade. I guess it must have been a real culture shock to older residents when Woolco opened its doors in the newly-built Ards Shopping Centre in 1976 and it certainly changed my mother's shopping habits.

Previously shopping had been a Saturday morning exercise, precision-timed with enough left to be able to visit her mother in Raceview Terrace and then get home before the football fans heading for the match down the Portaferry Road started to clog up the town around the fire station, an unavoidable bottleneck on the way back to Drumawhey. Due to the parking restrictions (no unattended vehicles), Irene or me would be designated to sit in the car while my mother would go into the various shops: Morrison's Butchers for meat, Charlotte Heron's for fruit and veg, Hampshire's for the papers and our comics, Tom Killick's chemist, or the many other specialist shops the town had to offer for miscellaneous bits and pieces. There might even have been time for a speculative reconnoitre of the main shops in the town, Wardens and Glasgows.

For me Wardens had at least tools and other 'man stuff' to look at, whereas Glasgows with their haberdashery would have held no interest at all except for one thing which transformed it into an emporium of delight – their cash handling system. When a customer made a purchase and handed over their money the assistant would load the payment along with a hand-written docket into a small cylinder, which they would then insert into the end of a pipe located in a wooden glass-fronted cabinet. With a whoosh the cylinder would disappear and you'd hear it rattling away down the pipe followed only moments later by the sound of the rattle getting nearer before, with a thump the cylinder would reappear in the cabinet containing your change and a stamped receipt. It was absolutely magical and

Samuel Morrison's, one of the last traditional grocers in Newtownards

even if you had a wardrobe full of unworn clothes it would have been worth buying some more just to see the system in operation!

Of course, everything changed after the Ards Shopping Centre opened, offering late night shopping under one roof with easy parking and no need to bring a 'car sitter'. As a result, such trips for us became Friday evening affairs to which even Daddy might have been enticed to come along. Looking back I think it must have had a massive impact on the town centre, particularly bearing in mind the parallel disruption it was suffering from both the Troubles and the downturn in the local economy due to the shrinkage of the traditional textile industries.

As a teenager I was more focused on my next rugby match than closely monitoring the socio-economic impact of out-of-town shopping centres, so my memories may not be the most reliable but I don't recall Newtownards looking as down at heel as many other parts of the Province appeared to be at the time. Perhaps it was the nature of the shops in the town with the two biggest 'anchor' stores, Wardens and Glasgows, having core product lines that the big chains in the shopping centre were not competing with directly, which enabled the town centre to weather the initial storm. Quite likely an even bigger factor was the resilience of the shop owners who had deep roots in the town and who, unlike today's chain stores run by faraway-located bean counters, were prepared to 'tough it out' when things got hard.

Certainly there was a great sense of community in the town in the Seventies, which I became aware of when I was involved with the first-ever Regent House 1st XV to reach the Schools Cup final in the same year the girls' 1st XI hockey team reached their respective final. Members of our squad wore a distinctive red tie and several times in the run-up to the final I was approached in the street by strangers who wished us all the best, which made our defeat in the dying moments of the game all

Our captain, Alastair Moles, receives a commemorative plaque from Alderman John Scott, Mayor of Ards, at a Town Hall civic reception in April 1978. Included with other team members are Regent House headmaster Dr W. A. Maguire and Dr J. Cole, chairman of the school's management committee. 233-10-1

the harder to take. At least the girls won their final and there was some consolation the following year when we won the National Schools Seven-A-Side competition in London, coming out ahead of many of the top public schools in the UK.

For the final few years of the decade I temporarily moved away from Drumawhey to central London to study engineering at Imperial College in Kensington. Having already visited London a few times I thought with its excitement, the things to see and do and the sheer buzz of the city it would be the place for me, but I started to have misgivings from the moment I showed up with my suitcase at the registrar's office on the morning term started:

Me: "Hi I'm Tim Johnston – here's my letter of acceptance."

Lady at Desk: "That all looks in order, I'll mark you off."

Me: "Where's my room?"

Lady: "Which room?"

Me: "My accommodation."

Lady: "Well, wherever you've arranged it."

Me: "Was I supposed to arrange accommodation?"

Lady exits left to discuss with colleagues "you're not going to believe this …"

I think the moral of this incident, and indeed the underlying theme of this whole piece reflecting on my memories of the Seventies, is that 'you can take the boy out of Drumawhey, but you can't take Drumawhey out of the boy'. I may have got my degree at Imperial and since then have had the good fortune and opportunity to travel to many far-flung corners of the world on business and pleasure, but if I've learned anything at all over the years it's that for all the faults and problems our wee country might have, for me there's no better place in the world than the little piece of heaven in the Ards I'll always call home.

1970

Making the News in the Chronicle

Villiam Edmund Carter, of John Street in Newtownards, was awarded the British Empire Medal in the New Year Honours List. Principal doorman at Parliament Buildings, Stormont, he had joined the Royal Navy at 15 and served all over the world. He lost an arm in 1941 after the gunboat he was serving on was hit by German shelling in the North Sea.

Newtownards Borough Council announced that the town's new indoor swimming pool would be open seven days a week, including Sunday afternoons. Opposition to the decision was voiced by the Reformed Presbyterian Church of Ireland and by the newly-formed Newtownards branch of the Ulster Loyalists' Association, describing it as a "departure from the teaching of the Scriptures which the vast majority of the people of this Borough enjoy and cherish."

The New Year saw redundancy facing 64 staff members out of a total labour force of 400 at Short Bros and Harland's Hawlmark factory in Newtownards. Fears were voiced that an ongoing credit squeeze was causing a slowdown in sales of the acclaimed Shorts Skyvan, which had a major impact on the local factory.

Ballywalter's southern district postman, Albert Cromie, retired at the end of January after 13 years in the job "to make way for the new mechanised delivery service" (as the Chronicle reported it). Postmistress Mrs S. Denkowski, representing the fifth generation of her family in the village

Post Office, presented a bouquet of flowers to Mrs Cromie, while her husband received a "wallet of notes" from Gilbert McBride, co-organiser (with Val Harrison) of a presentation function for Mr Cromie.

Berkshire International (UK) Ltd., the first American-based company to open a factory in Northern Ireland, and its subsidiary, Ulster Hosiery Ltd., announced expansion plans in February for their operations in Newtownards and Dundonald, providing in the region of 300 new jobs.

Brian Ardis (15), from Killaughey Road, Donaghadee, was awarded the Scout Silver Cross in February for saving the life of a young girl who had become trapped under a capsized dinghy in Donaghadee Harbour. He and a friend, Harold Moore, also 15, dived fully clothed into the dark waters to rescue the child, taking her to the safety of her father's cabin cruiser.

Donaghadee man Harry McNarry retired on 19 February after serving as an Ards Hospital ambulance driver for 16 years. During the Second World War he had been Donaghadee Urban Council's main driver and he was also transport officer in charge of all the town's ambulances. He rendered invaluable voluntary service during the German bombing of Belfast in 1941.

The final service at the century-old Greenwell Street Presbyterian Church in Newtownards prior to its demolition was held on Sunday 22 February. Subsequent services were held in the Memorial Hall, pending the erection of the replacement church costing approx. £100,000. The farewell service was conducted by two ministers who were brought up in the congregation – the Rev. H. D. McMorran, of Duncairn Presbyterian Church, and the Rev. J. M. Maddock, of Newington Presbyterian Church, both Belfast.

Holywood TA Centre was the venue on 20 February for the final parade of the Newtownards District of the Ulster Special Constabulary (the sub-districts being Newtownards, Bangor, Comber, Donaghadee, Portaferry, Dundonald and Holywood).

The new Regiment
Find out about us and come and join us.

The Ulster Defence Regiment ARMY

Two six-year-old Newtownards boys, Philip McMullan, Old Priory Close, and Christopher McCluskey, Ardmillan Crescent, saved a five-year-old girl from drowning on 11 March after they pulled her from the fast-flowing waters of the local canal. Maria Smyth, from Lisbane Drive, had lost her footing close to where the water emerged from a culvert into the main stream, further strengthening local demands for improved safety measures.

Portaferry man Nicholas (Nicky) Curran, who had been building boats of every kind since the late 1930s, completed a 19ft. general purpose vessel from mahogany and oak for the locally-based Queen's University Marine Biology Unit. Aged 52 and from Shore Street, Nicky was viewed as one of a fast-dwindling number of people in Portaferry who had a long association with boats and the sea.

The Distinguished Service Medal of the Girls' Brigade was awarded in April to Lesley Henry (15), a member of 37th Company (Shore Street Presbyterian Church, Donaghadee) following her successful efforts to save a Downpatrick girl from drowning at Silver Strand, Wicklow, in July 1969.

Newtownards Swimming Pool opened to the public for the first time on 6 April and first boy to take the plunge was David Savage from Windsor Avenue. The main attraction was the 25m. pool capable of holding 200 swimmers and varying in depth from three feet at each end to six feet and six inches in the middle. In addition there was a 200-seat spectator area.

During the first week 1,800 swimmers visited the pool each weekday and Saturday, with 800 attending on the Sunday afternoon. The official opening ceremony, performed by the Governor of Northern Ireland, Lord Grey of Naunton, took place on 7 May.

The Rev. J. E. Jones, who served as minister of Second Comber Presbyterian Church for 42 years, was honoured by the congregation on the occasion of his retirement. During a presentation function at the church in early April he was praised for his long and devoted ministry.

In preparation for the introduction of decimal currency in February 1971, local company Debretta Ltd. issued each staff member with decimalised pay slips as well as a card by which they could convert the old currency into the new. It was also the company intention to change over their method of accounting to a completely decimalised system on 1 June 1970.

Twenty-two year-old Valerie Lemon from Ballywalter was voted Miss Ulster Television 1970, giving her a place in the Miss Great Britain competition which was being staged in Morecambe that summer.

The new principal of the Model Primary School in Newtownards was former pupil Charles McLean Ferris, who had been on the teaching staff for 22 years. He was taking over from retiring principal Samuel Stevenson.

Dr Elizabeth Long, wife of local MP Captain William Long, was re-elected as chairman of Donaghadee Urban District Council on 1 June. There was speculation she would be the authority's final chairman before the reorganisation of local government.

A two-week national dock strike in July had a profitable 'bootlegging' spin-off for fishing boats based in Donaghadee and Portavogie, with many crews keeping up an almost continuous 'bacon and egg' run between the two ports and Scotland. They were making up to £100 per trip, but at the same time they were incurring the wrath of the striking dock workers. An articulated trailer with its load of bacon was thrown into Portavogie Harbour on 23 July, while shortly afterwards thousands of eggs were smashed after two lorries were ambushed between Ballyhalbert and Ballywalter.

Donaghadee Urban District Council voted in early August to force mobile ice cream salesmen to move on if they remained parked for too long at the one spot. The action was taken after Cllr John Scott complained that a Mr Softee van was parked for two-and-a-half hours on the Parade the previous Sunday afternoon. He said it was unfair to existing businesses in the town, which paid rates and taxes for their properties.

Three widowed Comber sisters were reunited for the first time in 50 years after Mrs Lily Brown (née Hamilton) travelled over to Canada to meet up with Mrs Minnie Hope and Mrs Susan Woods in Toronto. Mrs Hope and Mrs Woods had both emigrated to Canada at the same time in search of a new life.

The new one-way traffic system took effect in Newtownards from 8.15am on Sunday 23 August. It provided clockwise circulation along Regent Street (from Gibson's Lane), Frances Street (to Castle Place), High Street and Mill Street (to Gibson's Lane). Both Lower Mary Street and Meetinghouse Lane became one-way running southwards, while the Frances Street entrances to Conway Square were closed to traffic as a result of the changes.

Fears the sonic boom from Concorde's first Irish Sea test flight on 1 September would cause widespread damage to property along the Ards Peninsula proved to be unfounded. Indeed, a 14-member team from the Mechanical Engineering

Department at Queen's University, who installed testing equipment in a number of old buildings (including the Temple of the Winds at Mountstewart), reported that the noise and waves created by the boom were so slight their recordings were "almost negligible."

Former Ballyeasboro man John McVeigh returned there in mid-September from his home of 50 years in Kansas City to officially open a new hall at St Andrew's Church in memory of his late parents and sister. His father, James, had been the longest serving churchwarden at the Ballyeasboro church, while his sister Minnie taught in the Sunday School and was involved in church activities for over 50 years. Despite living so far from Northern Ireland, Mr McVeigh contributed many thousands of pounds towards the construction of the new building, named the McVeigh Hall.

The Whitespots animal shelter, representing the culmination of two years of hard work by the Bangor and Ards Circuit of the USPCA, was officially opened on 21 September by the charity's president, South Belfast MP Rafton Pounder.

A Newtownards branch of PACE (Protestant and Catholic Encounter) was formed at the beginning of November, largely comprising, at the outset, members of the former Ards Civic Association. It had been launched the previous year to raise funds for the "relief of distress among the innocent victims of rioting in Belfast."

According to Regent House headmaster Dr W. A. Maguire, speaking at the annual prize day on 29 October, the total number of pupils had increased to a record 1,131, which represented "saturation point." It meant, he said, that the "miracle of putting a quart into a pint pot is being performed regularly at the school."

A weekend of commemoration and thanksgiving was held at Comber Methodist Church in early November to mark the 150th anniversary of Methodism in the town. Two former superintendent ministers of the Newtownards circuit, the Rev. Walter Bingham and the Rev. George Watson, participated in the special services.

Unionist Robert J. Brown was elected onto Newtownards Borough Council in November as a representative for Castle Ward in succession to Cllr Clifford Crothers, who had resigned. Mr Brown defeated Labour opponent Ken Young by 331 votes to 100 in a by-election.

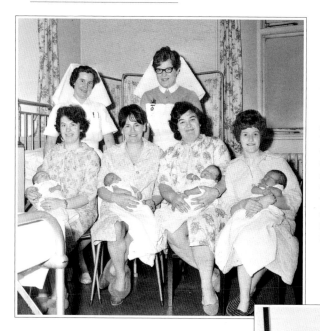

Four proud mothers pictured at Ards Hospital with babies born on New Year's Day 1970. From left: Mrs Doreen Agnew, Newtownards, with daughter Pamela; Mrs Claire Breen, Cloughey, with son Christopher; Mrs Sarah McCracken, Newtownards, with son Stephen, and Mrs Teresa Doran, Portaferry, with daughter Tanya. Included are Staff Midwife Addy and Staff Nurse McAlonan. 217-2-3

Mrs B. Scott, chairman of the Tufty Club Association for Northern Ireland, reads a story to children from the new club at Londonderry Primary School, Newtownards, in January 1970. 217-18-3

Sandra Beattie (22), from Main Street, Ballywalter, was crowned 'Miss Blaxnit' in January 1970 at the firm's annual dinner in the New Mount Royal Hotel, Donaghadee. 217-41-1

Members of the 23rd NI Girls' Brigade team (Newtownards Methodist Church) who won the Ards District PE competitions in January 1970. Back row (from left): Miss P. Savage, Mrs G. Elliott (pianist), Mrs J. McCahon. Centre: A. Dunn, J. McAuley, S. Conway, A. Hawkins. Front: M. Spence, A. Spence, F. Thompson and V. Mayne. 218-20-22

Mr Samuel Gibson (left), who retired in February 1970 after serving for 42 years as secretary to Newtownards Baptist Church, was honoured by the congregation at a presentation function. Picture shows elder Mr H. Hawe (right) handing over a silver tea set and watch on behalf of the congregation as other church officials look on. Included (from second left) are: Mrs Gibson, Pastor J. Ravey, the church's first pastor, Pastor N. Baird, Mr A. Oliver, elder, and Pastor W. Wilson, first secretary. 218-70-2

Members of First Comber Scout Group in February 1970 pictured at their annual Gang Show in the church hall. 218-59-1

Members of 106th NI Girls' Brigade (Ballygowan Presbyterian Church) are pictured at their annual Company meeting in January 1970. 218-61-1

Comber Secondary School won the local home safety quiz in mid-February 1970 by defeating Newtownards Further Education College by 36 points to 34. Back row (from left): Mrs S. Gunning (scorer), Mr S. R. McLawrence (quizmaster), Mr William Boal (committee chairman), Mrs F. Dorrian (timekeeper). Middle (Newtownards team): Wilma McDonald, Heather McLeavy, Heather Giffin, Margaret McKee. Front (Comber team): Margaret McDonald, Muriel Hiles, Lily Gibson and Maurice Gamble. 218-75-3

Members of Portavogie Presbyterian Church's Christian Endeavour group with leaders and the minister, the Rev. T. A. Houston, at the CE's birthday party in April 1970. 221-82-3

Children from St Patrick's Church, Ballyphilip, received their First Holy Communion in May 1970. 225-78-3

Noel McBlain, Charles Sibley, Junior Hedley and Dan Magowan, all pupils at Scrabo Secondary School, put in some training in May 1970 before undertaking Duke of Edinburgh Award tests in the Mournes. 225-41-2

The children's choir from Granshaw Presbyterian Church at their annual children's day services in early June 1970. Included are Mr W. J. McKibbin, Sunday School superintendent, and the Rev. Kenneth Smyth, special speaker. 226-97-2

Children from Newtownards Model Primary School applaud as retiring principal Mr S. Stevenson receives a wristwatch from the staff and pupils at the end of June 1970. 228-42-2

Policemen's wives from Newtownards and district pictured before leaving the town for a bus run to the Mourne Mountains in June 1970. 227-21-2

One-year-old Donna Clare Dugan, from Carrowdore, was crowned 'Rose of Clandeboye' at the famous estate's annual fete in early September 1970. 230-40-2

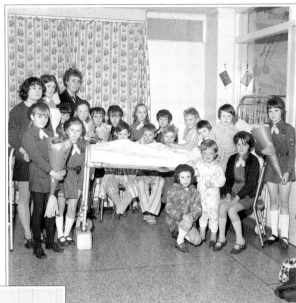

Members of the Second Newtownards 'B' Brownie Pack presented Halloween gifts to patients in the McKelvey Pavilion at Ards Hospital in early November 1970. Included are patients Greer McConnell, Garth Maxwell, Clifford Gourley, John Paden, Susanna Brady, Jennifer Napier, Martin Armstrong, Brownie leader Mrs McCallen with assistant Joyce White, and Nurse Thornton. 232-44-2

Mrs Sadie Harkness, of Bangor Road, Newtownards, who was convalescing in the Merdyn Nursing Home, Holywood, received a certificate of appreciation for her services to the British Legion Poppy Appeal from Mr Herbie Mateer, a local member of the Legion's National Executive Council, in November 1970. Mr Mateer, who was vice-president of the Newtownards branch and chairman of its services council, also presented Mrs Harkness with a bouquet of flowers on behalf of local poppy sellers. Looking on is son Tom Harkness, a member of Newtownards Borough Council. 233-26-3

Mr and John Finlay, of Newtownards Road, Cottown, cut a special cake to mark their golden wedding anniversary in December 1970. Mr Finlay was married to the former Miss Rose Alexander by the Rev. Wilson Marshall in Groomsport Presbyterian Church on 8 December 1970. The couple had two daughters and seven grandchildren. 234-84-13

Members of the cast of Millisle Parish Church Sunday School's nativity play in December 1970. 235-28-1

Head girl Irene Boyd and head boy Jim Reid present a silver tray to retiring Donaghadee Secondary Intermediate School headmaster Mr H. A. Reilly in late December 1970. Included are members of staff. 235-74-1

1970

Sport in the Chronicle

Comber light heavyweight boxer John Conway was beaten on points at the National Junior Championships in Dublin at the end of January. He lost to Dublin Garda Billy Cooper, from Crumlin, with one press report describing the winner as "the most amazed fighter on the night, when the judges awarded him a majority decision over Conway."

Ards FC officials hoped to begin work on the first stage of a new building programme during the approaching close season and to have it completed in time for the beginning of the 1970-71 season. The work would involve the construction of a new pavilion, boardroom and offices.

Conlig A, under manager Jimmy Currie, became Bangor Darts League champions in late February following a 6-4 victory over Belzar in the village. John Crawford won the last game to clinch the title.

Movilla Netball Club member Joan Compton was selected for the first-ever Northern Ireland under-21 team in a fixture against Wales on 28 February. The game took place in Wrexham and the Northern Ireland girls won an exciting encounter 25-22.

Ards manager George Eastham was sacked by the club on 10 March after he refused to resign. His dismissal came with three months' wages. During his two spells with the club they had won the Irish League, Irish Cup and Gold Cup. He was replaced by fans' favourite Billy Humphries, who within weeks had the additional thrill of being selected as Ulster Footballer of the Year.

Regent House fell short of reaching the Schools Cup final for the first time in early March. After beating holders Bangor Grammar School in the third round, they drew 3-3 with Rainey Endowed School in Magherafelt in the semi-final but lost the replay at Newtownards by 11-6.

The Movilla Minor Boys team won the Northern Ireland Minor League Table Tennis Championship at the Wellington Hall in Belfast on 14 April. Under coach Clifford Thompson, the team members, all aged 12, were Michael Fry, John Boyce, John Carson and Joe Smyth.

The Private Greens League flag was unfurled at Comber Bowling Green for the first time in the club's 47-year history, following the election in April of long-serving Comber club member James Boyce as president of the Private Greens League. By tradition the green, blue, white and red colours were flown at the home club of the current PGL president.

Ards IIA retained rugby's Forster Cup with a 9-6 victory over BRA Former Pupils IIIB at Ravenhill on 25 April. Scorers for Ards were Clarence Hiles (two penalties) and Jimmy McAllister (try).

North Down's Paul Gilliland scored 108 runs in a friendly match against Muckamore at Comber on 25 April. The club notched up 170 runs, giving them a 90-run victory over their opponents.

Ards FC lost out to local rivals Bangor in the final of the County Antrim Shield on 22 May. It took a total of four games, three of them ending in 1-1 ties, until Bangor finally came out on top with a 3-2 victory.

Reflecting the mounting impact of the Troubles on social life in Northern Ireland, Sheffield Wednesday cancelled a planned pre-season friendly against Ards. However, Stoke City, including legendary England goalkeeper Gordon Banks, did make the trip to Newtownards on 27 July and notched up a 1-0 victory over the home side.

Seventeen-year-old Sean McCleery, from Steele Dickson Avenue in Portaferry, landed a 110lb spotted ray skate while fishing in Strangford Lough on 5 August.

During a league cricket fixture between Donaghadee and Greenisland on 29 August, the former's opening bowler, Ivan Reid, bowled 13 maiden overs (out of 14) for four wickets, with just one run conceded. Donaghadee won the match by 60 runs. That same season saw the club securing the Section B Qualifying League Championship.

London journalist Kevin Murphy swam the North Channel, from Orlock Point near Donaghadee to Portpatrick in Scotland, in 11 hours and 21 minutes on 11 September, beating the old record set by Tom Blower in 1947 by an amazing four hours.

The new Ards FC pavilion, built at a cost of £10,000, was officially opened on 21 September, prior to an Ulster Cup fixture between Ards and Glentoran. The visitors won 3-0.

Newtownards golfer Rodney Hutton (23), a former Ulster and Leinster Boys Champion, turned professional in late October, joining Malone Golf Club as Assistant Professional. He was renowned as an all-round sportsman, having also played cricket for Downpatrick.

Ballycran GAC's new £30,000 community centre, comprising a hall and several ancillary rooms, was opened at McKenna Park on 27 December by Sean O Siochain, general secretary of the Gaelic Athletic Association.

Comber Rifle Club chairman Mr W. R. Potter (front, second from left) with some of the chief guests at their annual dinner, which was held in March 1970 at the Andrews Hall.
220-59-1

First Comber Presbyterian Church's badminton team won Division Six, Section B, of the Belfast and District Presbyterian League in late March 1970. Back (from left): Raymond Haliday, Colin Magowan, George Roddy, William McClements, David McVeigh. Front: Ann Blackstock, Florence Fisher, Helen Malloy, Hilda Fisher and Jane-Mary Cathcart.
220-58-1

Members of the Ards 3A rugby team, winners of the Forster Cup in May 1970. Back (from left): I. Coulter, M. Hodgins, J. McAllister, K. Christie, D. Thompson, J. Mahon, F. Orr. Centre: R. Finlay, C. Hiles, B. Hutchinson (captain), J. Hamilton (chairman), W. Shaw. Front: D. Hanley, D. Heron, J. O'Kane and M. Davidson. 223-95-1

The darts team from the Village Inn, Kircubbin, winners of the Portaferry and District Darts League in early May 1970. 224-6-1

The Ards cricket team in May 1970. Back (from left): J.Crowe, R. Mowat, S. Alexander, J. Boal, I. McLean, R. Keenan. Front: D. Trolan, A. Wright, J. Anderson, R, Dunn (captain) and J. McMillan. 224-82-1

Ballygalget Mitchels hurling team pictured after the opening of their new park in mid-May 1970. 225-50-1

Millisle's cricket team won the Woburn Cup in early August 1970. Back (from left): John McAvoy, Stephen Wilson, Phil Gwynne, John Stannage, Garth Armitage, Jack Kennedy, Laurence Brown. Front: Bill Wilson, Jim Wilson, T. J. Kennedy (president), George Wilson (captain) and Tom Beggs (vice-captain). Not included in the picture is David Munn. 229-19-1

Ballywalter's young soccer players won the Lower Ards Junior Knock-Out Cup in October 1970 and celebrated their success by gathering at the local Grand Prix Hotel. 231-91-1

Members of Movilla Netball Club at one of their Wednesday training sessions in October 1970. 232-49-1

The Ards Ladies bowling team won the Junior National Championship and the Private Greens League in October 1970. Back (from left): A. G. Dorman, B. Davison, M. Adamson, E. Coffey, K. Rice, A. B. Dorman. Front: J. Woods, M. McMaster, E. McCullough (president), F. Moore, E. Grimes and P. Adams. 232-29-1

The Rosemount senior soccer team from Greyabbey, winners of the Lower Ards Summer League Cup, at a presentation function in October 1970. 232-95-1

Dessie Reid

remembers ... The Fire Service and the Chronicle

As the fire appliance sped up High Street an urgent voice came over its cab radio: "Fire control from Newtownards One – from Section Leader Allen – make pumps three, building used as cinema well alight." It was late in the evening of Monday 10 October 1977 and the town's Regent Cinema was about to succumb to the Troubles.

A few minutes later Newtownards Two, of which I was a member, arrived at the scene to witness flames already leaping through the roof of the cinema and threatening the nearby Scrabo Electrical Engineers in Regent Street, as well as the betting shop in Gibsons Lane. As he had done on so many times before in my fire-fighting career, officer-in-charge Section Leader Robert (Bertie) Allen, later a well-deserved recipient of the British Empire Medal, soon had us getting to work in well-practiced drills.

However, even with the help of Bangor and Belfast colleagues, the 'Regent' had shown its last movie. The cinema's two projectionists, the late Bertie Beattie and the late Jimmy Mullan, were devastated by the loss of the cinema, and their jobs. However, Scrabo Electrical and the 'bookies' still stand today as testament to our endeavours.

When I joined the Newtownards retained section in February 1960 I was the youngest on station at 19. The then Portaferry Road fire station is now the current Northern

Dessie Reid joined the Newtownards Chronicle in May 1955 as an apprentice compositor, becoming a linotype operator before retraining on computers.

Dessie also contributed columns to the Chronicle, namely *Focus on Ards Folk* and *Around and About.*

In February 1960 he received permission from his employer to join the part-time ranks of the Newtownards Section of the then Northern Ireland Fire Authority. There followed an amazing journey of 26 years, during which Dessie was involved in minor and major fires, minor and major incidents, not to mention many amusing incidents. If asked he says he would do it all again!

In 1975, Dessie was promoted to the rank of Leading Fireman and he holds the Fire Brigade Long Service and Good Conduct Medal.

From left: Firemen L. Crone, T. White, D. Reid, F. Barclay, H. Bowman
Photo courtesy of Dessie Reid

Ireland Fire and Rescue Safety Centre. It was in August 1961 that we moved 'next door' to what is the present station. My training commenced at station level under the watchful eyes of experienced Leading Firemen John Kisby, Jim McDowell (later to become Sub-Officer in charge with a BEM to follow), Peter Rollo and Jim Finlay, all now sadly deceased. Guidance was also forthcoming from the ever willing late F/m Lex Crone, as well as the Mitchell father and son duo. Regrettably, Hugh (Sen.) passed away within a few months of my joining the brigade. I underwent specialised training at Fire Brigade HQ in Lisburn, where many ladder descents were made from dizzy heights off the training tower with no safety lines whatsoever. Today, I much prefer to keep my feet on the ground!

For some years now Newtownards has been manned during the day by full-time firefighters, ably backed up by part-time personnel. Throughout my time of service the station was manned part-time with personnel hailing from all walks of life. We were mobilised by a siren which was situated firstly on top of the retort building which was once a feature at the Mill Street gasworks, and then on top of the fire station roof itself. In later years we were issued with personal alerters (bleepers), which were a great step forward.

On responding to a call-out it was the duty of the first person into the station to ring the local police for the address of the incident. One particular morning, on charging out of my place of employment, the Newtownards Chronicle in Frances Street, I did just that. A voice answered, 'Police station,' to which I replied, 'I know it's the police station, could I have the address of the fire please?', or words to that effect. The voice repeated, 'Police station," adding, "the fire is in the police station." It turned out to be a minor affair but a week later breathing apparatus was required to source a serious outbreak in the then courthouse in Regent Street.

The 1970s were busy indeed for most fire stations in Northern Ireland with Newtownards being no exception. The Town 'n' Country in Regent Street was a major blaze (also 1977), while local firefighters also acquitted themselves admirably in Bangor on Saturday 30 March 1974 when Wellworths, Woolworths and the Co-op were all ablaze.

Being a perimeter station to Belfast, Ards firemen were called into the city on many occasions as back-up. Plenty too were the chimney fires in winter and gorse fires in summer. Nor was our 'patch' without its share of lives lost in road traffic accidents and other incidents.

To say I rubbed shoulders with many amazing characters in our local fire station would be an understatement. L/Fm Robert Bowden, (deceased) was one such person. It's well documented that on one occasion while driving up the rough track to the lead mines in the station's Austin tender with trailer pump he got up from the driver's seat, walked round to the back of the open-backed appliance and starting chatting to the crew – that is until they caught on the vehicle was driverless! He also loved to tell the story (as only he could) about delivering coffins in Belfast for Sheals' coffin factory at Windsor Avenue, when he was stopped at an Army checkpoint during the civil unrest. A soldier insisted on inspecting his lorry's load, following which Robert was told to 'move along' in no uncertain manner!

Leading Fireman Robert Bowden (centre), who retired after 25 years' service as a retained fireman with the Fire Authority for Northern Ireland in Newtownards, is pictured with Divisional Officer Smyth, Station Officer Crawford, Sub-Officer Robert Allen BEM and other colleagues in August 1975. 60-14-115

The late L/Fm Tom White is another whose name is indelibly written into station folklore. 'Whitey' was regarded by us all as a very competent driver. However, his career was not without the odd mishap. Negotiating the narrow confines of Comber's Castle Street one fine day, with blue lights flashing and two-tone horns sounding, a parked car was just missed by the large emergency vehicle. Some time later, with the innocent car driver just about recovered from his ordeal, Tom reappeared in Castle Street on the return journey and, would you believe it, managed to strike the same car a glancing blow, much to the owner's dismay!

Also worth recalling is the morning Tom tried to suppress a yawn with the result his false teeth went skidding down a frosty unlit footpath. However, in the finest traditions of the Fire Brigade, his colleagues gathered round in his hour of need. Showing total disregard for their own safety and mustering all their skill and daring, they soon located the offending dentures which were hosed down and returned to their grateful owner!

From my own archives I can recall settling down one morning on one of the late Alex Rankin's chairs when he had his barber's premises in Conway Square. Hardly had his elderly assistant started to snip my hair than I heard the siren sounding in the distance. I flung the cloth away and sprinted out the door without a word, much to the bewilderment of my hairdresser and to the amusement of Alex. Apparently the hard-of-hearing assistant thought he had plucked a hair! We all had a good laugh when I returned next day to have my haircut completed.

Not all ominous callouts had a serious ending. We were once dispatched to the Dairy Hall playing fields where it was believed someone had been trapped. Two fire engines, an ambulance and a police car responded to what turned out to be a teenage girl well and truly stuck in a child's swing. On her speedy release the girl didn't know whether to laugh or cry!

But it all had to end sometime and so retirement came along in 1986 after what can only be described as both a challenging and rewarding 26 years. It goes without saying there would have been no Fire Brigade career without the consent and goodwill of the managing director and staff of the Chronicle. Time and time again on the sounding of the fire siren not only would doors have been opened for me but my bicycle would have been made ready for the dash to the fire station via Doctors Lane.

Sub-Officer Robert Allen BEM, Fireman L. Crone, Fireman H. Stanfield and Fireman F. Barclay represented the Newtownards Section of the Fire Authority of Northern Ireland at the Lord Mayor's Show in Belfast in May 1976. They took along this 1911 Merryweather Hatfield Trailer Pump, which had been lovingly restored by members of Newtownards Fire Station.
13-17-5

There was two-way traffic in my day!

When I look back on my early days as the firm's apprentice compositor, having followed my late brother Godfrey into the company, it was indeed a privilege to work under the supervision of the late Dick Cunningham, Norman Boal and Alec Haslett. True gentlemen all of them. I also worked for many years with colleagues Jimmy Boal (later manager), Gordon Orr, Wesley McClements (deceased), Davey Cairns, John Magowan, Sammy Moore and George Newell, to name but a few. Through time I progressed onto typesetting machines and in later years different computers.

When I became a journeyman at the age of 21 I remember buying a round of drinks for colleagues in the typesetting department. There are those who would say it was the last time I bought a round of drinks! When the late Mr John Alexander (managing director) came on the scene he of course wondered what was going on. When it was explained to him he emphasised to me that the years would now 'fly in'. He never spoke a truer word!

Because I showed promise at putting a few words together I was also allowed to contribute items to the columns of the Chronicle. I needed little excuse to write about some of the town's characters, including Joe Blake, Benny McAuley, Jim McMeekan and Maggie Berry. I was never happier than when researching articles on the Ards TT races, Ards Aerodrome and the town's railway. My one regret – after

Chronicle staff cricket team. Photo courtesy Dessie Reid

a couple of years of trying – was that my shorthand never got up to an acceptable speed. I tended to panic when I got behind and as a result I bought myself a tape recorder!

If pushed for a favourite contribution it would have to be an item on the local Field Marshal Sir Henry Wilson Memorial Flute Band, better known in some circles as the Back Deed Band. It's worth mentioning again that in later years the band's leader, Jimmy Oliver, didn't start the members with the traditional 'Band by the left quick march.' Rather he preferred to call out, 'Right boys, January, February, MARCH!' The band faded from the scene in the early 1950s.

In March 2006 I reached the big 65, bringing to an end a career with Alexander Newspapers which had lasted two months short of 50 years.

Big T

remembers ... Discos and Downtown Radio

Big T, alias Trevor Campbell, celebrates his 70th birthday in 2016, the same year that marks the 40th anniversary of the launch of Downtown Radio.

Despite starting his working life as a civil servant, a lifelong love for music saw him hankering for a career as a DJ. This became a reality on a part-time basis at local nightspots such as the T'nC in Newtownards in the early 1970s, before getting a full-time job with Downtown Radio when it was launched on 16 March 1976.

When the big stars visited Northern Ireland they would invariably include a visit to Downtown Radio on their itinerary for a studio interview with Big T. Memorably, he was able to introduce Johnny Cash at Downtown to his late wife and fellow broadcaster Lynda Jayne.

Today Trevor is the sole surviving presenter from those early days of commercial radio in Northern Ireland and he is still notching up enviable audience ratings.

The day Downtown went on the air we led with the news that Harold Wilson had resigned as Prime Minister. My old friend Don Allen, of Radio North Sea International fame, called to congratulate me on a successful debut behind the microphone, adding: "Harold always threatened he'd quit the day you got your own show!"

Forty years later I'm still there – the last presenter from the original team – and I've never regretted for a minute my decision to leave a secure job to take my chances with Northern Ireland's first commercial radio station.

I'd always been interested in music. Growing up in the 1950s, my parents had a radiogram and we were always listening to records. My uncle William had a radio and record shop, so we had an endless supply of 78s. Another uncle used to set up a microphone in my grandmother's parlour, which he plugged into the back of her radio in the dining room.

My party piece was to speak into the microphone and my voice would come out of the radio. It was the first microphone I ever spoke into and, like a DJ on the radio, I was unseen. I would make up news stories about the Queen and the Duke of Edinburgh and those public service announcements urging anyone knowing the whereabouts of a particular person to "contact their nearest police station or call Whitehall 1212."

My sister Norma, six years my senior, was a major influence on my musical education. There was no real music for young people on the BBC so she was really into Radio Luxembourg. That introduced me to music ahead of my contemporaries, artists like Elvis Presley, Tommy Steele, Little Richard and Jerry Lee Lewis.

By the time Radio Caroline came along in 1964 I was hooked on the idea of becoming a disc jockey. I made endless tapes, including my own jingles, but I thought they needed to be perfect so I never got round to sending them off. The very idea that I could become one of those people on the radio seemed ridiculous, which explains why by the beginning of the Seventies I was working in the Legal Aid office of the Civil Service.

One night the DJ at the Boat Club hadn't turned up and they were looking for someone to play the records at the disco. The organiser, having been told I would be ideal, called me up and asked if I wanted the job. I knew I would always regret not doing it so I agreed, without letting on I'd never really done anything like it, certainly not in public.

The most I ever got was maybe a few pints, but I loved the work and very soon my week revolved around those Wednesday nights at the Boat Club. After that a friend offered me the chance to do some discos for money, which led to appearances in front of as many as a thousand people at the King's Arms in Larne, the Deerpark in Antrim and Ballygally House on the Co Antrim coast.

I was approached in autumn 1971 by Jack Rodgers and Bob Lennon, who had taken over the King's Arms and also supplied entertainment for a new venue in Newtownards, the Town 'n' Country. Very soon I was there every other Saturday and then Thursday nights as well, playing pop and oldies with plenty of chat too.

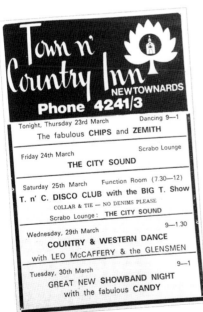

The promoter didn't think Trevor Campbell was a particularly great name for a DJ and he knew I'd been known as Big T at school so that was it. I didn't mind as it was printed in block capitals on adverts and stood out better than an ordinary name!

Doors opened at 7.30pm and by then the people were already queuing up. It was the early days of the Troubles and people from Newtownards were reluctant to travel to Belfast. City people also travelled in great numbers to Newtownards and to the T'n'C in particular.

Around that time I had my first taste of

Hendi (seated), John Paul, Paul Prenter and myself

radio broadcasting, thanks to Don Allen, who had a country show on Radio North Sea International. Don, who had previously been on Radio Caroline and Manx Radio, was a big country music fan and I found I loved the music too. Don offered me a job but it wasn't long before I was back in Northern Ireland. The boat was anchored four miles off the Dutch coast and the gales sometimes reached Force 10.

When Downtown started I was already presenting a Sunday afternoon show on hospital radio in Newtownards. I'd also had an approach from the BBC in Belfast, but they were only interested in offering me a late night Saturday programme. Don Anderson, who had been appointed programme controller for the new station, had heard and read about me. He rang to say he wanted to meet me with a view to having my own show on Downtown. We met in the bar of the Strangford Arms in December 1975, three months before the station went on the air. Within a couple of minutes he announced: "You're hired."

I immediately lost interest in my Civil Service job and handed in my notice. Construction work was still under way at Kiltonga – you had to go up a plank to get in the front door! I started with the lunchtime 'Dinner Spinner' show, as well as Saturday mornings and Sunday requests. I ended up being on every day of the week.

The other DJs included Hendi (Michael Henderson), John Paul (Ballantine) and Candy (Devine). We were all asked what specialist show we wanted to do and I

Members of the Downtown Radio ladies' football team before their match with a combined UTV and BBC team in May 1976, two months after the Newtownards-based station's launch. The match, which ended in a 2-2 draw, was organised under the auspices of Ballynahinch Civic Week. Back (from left): Mary McKegney, Cherrie McIlwaine, Pat Francis, Linda McAuley, Sally Boyce, Moira Orr, Wendy Austin, Janice (?). Front: Rosie Moore, Mary Robinson, Maggie Taggart, Phyllis Kelly, Mai Part and Maureen (?). Commentator was DJ Michael 'Hendi' Henderson (at rear). 41-15-4

said country music. It was very big in Northern Ireland at the time thanks to the showbands and also the influence of Radio Caroline and RTE. That meant a further hour and a half two nights a week.

There'd been a huge build-up in the press before Downtown went on the air. When 16 March arrived things went mad – we had to stop telling people to phone in because the switchboard was jammed. That first night I also had a country show from 8pm to 9.30pm and the phones went crazy again. Initial listening figures showed the country shows were getting higher ratings than some of the daytime programmes, which was unheard of in radio circles. Every survey since has shown the same.

My biggest worry – and I'd say it was the same for broadcasting colleagues who had left secure jobs – was that the public wouldn't like us, but thankfully they did. I've never much liked the sound of my own voice but people in shops started saying they recognised me from the radio!

We were a community station and the presenters made a point of getting out and about among the public. Roadshows played a big part in promoting our programmes around Northern Ireland. We also did considerable charity work, with the girls' football team proving particularly popular. It included future broadcasters like Linda McAuley, Cherrie McIlwaine and Wendy Austin.

Early days at Downtown. From left: Hendi, , Bill Smyth, myself, Candy Devine and Derek Marsden

Because of the Troubles, Downtown also had the UK's biggest regional newsroom with top-rated journalists like Eamonn Mallie, Gary Gillespie, David Sloan, Ivan Little and, later in the decade, Mervyn Jess.

After about three months the country show, which was receiving more letters and requests than any other programme on Downtown, was extended by 30 minutes. Paddy O'Flaherty (as Pat Brady) and then John Greer did an Irish country show on Sunday nights. I preferred to play American country – Elvis, Faron Young, Don Williams and Charlie Pride – along with the likes of Philomena Begley, Brendan Quinn, Gene Stuart and Frankie McBride.

My involvement with the T'nC ended when I joined Downtown but it wasn't the last of my appearances as a DJ at local nightspots. However, it was now one-hour guest appearances for triple the money I'd earned before.

I also worked with my late wife Lynda Jayne, who joined the station in November 1978. Most people assume we met at Downtown; in fact I'd had an eye for her when she was a presenter on UTV. We first met in 1977 at a charity event where we were both judging the talent competition. I invited her out for a drink and she agreed.

I'd parked the station's instantly recognisable Cortina Estate outside and a crowd of youngsters were standing round wanting my autograph, yet Lynda was the one appearing on television. She always loved telling people that story. That same evening she accompanied me to a cocktail-tasting competition at the Stormont Hotel. Our relationship developed from there, particularly after she joined Downtown.

Singer/ songwriter Bill Anderson once told me real happiness in life is being so good at your hobby that someone pays you for doing it. The fact I'm still here doing what I love suggests it was worth taking the risk when Don Anderson called me back in 1975. Downtown is essentially the same homely radio station it's always been and Northern Ireland is still the 'small big place' it's always been. That's the strength of any local radio station and I'm proud to have played my part.

Billy Kirk

remembers ... Cycling

The year 1971 was a critical, if not fateful, time in my life. Thirty-four years-old and married with five children, I'd worked since 1953 as a draughtsman in the aircraft industry. As a racing cyclist, beginning in 1954, I had achieved multiple Irish Championships and was record holder at 10, 25 and 30 miles, but my best years were over.

In April my employers, Short and Harland's, made 140 people redundant and I was one of them. It was a bad blow, but worse was to come. Around the same time, despite my evident fitness, an insurance medical found a non-functioning left kidney although, having resumed racing after a five year lay-off, and having done 25-miles in 61 minutes, my GP, Dr Cole, considered me very fit. With a young family to support, worries about health and employment naturally assumed major significance but the exertion and focus of racing provided a welcome escape.

By June I was keen for competition and I hatched a plan to ride in a race being held during the approaching Falls Road (Belfast) Fleadh under the rules of the National Cycling Association, a 32 County body not recognised by cycling's world governing body.

By taking part I risked suspension from my own cycling organisation, the Northern Ireland Cycling Federation. The two bodies did not recognise each other, or compete with each other – a surefire recipe for strife and recrimina-

Born in 1937, by the age of 14 Billy had lost both parents to the ravages of TB.

Always keen on cycling, Billy rode his first 10-mile time trial in 1949 and despite swearing "never again" he was hooked and went on to become a multiple Irish Champion, setting numerous national records along the way and representing Ireland at the World Championships in Amsterdam in 1959.

He retired from competitive cycling in 1963 to pursue a career in photography, culminating in working for the N. I. Tourist Board and having a selection of his work published in *Images of Belfast*, Blackstaff Press (1983).

However, his bicycle continued to call to him and he returned to occasional competition from the early Seventies. In 2006, aged 69, Billy proved that age can be just a number when he set a lifetime personal best for 25 miles, completing the distance in a remarkable 57 minutes 59 seconds.

Billy and wife Mary outside Forster Green Hospital in 1971

tion which should have no place in sport. However, I reckoned I could get away with riding in this Fleadh against riders who in all probability didn't know me.

Back in 1971 the Falls area was in chaos with barricades everywhere and bin lids banging day and night. I apprised event organiser Joe McAloon of my intentions and the need for secrecy. It sounds crazy but I even bought a false beard which, on reflection, I did not use. Despite some apprehension, I felt everything was falling into place. On the race morning, a Saturday in late August, my wife Mary and I, along with our five-year-old son Brendan, set off in our Ford Cortina for West Belfast.

We parked in Castle Street and made our way to the race headquarters on the Falls Road. Joe McAloon gave me a knowing wink to say all was well. No one appeared to recognise me. I was about to register as 'Liam Tuohy', a name suggested by old work colleague Bobby Delargy. However, Joe gave me the name 'Gerard Briggs' so I forgot about 'Tuohy.'

This was a completely new course and experience for me. The race would start at the Falls Road Baths, then on to Leeson Street, Raglan Street, Albert Street and ending back at the Falls. But it almost ended for me at the starting line. The famous Belfast 'crew cut' barber Rab Maguire, whose customers included world champion boxers Freddy Gilroy and John Caldwell, as well as myself, recognised me. Despite the earliness of the hour, Rab had already partaken of not a little liquid refreshment and couldn't quite grasp the fact that I wasn't Billy Kirk but 'Gerard Briggs.' How I regretted dispensing with the false beard! To compound matters former Newtownards Chronicle photographer Farnham Nixon was in the crowd doing a job for the Irish News. Fortunately, hidden behind my dark glasses, he didn't recognise me.

The 30 riders in the field were strangers to me, with the exception of the great Shay O'Hanlon, four times winner of the eight-day Ras Tailteann. However, also competing, as I later learned, were notables Davy McLarnon and Brian Holmes from Belfast and Colm Nulty from Co. Meath. I was in exalted company! This was the final day of the Fleadh and there was a carnival atmosphere. Pubs were doing a roaring trade as the sounds of fiddles and guitars and banjos mingled with tin whistles, uilleann pipes and drums.

Among the babble of voices in the heaving crowd of spectators I detected visitors from the USA, France, Germany, Holland and Spain. When the race started, the revellers, pints in hand, cheered all the riders on as they swept past on every lap. The race would be of one hour duration plus two laps. At the end of lap two Brian Holmes of the St. Agnes Club led, followed by Colm Nulty, pulling out a 50m lead. Impetuously, I joined them to form a three-man breakaway. It was a big, big exhausting effort for me and for 15 minutes I struggled for breath and wasn't able to take my turn at the front of the group. Fortunately I recov-

Brian McNally leads Billy Kirk in the Blaxnit Grand Prix 1971 at Mill Street turning into Gibson's Lane

ered strongly, took the lead and from then on did my fair share of the work.

It was an exciting race. As we flashed past The Old House pub I glimpsed blurred faces and smelled the pints of beer being swilled to the jingle jangle of musical instruments. The roars of appreciation from the crowd – "You're going to lap the rest of the bunch!" – inspired me. I was going so strongly I opened up a gap on my two companions. I afforded myself a little smile as I heard them shout to each other: "Close the gap on him! Close the gap!"

I later found out that organiser Joe McAloon, in the race director's car (an MG Midget!), was going ballistic as he realised I might possibly win the race. How was he going to report 'Gerard Briggs' as the winner and everyone then demanding to know who this 'Gerard Briggs' was and where did he come from? He needn't have worried. My sparkle and energy faded as we did indeed lap all the other competitors. Nulty won by half a length from Holmes, while I finished third, 10 lengths adrift.

After the finish Nulty and Holmes said to me, "You rode well but who are you?" I replied, "Only an old NICF time-trialist," but I did whisper my proper name.

After the prizegiving we retired to The Old House to enjoy music, song, beer and coffee. At the bar I bumped into Rab Maguire, a little more sober and sympathetic to me than before. We reminisced about the good old days and the personalities who frequented his famous barber-shop. Rab even took us round to the old and by then vacant shop, his business having moved to Smithfield. The chairs were still there, along with the mirrors, old fight posters, photographs and cuttings of champions Caldwell and Gilroy. Rab related to me the story of how he started in the hair-cutting trade in 1946. He and another chap applied for an apprentice's job at Esler's in Donegall Street and Rab got the position because he was reckoned to be the more talkative of the two – the other was Gerry (later Lord) Fitt!

Despite the stimulation provided by the day's racing, driving home I found the old anxieties returning – and with some justification. Barely one month later I was admitted to Forster Green Hospital where tests revealed my left kidney had been completely destroyed by tuberculosis and the right kidney was also diseased, although treatable. After six months of drug treatment it was the turn of the great renal surgeon Mr Joseph Kennedy, who operated for six hours in Belfast City Hospital to remove my kidney and ureter. He told me I had been infected from infancy, almost certainly through contact with my mother.

During my treatment and recuperation I had plenty of time to dwell on my past life – my childhood in a little cottage out the Donaghadee Road, the early passing of both parents from the disease, and my determination not to succumb but, rather, to lead a full and healthy life. As I recovered, my thoughts began to turn towards the future and what it might hold. I had no desire to return to the engineering drawing board, having seen too many old colleagues collecting their gold watch at 65 and retiring, very often, to an early death.

Life always has something to offer. Three months after my operation, having recovered from surgery, I cycled with Bobby Adair, a well-known Ards cyclist and builder, and my son Lennie to Portglenone to see a cycle race. It was a distance of 70 miles, which I managed easily.

As well as cycling, I'd always been a keen photographer and I decided to enrol at the College of Art in York Street as a mature student. I hoped we'd be able to survive on the proceeds of a little piece of property I'd sold in addition to a student grant. It would be tough going, not only for myself, but also for Mary and the children, but we would face it with resolute determination.

I completed my course, achieving an excellent Diploma in Art and Design in 1975, which led to several exhibitions and many book publications recording the way of life around the Shankill and Falls in the 1970s.

Life is good, life is what you make it and life is for living. At the time of writing this, 44 years have elapsed since that devastating diagnosis in 1971. At 78 years of age I ride my bicycle every day, often undertaking 40-mile round trips down our beautiful Ards Peninsula. There is always something new to see, something new to experience. And in the saddle-bag of my bicycle, always – a camera.

1971

Making the News in the Chronicle

A new hall for Millisle Presbyterian Church, built at a cost of £25,000, was officially opened on 4 January by Lord Dunleath and dedicated by Presbyterian Moderator Rt. Rev. Dr James Haire.

Lord Dunleath (second from right) officially opened the new hall at Millisle Presbyterian Church. Included are (from left): Clerk of Session Mr R. McWha, Moderator of the Ards Presbytery the Rev. T. A. Houston and Carrowdore minister the Rev. R. J. McCracken. 236-18-1

There was a British Empire Medal (BEM) in the New Year Honours List for Portavogie widow Eileen Eldred who had been looking after permanent foster children – those with no parents – for 25 years. The former nurse to handicapped young people was foster-mother to 13 children aged from nine to 18, having over the years fostered a total of 15 children.

Post Office staff went on strike in mid-January (it would last seven weeks), complaining the eight per cent pay offer to postmen, whose take-home pay was between £13 and £14 a week, came nowhere near the cost of living, which had risen by 12 per cent during the previous year.

Commerce Minister Roy Bradford announced on 27 January that export successes in recent years, coupled with a major diversification plan, would mean the creation of more than 150 new jobs for Black and Co. (Blaxnit) in Newtownards. The company's key export markets were in Canada, Scandinavia, the Middle East, the Far East and Japan.

> GREAT LOYALIST PARADE
> and PUBLIC MEETING
>
> # Dr. Ian R. K. Paisley, M.P.
>
> Queen's Hall - Newtownards
> TUESDAY, 16th FEBRUARY
> (DR. PAISLEY WILL LEAD PARADE)

In the run-up to the introduction of decimalisation on 15 February, the Down County Library Board announced a fines amnesty for all late books returned to libraries between 15 and 27 February. When fines were restored on Monday 1 March they were reduced from 3d to 2.4d (1p) per week.

The price of the Newtownards Chronicle rose from 8d to 4p (the equivalent of 9.6d).

Sir Ian Fraser, chairman of the Northern Ireland Police Authority, officially opened the new police station at John Street, Newtownards, on 28 January. Built at a cost of £90,000 it replaced the previous barracks at 19 High Street, which was used for 25 years.

> Ministry of Home Affairs
>
> CIVIL AUTHORITIES (SPECIAL POWERS) ACTS (NORTHERN IRELAND) 1922-43
>
> Notice is hereby given that the Minister of Home Affairs has made Regulations under the above Acts, dated 29 January 1971, entitled the Civil Authorities (Special Powers) Acts (Amending) Regulations (Northern Ireland) 1971 (SR & O 1971 No. 40). These Regulations make it unlawful for any person to print, publish, circulate, distribute, sell or offer for sale any document advocating certain specified unlawful activities of a subversive nature.

In early February the 20 part-time firemen in Newtownards were issued with pocket radios that emitted a 20-second 'bleep', which replaced the familiar wail of the town's fire siren.

The foundation stone for a new £45,000 hall at Strean Street Presbyterian Church in Newtownards was laid by Moderator Dr James Haire on 27 February. He said the Troubles in Northern Ireland showed how important it was for congregations to have premises for training themselves and the next generation in Christian faith and practice.

Speaking at the annual prize-giving ceremony for nurses of the North Down Hospitals Group in mid-March, Chief Medical Officer Dr Maurice Woods warned the public of the impending rundown of both Ards and Bangor Hospitals, with the transfer of patients to Dundonald. Unless they "make their MP's life hell," he said, they would "wake up some morning and find they had no hospital service."

Ards MP and Education Minister Capt. William Long pledged his support to new Prime Minister Brian Faulkner when he addressed the annual meeting of the Ards Unionist Association in the Queen's Hall, Newtownards, on 25 March. "In Brian Faulkner," he said, "we have someone who has all the qualities of leadership, intellect and determination needed by anyone in that position."

Plans to build an exact replica of the old Ards TT racing pits at Quarry Corner, Dundonald, as a tourist attraction – at a cost of £3,500 – were revealed at Newtownards Town Hall on 6 April by Lord Dunleath, chairman of the Ulster TT Commemorative Committee. The annual Ards Circuit TT was held for nine years, the last being in 1936.

Comber native Patrick Toman (20), whose mother still lived at Brownlow Street, paid a six-week visit to the town while on leave from the Royal Australian Air Force. He had emigrated to Australia five years earlier with the intention of taking up a career in farming but instead joined the RAAF and had just spent more than a year serving in Vietnam.

Newtownards Borough Council announced its own three-week Ulster '71 celebrations between 13 May and 5 June, culminating in a parade and the Mayor's Show, emphasising the work going

on among youth in the town rather than its commerce and industry. However, a major industrial exhibition in the Queen's Hall would feature that side of Borough life, while the Chamber of Trade also had plans for a shopping week during the initial days of the celebrations.

Court sittings in Greyabbey and Comber were merged into an enlarged Newtownards Magistrate's Court from the beginning of May.

Short Bros. and Harland announced in late April that 110 employees at its Glen Works in Newtownards were being made redundant and the plant would close by the end of August. The Glen Works housed the company's general engineering division, which a statement said "cannot be maintained on a profitable basis."

The Abbeyfield (Donaghadee) Society's first purpose-built elderly people's home in the town was officially opened by Lord Grey, Governor of Northern Ireland, at Barnagh Close on 28 April.

North Down Rural Council's hopes of providing a learner swimming pool in Kircubbin received a setback in early May when the Down County Education Committee said it could not give an assurance "at this stage" of endorsing the plan. However, the Committee said it would welcome a discussion with Councillors on the matter.

The Ards Labour Party called on the local Borough Council in early June to restore free school milk to primary school children in the area, if necessary by making school milk a charge on the rates.

In the first Troubles-related incident of terrorist violence recorded by the Newtownards Chronicle, no one was injured when Ballywalter's war memorial was targeted by bombers on 28 June. Around one pound of gelignite was used in the explosion which blew in windows in two houses across the road from the war memorial, along with most of the windows in the adjoining Ballywalter Masonic Hall. The cenotaph itself was undamaged.

Plans to entice Belfast people with £120 grants to move out of the city to the 'growth town' of Newtownards were given a general welcome by Borough Councillors in early August. However, there was strong support for local people being given priority in the allocation of public authority housing. The grant scheme, promoted by the Stormont Government, included an additional £50 where resettlement was in a new subsidy house.

RENT and RATES STRIKE

The Ministry of Development wishes to make it absolutely clear to those who are refusing to pay rents or rates or are under pressure to do so that:

– failure to recover rent and rates can result in :—

delay in house repairs and improvements and even house building; reduction in services and redundancies among Council employees;

– the strike is not harming the Government—it is harming local people in the immediate areas concerned.

The Government is determined that :

1. Rent and Rates must be paid.

2. Arrears which will accumulate, will have to be paid.

LEGAL POWERS WILL BE SOUGHT TO DEDUCT MONIES DUE, INCLUDING ARREARS, FROM ALL FORMS OF STATE AND PUBLIC PAYMENTS.

In your own interest :

1. Pay no heed to those who call on you to hold back your rent and rates.

2. Do not let yourself be intimidated or pressed into supporting them.

3. Remember that it is you personally—not the leaders of this campaign—who will suffer the hardship which must inevitably follow and who will be faced with a heavy payment of arrears.

There was shock and horror throughout The Ards following the tragic death of Portaferry-born priest Fr. Hugh Mullan on 9 August, during one of Belfast's bloodiest days of the Troubles to date. Aged 40 and a son of Mr and Mrs John Mullan, of High Street in Portaferry, he was shot dead while on an errand of mercy.

Fr Mullan had been at home on the Springfield Road with another priest when he received a call to administer the Last Rites to a wounded man at nearby Moyard Park. As he was walking away he was hit by a burst of machine-gun fire.

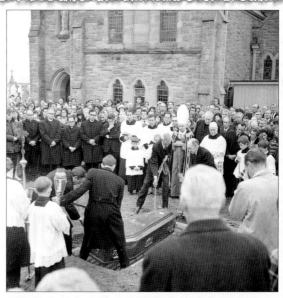

The Bishop of Down and Dromore, Dr Philbin, watches at the graveside at Ballyphilip, along with hundreds of mourners, at the burial of Portaferry-born priest Rev. Fr. Hugh Mullan, who was killed in August 1971 during a gun battle in Belfast. 244-81-2

He was educated at Ballyphilip Primary School, after which he went to sea for a year. He then resumed his studies at St Mary's College, Belfast, and afterwards at St Malachy's College. He entered Queen's University, obtaining a BA degree, and was ordained to the priesthood at Maynooth College in 1959.

Survived by his parents, two brothers and a sister, Fr Mullan was buried at Ballyphilip cemetery on 12 August, following Requiem Mass at Corpus Christi Church, Ballymurphy, and St Patrick's, Ballyphilip.

Electricity Board worker Harry Beggs (23), who died in a bomb explosion in Belfast on 25 August, had strong family ties to Ballywalter, where he was buried the following week. Although he had lived in Belfast all his life, his father, also Harry, was born and raised at Well Road and had worked as a blacksmith there for many years before moving to the city. Mr Beggs was also survived by an uncle, John Beggs, of Greyabbey Road, and an aunt, Mrs Samuel Dunbar, of Main Street, Ballywalter.

Bombers targeted the police stations at Comber, Dundonald and Saintfield within the space of a week in mid-September. A number of officers and a civilian were injured and damage was caused in the three blasts.

Newtownards made history on 24 September when the 500th Abbeyfield House in the British Isles was officially opened in the town by Sir Robin Kinahan, Abbeyfield's Northern Ireland regional president. The £8,000 building, located at Greenwell Street, provided accommodation for seven people and a housekeeper. It was named the Dr Edmund Quiery Memorial Abbeyfield House after the founder member of Newtownards Lions Club and an enthusiastic supporter of Abbeyfield.

The Town 'n' Country Inn at Regent Street, Newtownards, opened its doors to the public from the end of September. Its programme of entertainment included cabaret and C&W music on three nights in the Scrabo Lounge and the Harteford Bar and Buttery, while for young patrons there was a Saturday night T 'n' C Disco Club with DJ Big T.

Addressing a 'Loyalist Solidarity Demonstration' in Conway Square, Newtownards, on 1 October, the Rev. Ian Paisley, Protestant Unionist MP for Bannside, urged Protestants throughout Northern Ireland to follow the lead of their East Belfast counterparts and barricade their own areas, "closing them off against gunmen." He also urged his followers to boycott goods from the Republic of Ireland, including butter and sugar, and to refuse to handle Irish coinage, which he branded "foreign money".

The Croagh Patrick Hotel at Millisle Road, Donaghadee, fell victim to an economic downturn within the tourism industry, caused by the ongoing Troubles. It closed its doors in the autumn after operating with limited success for around two years. The hotel reopened under new management the following April (1972) and by late 1974 was operating as the Old Forge Hotel.

North Down Rural District Council voted against a proposal in early November to replace the Strangford Lough ferry service with a bridge or barrage as a 'more sound long term investment'. Instead, the members decided to endorse Down County Council's request for a second vessel to provide a more regular and reliable service.

The former Rockview Motors premises in Donaghadee were extensively damaged by a bomb on 7 December. No one was injured by the blast which was aggravated by a fire involving five old cars which had been sprinkled with petrol or paint thinner.

The Old Cross, one of the most outstanding monuments in Newtownards, was presented to the local Borough Council by Lady Mairi Bury as a gift. Under the terms of the accompanying covenant the authority was not allowed to move the cross without the permission of Lady Bury or her heirs.

Unionist Sam Moore was elected in early December by the voters of Victoria Ward to fill a vacancy on Newtownards Borough Council, occasioned by the resignation of former Mayor Norman Francis. He defeated Labour candidate Jack Sharkey by 644 votes to 123 in a by-election.

Conlig was proposed as the ideal location for a new hospital to cover the major towns of Bangor and Newtownards, as well as the surrounding area. The suggestion was made at a meeting of the North Down Hospital Management Committee in mid-December and gained considerable support, given the ready availability of land.

On 29 December 31-year-old Norwegian pilot Torolf Sogn became the first person to fly a glider for over five hours over Scrabo Hill in Newtownards. His flight, lasting five hours and 16 minutes to be precise, was achieved in a Skylark 3B glider dating from 1958, despite repeated warnings that it would not be possible because of the area's difficult topography. The pilot was a post-graduate student at Queen's University and chairman of the University's Gliding Club.

Mr and Mrs Thomas Byers, of Kearney Road, Portaferry, celebrated their golden wedding anniversary on 5 January 1971. The couple, who were married by Fr. John McAleese at St Patrick's Church, Ballygalget, had one daughter, seven sons and 33 grandchildren. 236-10-3

Mrs V. Dynes, who presented the awards at the Kircubbin, Portaferry and District Ploughing Society's annual prize distribution, in the New Locarno Ballroom, Portaferry, is pictured in February 1971 with cup winners and officials. Included are: T. McKeating, C. McGrattan, W. Hunter, W. Johnston, treasurer, J. Smyth, chairman, H. Brice, vice-chairman, J. Crawford, secretary, H. McNally, B. McNally and G. Gilmore, committee members., 237-12-1

The first three policewomen in Newtownards took up duties in late January 1971. From left: W/C Josephine Haire, Sgt. Muriel Price and W/C Jacqueline Patterson. 236-91-1

Pupils of St. Finian's Primary School, Newtownards, pictured at their first annual party in January 1971. It was organised by the parent-teachers association and held in the assembly hall. 236-49-1

Two foundation members of Donaghadee Women's LOL 57, Mrs Alice Keith (left), Worshipful Mistress, and Mrs Rebecca Bunting, cut the Lodge's 50th anniversary cake at a celebration in the Copelands Hotel in March 1971. 238-1-2

The Millisle Players staged The Kidnappers in February 1971. Back (from left): Sinclair Garland, Thomas Waugh, John Keenan, Charles Garland (playwright). Front: Wendy McCutcheon, Grace Seymour, Martha Adams and Helen McKeag. 237-29-3

Robins from First Comber Presbyterian Church are pictured at their annual display in the church hall in March 1971. 238-14-2

Ulster athlete Mary Peters (a year away from winning Gold at the Munich Olympics) is joined in March 1971 by young models who took part in a 'Tots to Teens' fashion show in the Queen's Hall, Newtownards. The fashions were presented by Rosemary's of John Street, in the town. 238-32-1

Seventeen-month-old Brian McConnell, son of Mr and Mrs Hugh McConnell, of Hogstown Road, Donaghadee, won a giant Easter egg in a ballot held in aid of mentally handicapped children in April 1971. 239-43-3

Members of Portavogie Junior Christian Endeavour pictured with their minister,
the Rev. T. A. Houston, in May 1971. 240-37-1

The Worshipful
Master, officers
and members of
Loughries True Blues
LOL 1948 pictured
on 12 July 1971.
243-71-2

Mrs Ross, wife of Movilla Secondary School headmaster Mr G. R. Ross, presented the awards on the final night of the Newtownards Irish Dancing Festival, which was held in the school at the end of July in 1971. She is pictured with the prizewinning dancers, along with adjudicator Miss Irene McCann, accompanist Miss M. Griffin and some of the dancing teachers. 243-37-1

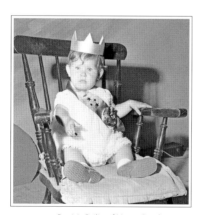

Patricia Bailie, of Manse Road, Carrowdore, won the one to two years section of the Ulster '71 bonny baby contest at Greyabbey in August 1971. 244-95-1

Lord Dunleath prepares to set off on a commemorative lap of the Ards Tourist Trophy Race circuit in September 1971 at the opening of the Dundonald TT memorial by Lord Grey, Governor of Northern Ireland. 246-22-2

Ballygowan Pigeon Club members with trophies at their annual dinner in the Town 'N' Country, Newtownards, in November 1971. 248-14-2

Pupils of Moneyrea PS who took part in the school's Christmas concert in December 1971. 248-89-2

Members of Newtownards Gateway Club with officials from the local Lions Club, who organised a Christmas party at the Mill Street recreation hall in December 1971. 249-28-1

Norman McBriar, Ronald Mottram and Jim Baxter, all members of the St Mary's (Comber) Venture Scouts, with the County Down Challenge Shield which they won in December 1971. 249-51-2

Members of the Killaughey Mission Hall Sunday School choir sing carols during their Christmas party in December 1971. 248-87-2

1971

Sport in the Chronicle

A̳rds British Legion darts player Ron Drain achieved a 13 darts finish in a match against Killain. After 11 darts he needed 18 but had the misfortune to hit a double one, leaving him needing 16. This he achieved with his 13th dart. Had he managed the feat in 12 it would have been an all-time record for the Vintners League.

Ards Rugby Club launched an appeal to raise £30,000 in mid-January towards the development of three full-sized pitches and a new pavilion on a nine-acre site at Comber Road – a project which, it was stated, would over-shadow any previous effort by the club or, indeed, by any other sporting body within the borough. In May it was agreed unanimously the new ground would be named Hamilton Park after hard-working chairman John Hamilton.

Ards Rugby Club chairman John P. Hamilton cuts the first sod for the new pavilion on the Comber Road in early January 1971 as (from left) Archie Moore (IIIA XV captain), Dennis S. Nash (treasurer of the fundraising committee), Bert Jordan, Sam Orme (club secretary), Wilson Moore and Davy Heron (club coach) look on. 236-23-3

Fourteen-year-old Margaret Dorrian brought honour to Newtownards when she won the girls' title at the Irish Open Table Tennis Championships at Balmoral on 16 January. She became the first Newtownards girl to win an Irish Open title since Margaret Finlay in the 1962-63 season. By March she was playing on the Ulster senior team. Her coach was Movilla High School teacher Clifford Thompson.

The first round of the Irish Cup on 13 February featured matches involving two sides from Newtownards – Ards FC and Ards Rangers, the latter having qualified for the competition with an earlier victory over Banbridge Town. However, both sides were defeated, the seniors by Chimney Corner (2-0) and the Amateur League side by Glenavon (6-0).

History was made when Ards RFC met North in the first round of the Senior Cup on 6 March. With 13 Senior clubs in Ulster rugby it had been decided to invite three Junior sides, among them Ards, to make up the 16 needed for the draw. It was also the first occasion a leading Irish Senior club had visited Newtownards with a full-strength side (any previous encounters had been, for the most part, pre-season friendlies). For the record Ards lost the encounter 36-3.

Ards II won the Intermediate Cup after defeating Chimney Corner (the same side that had defeated their senior counterparts in the Irish Cup earlier in the year) in a replay at Cliftonville on 13 April. The first game had ended 1-1 but three goals in the final 10 minutes of extra time in the replay gave Ards II a 4-1 victory.

Ards Rangers II won the Amateur League's Cochrane Corry Cup on 12 May with a 3-2 victory over Queen's University II at Cliftonville. Goalscorers were Bobby Murphy, Junior Taggart and Bill Taggart.

Donaghadee cricketers travelled to Downpatrick on 22 May and notched up a victory in their very first match in the NCU Junior Cup, defeating the home side by 41 runs.

Ballydrain Harrier Armour McAleer took part in August's rain-swept Northern Ireland Marathon along the streets of Belfast, which attracted just nine runners. He completed the 26 miles and 385 yards in 2 hours and 43 minutes, some three minutes faster than the previous year.

The mid-August opening of the 1971-72 Irish League season, including the B Division, was temporarily postponed because of the deteriorating security situation in Belfast and Londonderry. By the following week Ulster Cup fixtures were going ahead outside Belfast – which commenced with a 3-2 home defeat for Ards at the hands of Linfield.

Marilyn Dawson from Greyabbey, riding Clare Cottage, was a member of the Irish team that won the European Junior Team Showjumping Championship at Hickstead on 14 August. Ireland, in their first-ever win, defeated Germany in a jump-off after both teams finished with eight faults.

North Down cricketers secured the Senior League Section II title on 14 August with a 71-run victory over Holywood at Comber. They completed their season the following week with a tenth win out of 10 games.

Ards FC were beaten 1-0 by Ballymena United in the City Cup final at the Oval on 4 December. The team had been plagued by injuries in the run-up to the match – their first-ever appearance in the final of the competition.

Members of the First Donaghadee Boys' Brigade volleyball team, winners of the Northern Ireland Cup in late February 1971. From left: Harold Moore, Charles Neill, Trevor Murphy, Michael Miskimmin and Drew Taylor. 237-63-1

Ballywalter United, winners of the Conlig Winter League in early March 1971. Back (from left): L. Dorrian, G. Davidson, S. Beattie, W. Beattie (manager), J. Eccles, D. Donnan, J. Flannagan (trainer). Front: R. McCready, J. Gunning, N. Donnan, H. Simpson (captain), C. McConnell, A. Cromie and I. Gunning. 237-94-3

Portaferry Minor hurlers played Ballycran in a challenge match during Portaferry Carnival Week in June 1971. 242-16-1

Trophy winners from Ards Swimming Club's annual gala, held in June 1971. Back (from left): Michael Copeland, Pamela Foster, Paul Lampe, Patricia Belford, Tara Watts. Front: Karen Clements, Barbara Forsythe, Ashley Morrison and Stephen Gunning. 241-69-3

Young soccer players from Comber Primary School won the North Down Primary Schools League in June 1971. Back (from left): Brian Patton, Jim Wilson, Rodney Jess, David McVeigh, Morrow Horner, Samuel Jamison, Stephen Russell, Desmond Savage. Seated: Stephen Barry, Gary McKibben, Mr J. W. Sandford (coach), Gary Savage (captain), Alastair Moles, Philip Maxwell, Robin Haire. Front: Stephen Potter and Christopher Tompsett. 242-89-1

Londonderry Primary School swimmers won the Festival '71 Perpetual Challenge Cup at Newtownards Swimming Pool in June 1971. 241-90-3

Members of Ards Amateur Swimming Club had reason to celebrate in September 1971 when they recorded their first win as a team, defeating Bangor by 412-408 points. Girls – R. Moore, P. Belford, S. Catney, D. Ennis, D. Kirk, D. Maxwell, K. McBride, K. McKnight, K. Clements, S. Boyd, H. Gunning, M. Groves, E. Groves, C. Groves, J. Montgomery, W. Ambrose, S. Whitla, S. McNickell, E. Monan. Boys – P. Lampe, T. McClung, D. Bellerby, S. Gunning, A. Catney, M. Copeland, B. Montgomery, A. Forsythe, T. Morrison, A. Morrison, L. Kirk, I. Hall, R. Ennis, D. Boyd, G. Clements and T. Graham. 246-77-1

Members of the newly-formed Comber Boys FC listen intently in November 1971 as secretary Jim Sandford outlines tactics for their next match. Included is team manager Clarence Hiles. 247-72-2

Louis Dempster, president of the newly-formed Comber Boys FC, presents Alastair Moles with the trophy for winning a penalty kick competition in November 1971. Included are (from left): William Strain, third, Philip Maxwell, second, and Robert Shanks, fourth. 247-95-3

Brian McDonald

remembers ... Industry

By the mid-1960s competition from cheap foreign imports was impacting adversely in Newtownards, as well as elsewhere in Northern Ireland, with factories receiving fewer orders for their goods. Many responded by cutting their workforces but very soon factory closures became the order of the day; as the new decade dawned Newtownards had an unemployment rate of 6.5%.

The outbreak of the Troubles, the abolition of the Northern Ireland Government at Stormont and the political instability these events caused, also contributed to the problems faced by factory owners during the 1970s.

As early as January 1970, Short Bros. and Harland announced that 64 men out of a total local workforce of 400 were to lose their jobs. The company stated this was due to a slowdown in sales of their Skyvan aircraft due to the credit squeeze in the United States and the depressed state of the international air market.

As the year went on, Shorts was facing the possibility of losing more workers – indeed the very future of the factory itself was in doubt. By September the company had announced that no aircraft were being built in Newtownards. Members of the workforce were kept employed on other projects, the most important being the manufacture of the Shortland armoured car, which was based on a Land Rover chassis. They announced that 100 had been sold for

Brian McDonald was born in Dublin but returned to his father's native Newtownards while Brian was still an infant and he has lived there ever since.

In parallel with his career in primary school education, Brian has always had a keen interest in local history and has been a member of Ards Historical Society since it was founded in 1967. He has held various offices in the society and has been involved in the publication of many leaflets and booklets on local history as well as being a well known speaker on various historical subjects.

Retirement has allowed Brian to continue to pursue his many interests – something he hopes to be able to do for many years to come.

export, with Thailand being a major customer. Production, however, was slow and the company looked at other ideas to keep the factory operating.

Northern Ireland Carpets survived by merging with the Belfast Ropeworks Co., while the Ulster Print Works was taken over by a Lurgan company. Closures continued. In 1972 Associated Portland Cement Manufacturers decided to close the Irish Roads (Belfast) Ltd. quarry at the North Road in the town. They said the facility had been operating at a severe loss for some time and would close at the end of January with the loss of 98 jobs.

In April, Walkers Mill announced it was closing due to increasing unprofitability in flax spinning. It had been in the town since 1864 but would close by the beginning of July with the loss of 120 jobs.

However, all was not gloom and doom as far as jobs were concerned. Back in February 1970, Berkshire International (UK) Ltd., which manufactured ladies' hosiery and knitwear at their factory on the Donaghadee Road, announced a major expansion plan. They hoped to create 300 new jobs over the next year at their factories in Newtownards and Dundonald and to take over an empty factory at Comber Road in Newtownards.

Ulster Print Works

In 1972 the Ulster Print Works advertised for male workers due to a further expansion of their business and in that same year a Lisburn firm, Franklin Transport, took over an old factory on the Crawfordsburn Road with the promise it would create 50 new jobs.

However, in truth any hope of a jobs resurgence in the town would be short-lived. No new employees came forward, indeed companies such as Crepe Weavers, Ards Swiss Embroidery Works, Kayber Carpets Ltd. and Walker Caledon (tweed manufacturers) began to lay off workers.

In May 1976 the town was shocked by the announcement that Black and Co. (Newtownards) Ltd., which made men's socks under the name of Blaxnit, was in difficulties. Receivers were appointed and the future looked bleak for the company, which employed 300 people. In June it was announced the firm was integrating with Berkshire International (UK) Ltd. and that all the workers would be transferring to that company's Donaghadee Road factory. Some Black and Co. workers took strike action against this decision but the move went ahead and the names of Black and Co. and Blaxnit disappeared from the Newtownards industrial scene.

For many years Black's had advertised their products on the front page of the Newtownards Chronicle. When the company ceased to trade the advert was replaced by one for the Troubles-related confidential telephone line. A sure sign of the times!

As early as January 1972 the local authority had re-formed its Development Council, a body originally established in the 1960s

Blaxnit Management Team

with the aim of persuading companies to invest in Newtownards. They invited Northern Ireland Commerce Minister Robin Bailie to the town to discuss the problem. He made promises to do what he could but no positive decisions were made. Eventually a scheme was set up to build advance factories which would be ready for possible occupants.

These were usually grouped together in industrial estates and certainly succeeded in bringing new industries into the town. However, the factories were quite small, employed limited numbers and did little to solve the problem of unemployment in Newtownards.

The final two years of the 1970s saw a period of growth for V.F. Corporation, formerly Berkshire International, at their factories in Newtownards and Dundonald. In 1978 they employed 1,300 people and advertised vacancies for young school leavers. Further expansion took place in 1979. In August that year the company announced they were creating between 70 and 100 new jobs because of a growing demand for their products. That same year L. E. Pritchett and Co. Ltd., which employed 176 workers making milk and ice cream products, announced they were increasing production and needed 55 more employees.

The 1970s would, however, be remembered as a decade when the traditional manufacturing industries were gradually replaced by service industries. On 6 May 1976, the Ards Shopping Centre opened to the west of the town. It would eventually employ several hundred people who, in another time, would probably have worked in a factory. As the decade went on, the town saw building societies, solicitors and other businesses opening offices in the town. Many replaced long-established shops, bringing complaints from the Council, which was concerned about the impact this would have on the economic life of the town. In truth these changes would irrevocably alter the character of the town and lead to a time when Newtownards as a major industrial town was just a memory.

Mervyn Jess

remembers ... Growing up in Comber

Mervyn Jess, a BBC Senior Broadcast Journalist and published author (*The Orange Order*, O'Brien Press, 2007), was born in Comber in 1958 and attended Comber Primary School, Comber Secondary Intermediate School and Bangor Technical College.

He commenced his career in journalism with the *Newtownards Chronicle* in 1977. Three years later he joined Downtown Radio as a news reporter before moving to the BBC in 1988.

He is married to Lynn and they have two daughters. Mervyn's outside interests include music (playing and listening), soccer (mostly watching these days), reading and hillwalking.

Growing up in Comber during the Seventies, life was a world away from what was happening a matter of a few miles down the road in Belfast. For the most part the Troubles had little impact on the quiet market town. There were casualties of the violence, mostly families who lost loved ones serving in the security forces. There were a few incidents of a sectarian nature and a republican bomb exploded outside the town's RUC station but damage was minimal and there were no serious injuries.

The scale of death and destruction suffered elsewhere in Northern Ireland at that time was beyond most young people's comprehension, apart from what they read, heard or watched on the various news media.

As a young teenager I was more interested in what was happening in music than politics. Apart from school books, comics and the odd novel, my weekly 'must reads' were the New Musical Express and Melody Maker. At the age of 13-14 the music charts were of huge importance and I can still remember sprinting home from school at lunchtime every Tuesday in time to catch the latest Radio One chart rundown.

Like many teenagers at that time, I suppose music was one way of escaping the constant dread of everything else that was happening around us in Northern Ireland. While life in Comber was relatively normal, we knew that, taken in the wider context of where we lived and were growing up, it wasn't.

For a teenage music fan the fact that things were not normal was slammed home every time I read the back pages of the music press. Scanning the tour listings for top pop and rock groups of the time, none of them featured Belfast or anywhere else in the Province for that matter. A number of dance bands played the local hotels circuit, doing their best at churning out a cornucopia of covers, but we were starved of original live music.

In some perverse way this probably steered me and a few friends towards getting our own 'band' together. "Ladies and gentlemen, please welcome on stage… Copper Cactus!"

Only in the Seventies could anyone conjure up a name like that for a musical combo. Forty years later I can openly admit it came out of the deep recesses

Copper Cactus provided the music at a 10-hour sponsored disco for St Mark's Parish Church, Newtownards, in February 1976. From left: Michael Coey, Robert Watterson, Mervyn Jess and Leslie Savage. 84-20-126

of a T. Rex/ Marc Bolan-obsessed mind and I can safely say I was probably the only member of the band who liked it.

Prior to those heady teenage years 'on the road' playing gigs in dodgy pubs, church halls and Blue Lamp discos, there were other distractions. Procuring what was left of the lead flashing on the old railway station roof to use as weights for fishing in the Enler River was an early introduction to the town's rich history. The railway had ceased operations more than 20 years earlier but some of the old buildings, along with evidence of the tracks, still existed. We only had to ask our parents about 'the trains' to get the story in full technicolour detail. In retrospect I have wondered at times if the retention of the railway would have engendered amongst townsfolk a feeling of more connectivity to cities, towns and communities elsewhere. At that time I felt Comber was a place apart.

For a young person with aspirations to slip the confines of Comber and travel further afield, I need have looked no further than the monument dominating the town's Georgian square. On top of it stands a statue of General Sir Robert Rollo Gillespie, an officer in the British Army during the days of the Empire, who was killed fighting in Nepal. His dying words as he lay wounded are reputed to have

1st Comber Scouts, winners of the North Down Scout Football League in November 1973. Back (from left): K. Savage (coach), R. McQuiston (trainer), M. Coey, G. Smith, M. Jess, K. McQuiston, R. McElroy (official), G. Cowan. Front: B. McMillin, B. Quinn, R. Brown (captain), C. Montgomery and M. Heath. 268-66-1

1st Comber Scouts with Chief Scout's Awards which they received from District Commissioner Mr S. Watson in July 1972. From left: Patrol Leaders Mervyn Jess, Gary Smith, Michael Heath and Robert McQuiston. 257-30-1

been: "One shot more for the honour of Down." On the sides of the column are engraved the then (to me) unfamiliar names of battles he fought in far-off lands. What more does a boy need to fire his imagination?

I didn't need to enlist to get on the road. I joined a youth organisation instead. Growing through the ranks of the Cubs, Scouts and Venture Scouts presented opportunities for a range of Boys' Own-type adventures. Camping expeditions at home and overseas included travelling by boat, rail and bus to the bright lights of London, southern England and Switzerland. This was the stuff of legend for boys of our age and some of the stories are still recalled today when two or more of us get together, usually in McBrides pub in the Square.

Comber has grown considerably over the years, more in terms of housing than commerce. Unfortunately it has lost its established manufacturing industries along with many of its family-owned shops and businesses, while still managing to maintain its identity.

Its ancient name 'Comar' roughly translates as 'the meeting place of the waters'. Sited at the confluence of the Enler and Glen Rivers, the town has long been the beating heart of the famous Comber potato-growing industry. Over the decades the local community has become more multi-racial and pluralist but you've only got to scratch a Comber person to see where they're from. I proudly count myself as one of them.

Billy Humphries

remembers ... Ards Football Club

The Seventies proved to be the most successful period in the history of Ards FC. The club, under the guidance of an excellent board of directors, was on a sound financial footing and enjoyed the backing, both vocal and practical, of a number of flourishing supporters' clubs. On the field of play the 1st XI appeared in 10 major finals and finished second in the Irish League behind Crusaders in the 1972/73 campaign, a feat surpassed only by the championship success of 1957/58. Of those 10 finals, five ended in victory. The Reserves won the Intermediate Cup and were beaten finalists in the Steele and Sons Cup.

After being appointed player/ manager in March 1970 – my third spell as a player with Ards – my attention turned towards overcoming Chimney Corner in a County Antrim Shield first round replay. This task was eventually completed with a 2-1 win, setting in motion progress in the cup that led to the final and an encounter with old rivals Bangor. After a marathon series of games at Solitude we eventually lost 3-2 in a third replay. Although my first final as a manager ended in disappointment, at the end of the season I was named Ulster Footballer of the Year and the North End Ards Supporters' Club's Player of the Year.

During the close season my thoughts were already concentrated on the approaching 1970-71 campaign. Former manager George Eastham had left a strong nucleus of

Billy Humphries, whose name is synonymous with Ards FC, was born in Donegall Avenue, Belfast, in the shadow of Windsor Park. Thus his early allegiance was to local team Linfield.

He was the fourth son of James and Margaret Humphries, a younger sister completing the family – Alex, Samuel, Ronald, Billy and Beth.

Due to their parents' influence they participated in all the usual activities at St Simon's Church of Ireland, being regular attenders at Sunday School and at church services. Billy and Ronald were also members of the Church Lads' Brigade, with Billy attaining the rank of sergeant.

He attended St Simon's Public Elementary School, moving on to Fane Street Primary School (off the Lisburn Road). After passing the Qualifying Examination he was accepted into Annadale Grammar School. There he participated in most school activities and was, in time, a member of both the 1st XV rugby and 1st XI cricket teams.

After Junior Certificate he left school, his first job in a varied career being in the purchasing office of the Belfast Corporation Transport Department. Simultaneously he attended further education classes at Belfast College of Technology, completing a course with the British Institute of Management and obtaining a certificate in Personnel Management.

During Billy's move to Leeds United, he married childhood sweetheart June and they had two children, Julie and Martin. The couple now have five grandchildren – Victoria, Charlotte, Garin, Robbie and Lucy.

After returning from a professional career in English football, Billy joined Black & Co. (Blaxnit socks) as a personnel officer and enjoyed eight happy years there. After the company went into liquidation and was taken over by Berkshire International he was offered and accepted the position of manager of their wages department.

A year further on, Billy purchased a newsagent/ confectionery at Old Cross (junction of Greenwell Street and Castle Street) in Newtownards. He continued that successful and enjoyable occupation for another decade before selling the business.

He took up employment for the next nine years as a residential child care assistant at the Rathgael Training Centre, eventually retiring in 2000.

Billy and June now live in Bangor where he enjoys swimming and walking. He also meets up on a regular, albeit informal basis with old friends in Newtownards.

experienced players and my intention was to build upon that base. Billy Nixon, Billy McAvoy, Billy Stewart, Don Johnston, David McCoy and Barry Brown were all talented and had excellent playing records for the club. There were others who had given good service but I felt they would need to be replaced in the near future and the decision was taken to release them.

The team building started with Tom Coburn, from Lisburn, a young goalkeeper with potential. This was followed quickly by the signing of Syd Patterson from Glentoran, who although comfortable in either full-back position, also had experience as a centre-forward and performed effectively in midfield. Meanwhile, Billy Stewart declared his intention to leave the club, which was very disappointing news as I rated him an important member of the squad.

After a 4-1 home defeat against Shamrock Rovers in the Texaco Cup we achieved an excellent 3-2 win in Dublin but lost out on the aggregate score. The rest of the season proved largely uneventful apart from losing to Chimney Corner in the first round of the Irish Cup. I did, however, gain another player with Ray Mowat returning to the club after a spell with Distillery. He would give another 12 years' service and his 673 appearances for Ards remains a record. The 2nd XI provided us with our first trophy of the Seventies, defeating Chimney Corner 4-1 at Solitude to lift the Intermediate Cup. It was the same Chimney Corner side that had knocked the 1st XI out of the Irish Cup!

The 1971/72 season started promisingly. The team played with flair and the accent was on an attacking style of play. In the City Cup we were victorious in four of our five games, drawing the other one 1-1 with Linfield. We played Ballymena United in the final at the Oval but unfortunately a week before the game I sustained a knee injury and failed a fitness test. To make matters worse, 20 minutes into the final we lost influential central defender Billy Nixon with a similar injury. The defence had to be reorganised and with no substitutes then we played the remaining 70 minutes a man short. Despite being handicapped in this way we deserved something better than a 1-0 defeat.

Our season remained upbeat with another final beckoning. In the Irish Cup semi-final against Coleraine at Windsor Park we were leading 1-0 with seconds to go when a terrible misunderstanding in defence led to an equalising goal. Coleraine won the replay 1-0. Hardly having time to draw breath, successive wins against Ballymena and Glentoran saw us marching on to the final of the County Antrim Shield – a two-leg encounter at home and away against Crusaders. At Castlereagh Park we won handsomely 3-0 but the tables were turned in the second game at Seaview, with the home side's late rally bringing them level on aggregate. The tension was palpable as the match went to a penalty shoot-out. The Ards' penalties were all converted immaculately whilst Crusaders missed one of theirs. We were the new holders of the County Antrim Shield!

In May 1972 we advanced to the final of the Gold Cup following convincing wins against Glentoran and Distillery. Our opponents were Portadown and there was controversy over the choice of venue, with the organising committee in their wisdom deciding Mourneview Park, Lurgan, would be fair for both sides. The game finished in a goalless draw, which meant our supporters had to return a few days later to Lurgan – almost a home game for Portadown – to see us lose 2-1 after extra time.

I was fortunate and privileged to be named Ulster Footballer of the Year for a second time and also the North End Ards Supporters' Club's Player of the Year. There was great optimism as the 1972/73 season dawned with all the early signs being very positive. There was a new competition, the Carlsberg Cup, and resounding victories over Ballymena (6-0) and Bangor (4-1) saw us heading to Windsor Park for the final against our nemesis from the previous season, Portadown. Installed as favourites we did not live up to the billing, losing the game 3-0.

David Graham had come through from the Reserves and was showing considerable promise. Then in September we made two noteworthy signings – Maxie Patton from Glenavon on a free transfer (I could not believe my luck) and Dennis Guy, also from Glenavon. Maxie was an attacking full-back and Dennis was a prolific goal striker. The anticipation of pairing the latter with Billy McAvoy was mouth-watering. The transfer activity continued into December when goalkeeper Dennis Matthews joined us from Carrick Rangers. Also joining the first team squad was Killinchy 17-year-old Ronnie Cromie, elevated from the Reserves. He was an outstanding prospect and later justified the faith I'd placed in him. Our form was excellent throughout the season with just one point separating us in the end from League champions Crusaders. Finishing as runners-up – our best effort since winning the competition in 1957/58 – put us into the Europe and the draw for the UEFA Cup.

The following season, 1973/74, was guaranteed to be a special one. Our op-

The Ards FC contingent before leaving for Belgium and their game against Standard Liege in September 1973. 267-41-3

ponents for the club's first ever European competition would be Standard Liege, from Belgium, one of Europe's elite sides with almost a full team of internationals among their ranks. Before then we had added two players to the first team squad, Ronnie McAteer, returning to us from Linfield, and Dessie Cathcart, also from the Blues. We had also played another final – deservedly losing 3-0 to a good Crusaders side in the Carlsberg Cup – but then achieved excellent victories in the Ulster Cup against Linfield and Coleraine. The 6-0 scoreline in the latter game, against the season's eventual League champions, remains one of my favourite memories and proved the perfect preparation for the European tie on 12 September 1973.

That was a red letter day in the history of Ards FC. Castlereagh Park was looking resplendent: The newly built clubhouse and dressing rooms, replacing the old wooden structures which had served so long, were in place and with the green sward immaculate, conditions were perfect for attractive football. I walked onto the pitch an hour before the kick-off, accompanied by club chairman Billy McCully, and I could feel the hairs on the nape of my neck tingling. The terraces were already filling up and there was a buzz of excitement in the air. In the dressing room there was a sense of calm as the players prepared for the game. Like myself they were really up for the task ahead.

Before an 8,000-strong full-house crowd the game started with Standard Liege gaining the upper hand, passing the ball and impressively maintaining possession. Within five minutes they had taken the lead through danger man Josip Bukal and the omens did not look good. Nevertheless we settled in to our fluent attacking style of play and with Cathcart seeing a lot of the ball on the left wing the Belgians began to look increasingly unsure and realised the game was not going to be the walkover they might have anticipated.

An exquisite textbook move involving Mowat, Guy, McAvoy and myself tore the Belgians' defence to shreds and Cathcart provided the coup de grâce with a cracking shot from 20 yards. Five minutes later we were ahead after a penalty, awarded for a foul on Guy, was converted by McAvoy with nonchalant ease. The lead was well-deserved and we continued to harass the visitors' defence. However, shortly before half-time that man Bukal equalised and the game was on a knife edge. After the break the game continued at a great pace and the crowd became increasingly excited, realising an upset was possible. Ten minutes into the second half that optimism because a reality when the Icelandic referee awarded us a second penalty for a foul on Cathcart. This time the responsibility fell to McAteer who was itching to take the kick. Ronnie duly completed the task and Ards were ahead again. Both teams continued to fight for supremacy, with Ards holding firm and recording an historic 3-2 victory. The home fans invaded the pitch at the final whistle to acclaim their heroes and their sensational win.

Following a further Ulster Cup win, 2-1 against Distillery, it was off to Standard Liege for the return fixture. However, our journey from Dublin was interrupted shortly before we reached Brussels when our flight was diverted to London because of engine trouble. After a two-and-a-half-hour delay we safely reached our destination. The game, played in front of 30,000 spectators, proved an anti-climax as far as the result was concerned. The result of the two-leg encounter was still wide open at half-time but as the game entered the final quarter and Standard Liege were in the ascendancy, fatigue began to affect the part-timers' legs. The final result was 6-1 to the home side, with Bukal scoring four of them. The Ards players had done their town proud and the games were an unforgettable experience.

Back home we returned to our winning ways. We won our next two Ulster Cup fixtures, 4-1 against Portadown and then 8-0 against Cliftonville. Don Johnston failed to appear for the game at Solitude and we started with 10 players while Maxie Patton made a dash from the Reserves' game in Newtownards! In between these two games we had also despatched Cliftonville 6-1 in a second round Gold Cup tie. A 2-0 win against Glentoran followed and we were on the verge of winning the Ulster Cup. The necessary point was secured on 13 October when we drew with Crusaders. Players and fans alike were elated at our success.

We were quickly back at the Oval to play a hotly-contested Gold Cup semi-final tie against Glentoran, which finished 1-1 after extra time. It took another penalty shoot-out to settle the game and our players were equal to the challenge with another 100% success rate, the result being 5-4 in Ards' favour.

The all-conquering team of 1973-74. Back row (l-r): Patton, Nixon, Matthews, McCoy, Patterson, Tucker. Front row (l-r): Cromie, Cathcart, McAteer, Humphries, McAvoy, Graham, Mowat

The Oval was also the venue for the final and with an evening kick-off it was played under the floodlights. Old rivals Bangor were our opponents and they complained we had the advantage because we had also played there for the semi-final. What tosh! Billy McAvoy had picked up an injury and missed the game, which was watched by 8,000 fans in a fantastic derby atmosphere. In the first half we had the lion's share of play but the teams were all square, 1-1, at the interval. However, Ards raised their tempo in the second half and completely dominated the remainder of the game, which finished with a resounding 4-1 victory for us. Dennis Guy (2), Ronnie McAteer and Dessie Cathcart were our marksmen. It was our second trophy success inside three weeks.

In tandem with this ongoing period of success for the club, players were gaining representative honours. I was appointed manager of an Irish League XI to play a Canadian XI. David McCoy and Billy McAvoy both played important roles in a 6-4 victory, with the latter scoring two goals. Ray Mowat was selected for the Northern Ireland amateur team, which recorded a 2-0 win over England, and achieved a further cap in a 1-0 victory over Wales. Ronnie Cromie played in all three games of the British Youth Championship, with Northern Ireland winning the competition. Another of our young players, Jackie Warren, appeared as a substitute in one of the games. I received a further managerial appointment with the Irish League playing against the League of Ireland. Ards players David McCoy and Maxie Patton added to their League representative honours.

A celebration dinner and dance in the Town 'n' Country marked the golden jubilee of the club's first appearance in senior football back in 1923.

Our form in the Irish League was, to say the least, disappointing. Meanwhile, at the beginning of the New Year (1974) we were drawn against junior side Ballyclare Comrades in the first round of the Irish Cup. They were enjoying a successful season and I knew they would present a big challenge on their own patch. Due to heavy rain before and during the game we faced the Comrades on a mud heap of a pitch and the game quickly developed into a test of stamina, with the most-motivated team being the one likely to win. Trailing by a single goal for most of the match our perseverance paid off and with seconds remaining on the clock I managed to score a rare headed goal to equalise. The replay at Castlereagh Park was much more comfortable, resulting in a 4-2 win for Ards.

We were paired against Bangor in the second round and cup fever was the order of the day in North Down. Before a 4,000-strong attendance at Castlereagh Park, the game very quickly developed into a typical cup tie. Bangor gained the upper hand and led 2-0 at half-time. However, Ards came back with a vengeance after the break. Our attacking football so pressurised the Bangor defence that they folded in the last 25 minutes and we completed a remarkable 4-2 victory.

Glenavon were our opponents in the semi-final and in stark contrast to our poor league form we were on top form. We were quickly two goals to the good, both being scored by Billy McAvoy. Glenavon pulled one back but another two goals by Syd Patterson and Dennis Guy settled the nerves. A final 4-2 scoreline saw us marching on to the final against Ballymena United. Before that match, however, we were involved in the Blaxnit All Ireland Cup, which was sponsored by Newtownards-based hosiery firm Black and Co. Ltd. Our former chairman Harold Black was the company's managing director. Our first opponents were League of Ireland side Finn Harps, from Donegal. We secured a 3-1 victory at Castlereagh Park and then drew away against Drogheda United. Our attention then turned to the Irish Cup final.

On a sunny day in front of a 7,000-strong crowd – the attendance was affected by a bus strike – we took an early lead after a Dennis Guy header proved too good for the Ballymena keeper. We continued to dominate in a mediocre game until the break, only to see Ballymena equalising in the second half with a fluke goal when a crossed ball took an awkward bounce and eluded Ray Mowat defending our goal line. With the outcome of the game now back in the balance, Billy McAvoy calmed Ards nerves. A Ronnie McAteer pass split the opposition defence and Billy scampered away from the half-way line, rounded the goalkeeper and slotted the ball home. Ballymena argued it was offside but the television replay later proved the referee's decision to allow the goal was correct. Great elation followed the final whistle. We

Members of the North End Ards Supporters' Club had reason to celebrate in January 1974 after the club secured the Gold Cup and Ulster Cup in quick succession. 270-3-3

were Irish Cup winners for the second time in five years and there were joyous scenes on the streets of Newtownards when we made our triumphant return to the town.

No sooner had we recovered from our exertions than we were on our way to Drogheda for the next round of the Blaxnit tournament. Once again there was a large partisan crowd for the game, although it was clearly evident that our followers had made the journey south in impressive numbers. We were in complete control during the first half, taking a 3-0 lead and seemingly strolling to an impressive victory. Danny Trainor – later to lose his life in a car accident – was introduced to the proceedings by the home side after the interval and made an immediate impact on the game. With our defence facing a more aggressive approach by Drogheda United, our lead gradually evaporated and by full-time the sides were level. Having regained our composure and with no more goals during extra time, we faced up to another penalty shoot-out. Another 100% strike rate proved too much for Drogheda and we were through to another final.

Our opponents at Windsor Park were Ballymena United, it was our fifth final of a successful season and the players were very relaxed. After Dessie Cathcart put us ahead the result was never in any doubt, with further goals from McAteer and Patterson confirming our domination. It was truly an historic season for Ards FC. Dennis Guy was top scorer with 44 goals, which set a new club record in senior football. Maxie Patton had a magnificent season and was deservedly named Ards Player of the Year. The players and directors paraded through the streets of Newtownards holding aloft the four pieces of silverware and were warmly greeted by the large crowds that lined the route.

The beginning of the 1974/75 season showed all the signs of the trouble that lay ahead. For various reasons I had difficulty re-signing some of the players. In addition, our training preparations were hampered and for some players these proved inadequate for the season ahead. As a result of the re-signing issue, McAteer,

Cathcart and Matthews were not available for selection. Maxie Patton was also unavailable due to his suspension by the Irish Football Association for playing summer football. There were signals that Patton and top scorer Dennis Guy were not happy to continue travelling from Armagh and Portadown respectively and would prefer to play nearer to home. To add to our problems we were paired against PSV Eindhoven, one of the elite teams in Europe at that time, in the European Cup Winners' Cup.

The side I selected to face the Dutch was unrecognisable from the team that played during our four-trophy season and quite frankly was not up to the task. In the away fixture we were thrashed 10-0, although we fared considerably more favourably in the second leg, losing 4-1. By this time Alan Hay had joined the club but his career at Ards was brief, playing only a few games, while Bobby McKenzie arrived from Ballymena as cover for the unsigned Matthews. Results continued to be poor and there was little to be optimistic about in terms of team performances. In November Guy and Patton handed in transfer requests and left shortly afterwards. A team rebuilding programme would be necessary and that would take some time.

The 1975/76 season offered more cause for optimism, although our scoring capabilities were limited. Placing too much reliance on Billy McAvoy's efforts was not a healthy situation for the club. He was still scoring regularly, but losing Guy, McAteer and Cathcart was a massive blow. Incoming players Tommy Ferguson (Carrick) and Alan Larmour (Linfield) plus the return of Don Johnston strengthened the team, while the strike force was enhanced with Tommy Armstrong's arrival. An outstanding performance against League leaders Coleraine saw Ards winning 3-0, a result which pushed them off the top and was a welcome boost for morale.

On the down side, our influential and talented long-serving central defender Billy Nixon was playing less regularly and was close to retirement. His 500 appearances for the club bore testimony to his ability and loyalty to the club. At the end of the season (in which we finished seventh in the Irish League, an

Various Ards FC supporters' clubs made a combined presentation in November 1976 to Billy Nixon, marking his 500th appearance for the club. Included are Mrs E. Russell, chairman of the Special Efforts, T. Duncan, vice-chairman of the Abbey Arms ASC, D. Mateer, chairman of Movilla ASC, H. Owen, chairman of the Fox and Hounds ASC, H. Black, chairman of Hartford ASC, and Billy Alexander, chairman of North End ASC. 48-13-19

Billy Wallace of Ards Tyre Service presents a sponsorship cheque in November 1978 to Ards FC Player of the Month Ray Mowat. Included is club manager and coach Joe Kinkead.
64-4-4

improvement on the previous campaign) I also announced my retirement. My years with the club had been happy and successful. I was comfortable there and had made many friends. I have always referred to Ards as my football home.

A decline in crowd numbers attending games in the 1976/77 season placed new financial constraints on the club. A new social club and dressing rooms were erected at Castlereagh Park, which all added to our expenditure. Activities on the field were suffering the same fate. A new generation of young players were appearing for Ards – Alan Dornan, Tom Kennedy, George Gibson, Steve Allen, Frank Houston, Russell Welsh and Ronnie Mudd, to name a few – and were showing promise.

On the down side, Billy McAvoy put in a transfer request and I was aware the club he intended to join was Ballymena United. Billy had given long service to Ards and his goal-scoring exploits were legendary. He will always be remembered for that amazing record-breaking four-goal feat in the Irish Cup final success of 1970. In the interim period Tommy Armstrong would fill the gap and after a slow start he finished second in the goal-scoring chart for the 1977/78 season.

During the final years of the decade Ards continued to play inconsistently, with many mediocre performances being mixed with excellent displays. Finding a regular striker was proving elusive to the manager of the time. Joe Kinkead had made a gallant effort in that position and later a Billy Nixon/ Alfie Wright partnership was unable to find the key for past successes. With the approach of the 1980s, Ards FC could nevertheless look back with pleasure and reminisce about the most successful period in the club's history.

1972

Making the News in the Chronicle

Ninety-eight workers lost their jobs at the beginning of the New Year with the closure of the Newtownards quarries operated by Irish Roads (Belfast) Ltd. The shock decision was taken by parent company Associated Portland Cement, which revealed the business had been operating at a severe loss level for some considerable time.

Donaghadee Urban District Council agreed on 10 January to introduce a one-way traffic system, encompassing High Street, Bridge Street, Shore Street and New Street. The plan had the approval in principle of the Ministry of Home Affairs, which suggested the introduction of traffic wardens on a seasonal basis would assist the Council with traffic management.

The first lifeboat in the fleet operated by the Royal National Lifeboat Institution to be fitted with an anti-capsize self-righting air bag took up operational duties in Donaghadee on 3 February. The vessel arrived at the local harbour following extensive trials carried out by the RNLI and the British Hovercraft Company.

A shortage of junior medical staff at the Ards and Bangor Hospitals led to a warning from the North Down Hospital Management Committee in early February that a number of services were at risk. Although local GPs stepped in to help maintain services at the two hospitals, an immediate impact of the junior medical staff shortage was the temporary suspension of the casualty department at Bangor.

The new building for Greenwell Street Presbyterian Church, Newtownards, completed at a cost of £95,000, was officially opened by long-standing church member Mrs W. K. McMorran and dedicated by Moderator Rt. Rev. Principal

James Haire on 12 February. There was seating for 800 worshippers, as well as ancillary rooms for the choir and minister (the Rev. T. R. Johnston).

Workmen clear up debris following the bomb explosion at the Tivoli Bar in Donaghadee. 250-40-2

Bombers targeted the Tivoli Bar in Donaghadee, which was owned by former boxing champion Freddie Gilroy. The explosion, on the evening of 27 February, caused extensive damage to the premises. The culprits had left 15-20lb of gelignite outside the bar, with the resulting blast also shattering windows in adjacent buildings. No one was injured and Mr Gilroy promised his bar would be back in business within weeks.

A two-day strike called by Ulster Vanguard on 27 and 28 March, following the (temporary soon to become permanent) suspension of the Stormont Government, met with an almost 100 per cent response from workers in Newtownards, where an estimated 1,500 protesters gathered at Conway Square. Vanguard leader Bill Craig had called for the strike to begin at 10am on the Monday, with the busy shopping centre becoming akin to a 'ghost town' within minutes of that time.

Workers staged mass walk-outs from factories, shutters were pulled down at shops and other businesses and there were reports of Tartan Gangs marching around the centre of Newtownards singing loyalist songs.

The strike was accompanied by six-hour electricity cuts every eight hours which threw domestic life, as well as any remaining industrial activity, into chaos. In addition, there were water shortages in many areas and petrol was in very short supply.

The end of March also saw the formation of the Newtownards branch of the Democratic Unionist Party with Roberts Owens serving as chairman,

Ulster Democratic Unionist Party.
LOYALIST RALLY
in the QUEEN'S HALL, NEWTOWNARDS
on MONDAY 14th FEBRUARY at 7.45 p.m.
Chairman : Mr. Clifford Smyth. Speakers : Dr. IAN PAISLEY, M.P.,
Mr. DESMOND BOAL, M.P.,' and other prominent Loyalists.
ENROLMENT FORMS FOR THE D.U.P. WILL BE AVAILABLE

MINISTRY OF HOME AFFAIRS
Civil Authorities (Special Powers) Act (Northern Ireland) 1922
Notice is hereby given that the Minister of Home Affairs has made a Regulation under the above Act dated 28 January 1972 entitled the Civil Authorities (Special Powers) Acts (Amending) Regulations (Northern Ireland) 1972.
The Regulation relates to the powers of inspectors appointed under Section 53 of the Explosives Act 1875 and enables an inspector to search any person or any place or premises for explosives or explosive substances unlawfully held in contravention of the Explosives Acts (Northern Ireland) 1875 to 1970 whether or not he has reasonable cause to suspect that an offence has been or is being committed under the said Acts.
Copies of the Regulation will be available shortly.

Irene Brown as secretary, Ian McDonald as treasurer, and the Rev. Ian Paisley as president.

It was announced in early April that 120 workers would be made redundant with the impending closure of the long-established Newtownards firm of George Walker and Co. The Castle Gardens Mill-based firm, which dated back to 1864, was going into voluntary liquidation due to the "accelerating unprofitability in flax spinning," stated the company.

Some 3,000 Orangemen defied a ban on parades by marching through Newtownards on 22 April and then gathering for a 'Mini-Twelfth' demonstration in Londonderry Park. The aim of the event, according to the local (No 4) District of the Orange Order, was to show their numerical strength in the area. Police took the names of a number of participants.

Hopes were high for the boat-building industry in Portavogie, with the launch of a new £30,000 fishing boat, constructed by the local Shipbuilding Yard. The 25ft vessel was built for Ardglass fisherman Frank Zych and was named Polonia by his nine-year-old daughter Christine.

There was an OBE in the Queen's Birthday Honours List for Newtownards man Will S. Edgar in acknowledgement of his services to the Boys' Brigade movement over more than 50 years. A founder member of 1st Newtownards Company, the Gransha resident was also well known as one of the proprietors of Edgar's shop at High Street in the town.

The Ulster Defence Association staged a 'show of strength' over the weekend of 9-11 June by erecting barricades to create 'no-go areas' in Newtownards, Conlig, Comber, Greyabbey, Portavogie, Ballywalter, Millisle, Carrowdore and Donaghadee. A number of men guarded a checkpoint on the Newtownards to Comber carriageway on the Saturday night, while for a time Millisle was completely ringed by checkpoints, with long queues of traffic building up at a number of locations.

There was a similar episode at three Donaghadee housing estates in early July, with the Chronicle's local correspondent noting: "The residents co-operated fully with the UDA without incident. 'A' Company would also like to thank the many ladies who provided tea during this 48-hour period."

Two new tenants associations were formed for residents in major Newtownards housing developments – Glen Estate, chaired by Mr Jack Sharkey, and West Winds, chaired by Mr J. McClelland.

After months of indecision it was agreed by Newtownards Borough Council on 3 July that traffic wardens should be introduced in the town "without delay." It was hoped the cost would come from Central Government sources as the wardens were being employed for security reasons.

Jacqueline McKee, from Abbey Gardens in Millisle, received a Certificate of Merit from the Down County Education Committee in early July to mark her seven years of unbroken attendance at Millisle Primary School.

Although there were no immediately local victims of the Bloody Friday bomb blasts in Belfast on 21 July, around 750 workers from a number of Newtownards factories gathered for an impromptu memorial service in the Queen's Hall the following Wednesday. Clergymen representing the town's Anglican, Methodist, Presbyterian and Catholic churches, conducted the service, their key message being: "Return not evil for evil." A wreath in memory of the victims was laid at the Newtownards cenotaph.

The Queen's Award for Industry was presented to Donaghadee Carpets Ltd. on 18 August by the Governor of Northern Ireland, Lord Grey of Naunton. It was received by managing director Mr R. T. Halliwell, with Mr J. A. Lewando, chairman of owners the Carrington Viyella Group, also in attendance.

Security forces in Donaghadee in the aftermath of the explosion at St Comgall's 73/2a-57

St Comgall's Roman Catholic Church in Donaghadee was targeted for a no-warning bomb attack on 25 August. Six people, five women and a man, were taken to hospital for treatment. The women were suffering mainly from shock but the man, who was out walking his dog, received severe facial cuts. His pet was killed. Extensive damage was caused to the church, with the vestry demolished and a number of doors and stained-glass windows shattered and broken.

Parish Priest Fr Seamus Clenaghan was full of praise for the work of the RUC, Army and Fire Brigade in the aftermath of the explosion. He said there was no question of animosity or recrimination against the perpetrators as that would be contrary to their Christian teaching.

The traditional annual harvest fair at Conway Square in Newtownards, scheduled for 23 September, was cancelled by the Borough Council on security grounds (the venue being located within the police-imposed Control Zone). There was no fair the following year.

North Down Rural District Council and Newtownards Borough Council formally handed over control of housing functions to the newly-created Northern Ireland Housing Executive at the beginning of October.

Terrorists targeted the home of Ards Parish Priest Fr Robert Murphy on the night of 12 October. Windows and doors in the North Street property were damaged but no one was injured. Eight local Protestant clergymen condemned the attack as a "senseless and callous deed, which could have no other purpose but to stir up bitterness among members of a community which has prided itself on its good relationships."

Retired former British and European bantamweight boxing champion Freddie Gilroy, then aged 36, announced the sale of the Tivoli Bar in Donaghadee at the end of October, and his intention to emigrate to Australia.

"I must think of my family," he said. "All I want for them is the chance to grow up in peace and to become good citizens. Frankly, I see no future for them here and that's why we've decided to pack up and go."

The new owner of the Tivoli Bar was Freddie's brother-in-law Jack Banford, who played football for Ballyclare Comrades.

Clergymen from the Presbyterian, Anglican, Methodist and Roman Catholic churches in Newtownards took part in a service on 28 October to unveil and dedicate a new recreation hall for the town's Royal British Legion branch. The £11,000 building, located behind the RBL headquarters in Court Square, was named the Blair Mayne Memorial Hall, after the late Newtownards war hero. A commemorative plaque was unveiled by his sister, Mrs Frances Elliott.

A new confidential telephone line, with the number Newtownards 4567, was installed in the local police station to allow members of the public to provide, in confidence, information about murders, explosions and other serious terrorist-related crimes in the area. Messages were automatically recorded and no questions were asked.

The Government also offered, in tandem with similar services being introduced around Northern Ireland, a reward of £50,000 for information leading to the arrest and conviction of people responsible for murders and explosions.

The Alliance Party formed a Newtownards branch at a meeting in the Town Hall on 14 November. The party already had branches covering Donaghadee, Millisle, Kircubbin and Portaferry.

Retired nurse Miss Margaret McBurney, a native of Hill Road, Comber, celebrated her 100th birthday at the Hampton Park Nursing Home in Belfast on 20 November. Two nieces, Helen and Evelyn McBurney, still resided in the family home at Comber.

A group of hot-air balloonists from the Dublin and Belfast Ballooning Clubs created history on 26 November by completing the first balloon crossing of Strangford Lough, their journey having commenced from the Demesne in Saintfield. Among those taking part in the flight was Newtownards Chronicle journalist Des Ekin.

The balloon he was in snagged electricity wires after being caught by a freak gust of cold wind and rain, forcing the craft to land in a field at Crossnamuckley, two miles from Newtownards, and after it had crossed the Lough. No one was injured.

A Newtownards man was the victim of a suspected sectarian murder in Belfast on 6 December. The hooded body of 32-year-old heating engineer Samuel White, of Carrigbeg Avenue, was found by an Army patrol in an alleyway at Lisbon Street in the nationalist Short Strand area.

A Protestant, he was married with a young child. He had been severely beaten and stabbed in the chest. According to the Belfast Telegraph Mr White was, at that time, the 106th victim of sectarian assassins.

Newtownards Borough Council decided by the narrowest of margins – the chairman's casting vote – to allow the town's Dam Bottoms to be developed into a full wildfowl sanctuary by the Strangford Lough Wildfowlers' Association. An alternative plan, to develop a dual-purpose park with tame birds and access to the public, was defeated.

Some of the babies which were born at Ards Hospital on New Year's Day in 1972 with their proud mothers. From left: Mrs Ann Ritchie, Newcastle Road, Portaferry, with Seamus; Mrs Sandra Frazer, Lisbarnett Road, Comber, with Leon; Mrs Deirdre Spicer, Fresham Road, Rosehill, with David; Mrs Sandra Marshall, Moneyrea Road, Comber, with Susan, and Mrs Agnes Bailie, Harbour Road, Ballyhalbert, with David. Included are Staff Nurse Lilian McAlonan and Staff Midwives Gertrude Roddy and Margueretta Nesbitt. 249-81-3

King Felix (William Hawkins) and Queen Karen (George Mayne) smile at their daughter, Princess Tina (Anthony Forsythe), watched by attendants Roberto (Colin Trueman) and Blairo (John Smith) and the King's personal attendant Pintos (Gary Trueman) in a scene from 5th Ards BB's pantomime The Sleeping Beauty in January 1972. 249-86-1

Programme sellers at the Kircubbin and Portaferry Ploughing Society's annual competition in January 1972. From left: Gregory Johnson, Dorothy McKeating, Seamus Fay, Margaret Brown and Pat Johnson. 250-52-2

Members of 3rd Ards Cub Scout Pack were given a talk on road safety by a representative from the Road Safety Committee in late January 1972. With the boys are leader Miss F. Irvine and assistants Miss A. Murdoch and Mrs R. Dunn. 250-83-3

The Tivoli Bar in Donaghadee, owned by former boxing champion Freddie Gilroy, was targeted by bombers in February 1972. 251-40-3

Norman Scates, chairman of Comber Rec. FC, presents an inscribed pocket watch to retiring groundsman Bobbie Bailie in March 1972. Included are members of the club. 251-77-1

The Robins from 1st Comber Presbyterian Church at their annual display in March 1972.
251-100-1

Mrs Silcock, wife of Milk Marketing Board representative Joe Silcock, is pictured in April 1972 with prizewinners from Ballywalter Presbyterian Church Indoor Bowling Club's open pairs tournament, which was sponsored by Bangor Dairies.
252-21-1

Young Wives of Scrabo Presbyterian Church who provided tea and entertainment for senior citizens from the West Winds Estate in April 1972. Included is the Rev. G. McK. Eagleton, minister of Strean Presbyterian Church. 253-84-1

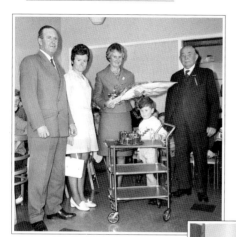

Miss P. Cully (with flowers) retired as principal of Ballyeasboro Primary School to take up the same position at Portavogie PS in May 1972. At a farewell function she was presented with a trolley, silver tea set, cheque and bouquet by the staff, school committee and parents of Ballyeasboro PS. Included are (from left): Mr D. Adair, school committee; Mrs K. McIvor, principal of Portavogie PS; Ian McCormick, who presented the bouquet, and Mr R. Gibson, representing the County Down Education Committee. 253-73-1

Officials and members of the newly-formed Bowtown Road Ratepayers' Association in May 1972. 254-36-3

Officers and members of 1st Portavogie Junior and Senior BB Sections at their annual display in May 1972. Included are the Rev. T. A. Houston (chaplain), the Rev. N. M. Heaney, the Rev. W. F. A. Bell and RUC Inspector T. C. Fergie with Mrs Fergie. 254-79-1

The combined senior choir of Newtownards schools with conductor Mr T. G. Odell at the annual Festival of Music and Dancing in the Queen's Hall, Newtownards, in May 1972. 255-17-1

1st Ards Cub Scout Group won the Dora Baxter Challenge Flag for County Down and the Newtownards and District Cup in June 1972. 255-38-3

Christina Mateer, from Ballymacreely, Killinchy, was presented with the Armagh Agricultural Society's Cup in June 1972. Owner of The Apple Blossom at Knock, she gained four firsts and four seconds in the home industry section at the Armagh Agricultural Society's annual show. 255-94-2

Spectators watch winner Desmond Brown in action during Ballywalter Festival Week's barrel race in June 1972. 256-25-3

Swimmers from Portavogie Primary School who won 13 medals, eight of them gold, at the Ulster Minor Swimming Championships, which were held at the Ballymena pool in June 1972. Back (from left): Gillian Thompson, Jeremy Kelly, Rodney Ennis, Barry Thompson, Naomie Donnan. Seated: Hazel Donnan, Karen McBride, Ashley Morrison (captain), Laura Bell and Gillian Ambrose. 256-32-2

Local postmaster Capt. R. A. Drennan presents Victoria Primary School pupil John McClintock with the Northern Ireland Trophy, donated by the Educational Advisory Committee of Ulster Savings, in June 1972. The school won the award for their set of scrapbooks depicting their chosen subject, 'Leisure Time in Newtownards.' Included is County Down Savings organiser Mr W. I. Thompson. 256-83-1

Officers and members of Cloughey Rising Sons LOL No. 1907 following the unfurling of their new banner by Mrs David Johnston, wife of the No. 11 District Master, in July 1972. 257-3-2

The choir from St. Mary's Primary School, Comber, won their class in the Under-12 section at the Comber Festival Week talent competition, held in the Andrews Memorial Hall in July 1972. They were also awarded the Festival's top award, the Carlisle Cup. Included is principal Mrs Ann Falls. 257-36-2

Ards Amateur Swimming Club members with the Inter-Club Cup which they won against neighbours Bangor in August 1972. They were also runners-up in the Provincial League. 258-8-3

Spectators and competitors watch the presentation of awards following the annual pram race at Portaferry in July 1972. 56-7a-56

Cup winners from the Newtownards Cage Bird Society's annual show in October 1972. 260-3-1

Prizewinners and officials of Donaghadee Pigeon Club who attended the annual dinner dance in the New Mount Royal Hotel, Donaghadee, in October 1972. 91-12-58

Boys and girls of the St Mark's Cadets took part in a programme of songs and poems in November 1972 to celebrate the silver wedding anniversary of Her Majesty the Queen and HRH the Duke of Edinburgh. 261-24-3

Children from the nursery school at Portaferry Road, Newtownards, enjoying their Christmas party in December 1972. 262-22-2

Pupils from Ballykeigle Primary School took part in a performance of 'The Sleeping Beauty', specially written and produced by principal Miss Shannon, assisted by Miss J. Rea, in December 1972. 262-44-1

1972

Sport in the Chronicle

Ards lost to neighbours Bangor in the Towns' Cup final at Ravenhill on Easter Monday (3 April). The only score in the game was a penalty kicked over by Con McCall for Bangor.

Ards FC's player/ manager Billy Humphries was named 'Player of the Year' in late April by the Northern Ireland Football Writers' Association. He received the award from chairman Malcolm Brodie.

Ards RFC won the Junior League Championship for the first time in their history on 3 May, defeating Instonians IIB in the Past Players Cup final at Ravenhill. The winning margin was 25 points to 4.

North Down, promoted to cricket's Senior League Section 1, lost their first match on 6 May at the hands of Queen's University. They bounced back the following week with a 119-run victory over the RUC.

Ards had a major scare in May's two-leg final of the County Antrim Shield. Having secured a comfortable 3-0 victory over Crusaders in the first leg at Castlereagh Park (through goals by Dave McCoy, Brian McCaughtry and Syd Patterson), they went on to lose the second leg, at Seaview, by the same margin. However, the match was settled with a penalty shoot-out by the narrowest of margins, five to four, with Billy Nixon taking the last one to ensure victory for Ards.

The club almost achieved a trophy double to end the season, losing out in the Gold Cup final replay against Portadown on 24 May by 2-1 following a 0-0 draw in the first game.

Ards lost 3-0 to Portadown in the season-opening Carlsberg Trophy final at Windsor Park on 16 August. By way of consolation they received £500 in prize money from the sponsors.

Ashley Morrison from Ards Swimming Club was named Ulster boy swimmer of the year at a meeting of the Irish Amateur Swimming Association's Ulster branch at Queen's University on 2 December. His proud coach was Gilbert McBride.

Donaghadee golfer Jim Conway beat some 25,000 entrants to win the Ford Fiesta Golf Trophy in Majorca on 8 December. The final took place seven months after a local qualifying round was held at his home club and three months after the Ulster area final at Castlerock.

The Ards 2nd XI cricket team before their first round Minor Cup match against Bangor in May 1972. Back (from left): H. Sharpe, S. Dalzell, W. Ainley, G. Dunn, T. McMillan, A. Payne. Front: D. Aicken, L. Jones, J. Boal (captain), R. Keenan and R. Brown. 254-76-3

Members of the Greenwell Street Presbyterian Church 'B' badminton team, winners of Division 5 of the Presbyterian League following their defeat of Whiteabbey in the final at Finaghy in May 1972. 254-83-2

Boys and girls from Donaghadee Golf Club, who attended a summer holiday coaching session in August 1972, are pictured with club professional Billy Hackworth and Youth Committee members Brenda Capper and Maurice Bunting. 25-6a-57

St Columba's Secondary School, Portaferry, were Ulster schools' hurling champions in December 1972. 261-97-2

Dennis McBride (23), from Lisbane, Comber, sits on his new 250cc Suzuki motorcycle as sponsors Terry Boyd and Maurice Russell look on. They traded in Belfast under the name B. and R. Motorcycles and were sole local agents for Suzuki moto-cross machines. Dennis had enjoyed another very successful season, winning the Irish 500cc five-mile championship and the Inter-Cities scramble in Cork, amongst a number of events. 261-100-2

Ian Shields

remembers ... North Down Cricket Club

The Sixties had ended on a sad note for Comber-based North Down Cricket Club with the deaths of two club legends, James Macdonald and Gerry Spence, but there was hope on the horizon as many younger members were joining the club and it started to come alive.

Jim Barry was a 'no frills' straightforward chairman who led a vibrant committee with plenty of experience. It included Raymond Crosby, Willie Dempster, Robert Rowan and J. L. O. Andrews as club trustees, Willie Watt, a former 1st XI captain, Robert Foley and James Burgess, representing the supporters and business interests, while Billy Artt, Jimmy Boucher, Adrian Thompson, Sydney Elliott, Roy Thompson, Wesley Graham and Alan Reid were experienced cricketers sprinkled throughout the teams. Youth had its representation through Hammie Mills and Ian Shields.

Roy Thompson's crucial period as secretary, from the mid-Sixties to 1973, saw the club begin to blossom. He was actively involved in promoting North Down at every level and played for both the 1st and 2nd XIs as a batsman and wicketkeeper. The treasurer in the early roller-coaster years was the versatile Adrian Thompson, a high order 1st XI batsman, a useful medium pace bowler and a capable stand-in wicketkeeper, before Raymond Crosby took over the treasurer duties in 1972.

Although he successfully played tennis in his teens, Ian Shields had a natural ability at cricket that was nurtured at Regent House School under the watchful eye of the legendary James Macdonald and at The Green under the even more watchful eye of Willie Andrews.

Ian played in the North Down teams of the challenging Sixties and Seventies but like all great club players his career had longevity. That brought much more satisfaction and success in the twilight of his career and at age 69 he still turns out for the 4th XI.

The club had three teams and a midweek side and had a growing membership that raised hopes of a 4th XI. But the burning desire throughout the membership was to return to the premier senior league and, as the years passed, there was a growing realisation that something, or someone, was missing to enable the club to complete that transition. Section Two was competitive and to get back into the top tier it had to be successfully negotiated.

The North Down cricket team in May 1970. Back (from left): W. Dempster, G. Dempster, G. Norris, W. Wilson, W. Wishart, R. Thompson. Front: P. Gilliland, W. Artt (captain), M. Campbell and I. Shields. 224-83-3

1970 was a good example of just how tight Senior Two was, as North Down and local rivals Bangor finished joint top, leading to a play-off at Stormont. Unfortunately skipper Billy Artt missed the game, holidaying in Majorca, and the team could not reach the 132 Bangor total, losing by 29 runs with Brian King taking six for 31. Walter Montgomery, who had joined from Ards, was a bright light in an otherwise ordinary team effort, but his four for 36 was not enough to stave off defeat.

The talented Lawrence Hunter was a great acquisition in 1971. He missed the early games that season but from then until the end of the decade he was our best bowler by a long way. Otherwise it was a determined and relatively unchanged North Down 1st XI that stuttered into the 1971 season against the unfancied YMCA at The Green. Batting first the top scorer, in a poor total of 52, was Walter Montgomery with 10! But this was to be Walter's day as he then took six for 16 in 17 overs, overshadowing his great slow bowling team mate Willie Dempster, who took three for seven. YMCA were all out for 43 and this unlikely victory began a run of wins that culminated in a 100% record with the defeat of Armagh in September. Promotion and time for another celebration!

The 1972 season saw the team struggling in the big league, and it was a big league in every way consisting of 16 teams. Wins against Downpatrick, Donacloney, RUC and Laurelvale gave the team 13th place.

In another NCU reshuffle in 1973 the league was split into three sections, with

North Down in Section 2 and amongst the pacemakers for most of the season. The crucial tie was against nearest rivals Donacloney at The Green on 25 August and what a thriller it turned out to be. Batting first, the home side were decimated by an outstanding bowling performance from Michael Lumb who took eight wickets for 32 runs to leave North Down 77 all out with only Geoffrey Dempster and Lawrence Hunter scoring in the 20s.

Donacloney had scored 33 before they lost their first wicket and then Hunter and Wishart took control with four for 23 and four for 19 respectively. The figures tell only part of the story,

2nd XI League winners in 1973 – Back: Robert McVeigh (umpire), Jack McMillan, Wilmer McKibbin, Willie Wilson, David McVeigh, Jimmy Boucher, Sydney Elliott, David O'Prey (manager). Front: Derek McCracken, Peter Artt, Jimmy Galway (captain) Jim Barry (chairman), John Armstrong and Walter Montgomery.

Midweek League winners – Back: Robert McVeigh (manager), Derek Steen, Peter Allen, Wesley Graham, Jack McMillan, James Campbell, Wesley Campbell, David O'Prey (umpire). Front: Jimmy McKittrick, Jimmy Boucher, Alvin Maginness (captain), Peter Artt, David McVeigh and Wilmer Barker.

as the game was interspersed with good and dropped catches, run outs and near misses, and panic batting aplenty. The unsung hero was Walter Montgomery who, although taking no wickets, bowled five overs for three runs at the crucial stage, enabling a dramatic one run win that guaranteed promotion.

The 1st XI was a well-balanced side. Lawrence Hunter, Walter Wishart, Miller O'Prey, Adrian Thompson, Ronnie Elliott and Don Shields were augmented in the bowling by Walter Montgomery with his left-arm spinners. Denis Artt had moved from Collegians to The Green and was arguably the best wicketkeeper in the country at this time. His brilliance behind the stumps enhanced all the bowlers' performances and he was a useful contributor with the bat, although the bulk of the

Captains of North Down Cricket Club's various teams in October 1973 with the trophies won during the previous season. From left: A. Maginnis (Midweek XI), I. Shields (1st XI), J. Barry (chairman), J. Galway (2nd XI) and D. Steen (3rd XI). 268-48-3

runs came from Malcolm Campbell, Billy Artt, Ian Shields and Geoffrey Dempster.

From the relative obscurity of Loopvale in the Belfast Cricket League, Billy Dale had gone to Civil Service but in 1974 he came to The Green, thus beginning a long and distinguished cricketing career that saw him play through the not so good times, to later win senior league and cup honours.

It was still a struggle in the premier league although a sixth position retained premier status. However, that was to change in the most dramatic of fashions in 1975 when Woodvale's Ken Kirkpatrick pulled Lawrence Hunter's last ball past a well-patrolled boundary, to send North Down back into Section Two. It highlighted our plight of being too good for Section Two but not good enough to stay in Section One.

Another change of captaincy saw Hunter faced with the same highs and lows that Billy Artt and Ian Shields had had to deal with in previous years. A disappointing third place behind Ballymena and Instonians in 1976 was followed by another title in 1977, losing only two of the 14 fixtures. At Laurelvale in June, a young left arm bowler took two for 21 in his four overs and began a career that would be difficult to match in the annals of the club. Robin Haire's emergence was certainly one of the reasons why Hunter felt the side was ready to compete and remain in the top league.

The first three games in 1978 set the tone. Walter Wishart's six for 42 was matched by Simon Corlett's six for 49 at Ormeau and North Down lost by 16 runs. At The Lawn, Waringstown were 68 for six chasing 109 when the rain intervened and in another nail-biter at Comber the following Saturday, Woodvale won off the penultimate ball. With only one victory against the RUC to show for a lot of effort, another bitter relegation pill was swallowed at the end of the season.

The astute Sydney Elliott accepted the leadership in 1979 in another bid to win promotion, but diplomatic activities behind the scene were already taking place amongst some of the club's administrators who realised some new initiative was needed to give the team a competitive edge and end the up and down culture that had plagued the club for most of the Seventies.

Elliott's team won the league with another 100% performance, but on the negative side was Ken Campbell's departure to golf and fast bowler Brian Johnston's departure to new pastures. Both served the club well and deserved their winners' medals.

It was a new era and new names were becoming established, occasional players in the team. They included John Gilliland, Clarence Hiles, Jimmy Galway, Garson Mowat, Stephen

North Down Cricket Club's 3rd XI pictured in October 1974 with the trophy they received for winning Section B of the 3rd Division. Back (from left): D. Kirk, J. E. McMillan, D. McVeigh, W. J. McMillan, I. Dempster, R. McVeigh. Front: J. McKittrick, C. Hiles, D. Steen (captain), J. Boucher and W. Graham. 86-16-93

Barry, Peter Orr, Jack McMillan and Sammy Wilson.

MORE AGONY THAN ECSTASY IN THE SENIOR CHALLENGE CUP

There were more Challenge Cup games in the Seventies than any other decade since the war, but the RUC gave us a first round exit in 1970, Comber man Richard Barker causing the damage with five for 18. Bangor did the same the following year with six wickets to spare and Donacloney successfully chased 184 at the Factory Ground in 1972 to compound the agony.

The team travelled to draughty Mossley in 1973 to play nomads Cliftonville, the outcome being another last ball boundary defeat and further despondency. It wasn't until 1974 that some progress was finally made in the Challenge Cup and the old bogey was put to bed. A total of 160 proved good enough against Bangor, Walter Wishart and Derek McCracken being the key men, but Lurgan's Alan Johnston put paid to any hopes of further progress when he took eight for 21 in a comfortable second round win.

A lengthy cup run seemed years away but in 1975 the team set aside poor league form and played some really good cup cricket. A great eight wickets win at Lurgan Park, chasing 152 courtesy of Billy Dale's four for 25 and Malcolm Campbell's unbeaten 88, was followed by a Ken Campbell-inspired 32 runs win against the strong Downpatrick side at the Meadow. A semi-final tie at home to Civil Service was the reward and hopes were high of a possible cup final place in early August. On a glorious day at The Green, North Down's first six batsmen contributed to a 245 total and Brian Johnston, Ken Campbell and Walter Montgomery shared the wickets to secure a 100 runs semi-final victory.

The victorious North Down cricket team with the Jack Newell Shield, which they received in June 1975 after winning the RUC six-a-side competition. Back (from left): D. McCracken, B. Dale, C. Hiles, R. Crosby. Front: M. O'Prey, D. Artt (captain) and J. Galway.
48-1-110

For the first time in 34 years North Down would contest a Challenge Cup final but, sadly, it turned out to be a huge disappointment. Unlike North Down, Waringstown had won senior league titles and Challenge Cups regularly since 1970 and were hot favourites to win again. On a blistering hot Friday at Ormeau, Waringstown scored 192 for four, including a measured century from Jim Harrison, and North Down replied with a paltry 56, Bertie McGill taking four for 28. As a contest the game was over, but Lawrence Hunter's four for 40 and Jimmy Galway's three for 21 were fine bowling performances in Waringstown's 130 for nine in the second innings, which was matched by North Down's 135 for 6 when Denis Artt hit a defiant 66 runs.

Perhaps the cup final appearance rekindled the old competitive cup spirit, because there was another good cup run in 1976 with away victories against RUC, Woodvale and Cregagh setting up a semi-final clash with Waringstown at Comber. North Down's batting let the team down on their big day and the 110 total was never going to be good enough to test the best batting line-up in Irish club cricket and we deservedly lost by four wickets.

A year later the visit to Lurgan Park saw defeat defending 213 runs, an impressive total courtesy of a Don Shields 76 and Geoffrey Dempster with 56. Wins over RUC and Muckamore in 1978 set up another semi-final opportunity against Waringstown at The Green but, after so many cup defeats at the hands of the Villagers, there was a severe psychological barrier to overcome and a defeat was almost inevitable.

The decade finished with another cup defeat at Waringstown but it was the first round win against Saintfield at the Demesne that produced one of the most exciting games of the season. David Napier, later to captain North of Ireland to Challenge Cup success, and later still to play at The Green, hit a typical swashbuckling unbeaten 83 in the Saintfield total of 153 with Lawrence Hunter and Clarence Hiles taking four wickets apiece. Was it enough?

The Saintfield 'critics' on the bank certainly thought so when North Down slumped to 64 for six and one of our batsmen had packed his bag and headed home. The game looked lost, but Hiles, who had been caught off a 'no ball' in his vital 37 runs innings, won support from Robin Haire, Stephen Barry and Hunter. But Jimmy Galway and Hunter still had to scramble 15 runs from 16 balls to pull off an unlikely victory.

Two hours later, in Comber, our bemused opening batsman Adrian Thompson learned the team had won in his 'absence'. It was all part of a new spirit emerging at the club and although we didn't know it at the time, the decade ended with a scent of a Challenge Cup success that was carried into the Eighties by Sydney Elliott's team.

The pinnacle of success for North Down occurred in 1973 when, along with the 1st XI winning Section Two, the seconds, thirds and midweek teams each won their respective leagues. Remarkably, of the 52 league games played, only four were lost throughout the club.

The Seventies at North Down were characterised by relegation and promotion peaks and troughs for the 1st XI, but entering the Eighties in the premier section the club was not only determined to stay at the top, it was about to guarantee that status in a way nobody could have envisaged. The good times were just around the corner.

Anne Johnston

remembers ... The Women's Institute

Anne Johnston has been a member of Donaghadee Women's Institute for 50 years.

She has served on committee many times over the years and has held office as Secretary and President on several occasions.

At Ards Peninsula Area level she has served as Area Secretary and Area Chairman and has represented the Area for three years on the N. Ireland Executive Committee.

She was a member of the Ulster Countrywoman magazine sub-committee for nine years; three of these as Chairman.

A keen craftswoman, she was awarded a Gold Spinning-wheel and organises a weekly crafts class in Donaghadee.

During the early Seventies, as the mother of four young children under the age of 10, the monthly WI meeting was my 'night out'. In many similar households husbands took charge of the children for the evening to give their wives the chance to catch up with friends young and old. As WI members we enjoyed listening to something of interest from the speaker or maybe even learning a new skill.

Speakers included John Pepper of the Belfast Telegraph on 'Ulster Humour', Mr H. S. Orr on the changeover to decimal currency, Crosbie Cochrane advised us on 'how to turn your garden into a mini-paradise', Mrs Nancy Brown showed how to make her beautiful flower arrangements, and Mrs Anne Cooley demonstrated how to make corn-dollies. We could take part in the fun social half hour, enjoy a chat over a cup of tea, or maybe take part in a quiz. The monthly competitions were varied and challenging and included the oldest postcard, an old-fashioned cure, a limerick, three scones or even a decorated paper-hat. It was also reassuring, especially in the 1970s, that the meetings were non-political and inter-denominational. We could relax and enjoy the fellowship.

There were around 1,200 members in our Ards Area Group of 17 Institutes stretching from Dundonald and Holywood to Portaferry at the tip of the Ards Peninsula. The most senior Institute was Portaferry, which was formed in 1935, followed by Donaghadee in 1943, Dundonald in 1946 with the others during the 1950s and 1960s: Holywood (1950), Ballyhalbert (1951), Ballysallagh (1951), Groomsport (1953), Bangor (1955), Ballyholme (1956), Ballywalter (1956), Ballyblack (1957), Helen's Bay (1960), Ballyrogan (1961), Ballygrainey (1969), Ballymaconnell (1970), Ballyoran (1973) and Millisle (1976).

Area Group meetings were held twice a year in the Spring and Autumn in the Queen's Hall, Newtownards, where members were invited to come together and meet in a large group. A special speaker was invited and Institutes took it in turn to cater and entertain. Area competitions were held in crafts, photography and cooking skills. In November 1978 approximately 570 Area members met, with the minutes recording: "Undoubtedly the highlight of the evening was the talk given by Gloria Hunniford of Taste of Hunni fame. An enraptured audience listened to Gloria recount some of her experiences on the programme, choosing a few extracts from her newly published book." Supper was served by Ballymaconnell WI, Holywood WI entertained with a sketch and songs by Percy French, the floral display was by Groomsport WI and Gloria was presented with a jar of Ballywalter honey.

Many Institutes formed choirs or concert groups; for example Portaferry choir, Ballyrogan choir, Holywood choir and the Donaghadee 'Follies' group were well known and appreciated as entertainers in their communities. In addition, members have always been keen to support their own communities and during the 1970s there was a real shortage of libraries in the Ards area. Following pressure from WI groups, mobile libraries began to visit the smaller towns of the Ards such as Donaghadee; these later were replaced by town libraries. Many members also became involved in the 'Meals on Wheels' distribution in the area and gave valuable support to the opening of

Members of Ballyrogan WI Choir provided the entertainment at a party organised by Newtownards Round Table for residents of Loch Cuan House in January 1978. Included in the picture are Round Table chairman Colin Cunningham and Mrs O. McFadden, officer-in-charge at Loch Cuan House. 43-12a-51

Abbeyfield Houses.

Craft groups aimed to keep traditional pastimes such as lace-making, rug-making, toy-making, knitting, crochet and embroidery alive and, through the WI crafts syllabus, work produced was assessed for proficiency ribbons. If a member's collection of crafts reached the required high standard, a gold award was made in the shape of a spinning-wheel and these were coveted by all crafters. Mrs Thelma Goldring (Dundonald), one of the first members to gain the WI gold award, was a talented and experienced craftswoman who won many awards not only in WI circles but at the RDS in Dublin and then served there as a judge for many years.

The Ulster Countrywoman magazine sought to keep members informed as to what was taking place around the whole of Northern Ireland, giving ideas for future meetings, sharing recipes to enhance family meals, supplying craft and knitting patterns, printing articles of interest written by members and informing readers of forthcoming events and competitions.

Members were encouraged to send in items of interest. The following, which appeared in February 1972, was entitled 'Hiccups':

Here are some remedies for hiccups which may be found both helpful and amusing:–

Put your left foot in a bucket of cold water and breathe deeply.

Walk 10 yards balancing an egg on your head.

Hold your nose and bend to touch your toes 10 times.

Put your right elbow on the floor and walk in a circle keeping the elbow in the same position.

Breathe in and out while holding a paper bag over your nose and mouth.

Lie flat with a hot water bottle placed over the lower part of your ribs. This acts more quickly if your knees are drawn up slightly.

Here's another trick that really does work, but it requires the help of another person – Ask her to hold a glass of water to your lips, which you drink in the normal way, while you put your little finger into each ear!

Contributed by Mrs A. Ferris, Ballygrainey WI

Advertisements in the 1970s magazines included those for Hoggs, the Coal Advisory Service, Berkshire support tights and stockings, Adelboden Restaurant

Members of Portaferry WI celebrated the 40th anniversary of the Institution's foundation at a well-attended dinner in the Market House on 11 February 1975. From left: Miss M. Morrison, president from 1966-68; Mrs S. C. Cuthbertson, vice-chairman of the Federation; Miss J. Stronge, president from 1954-57; Mrs F. Lyttle, president from 1968-72 and again in 1975; Mrs E. H. Brownlow, president from 1940-42; Miss A. Savage, president from 1962-64; Mrs E. Elliott, president from 1958-62; Mrs Harry Anderson, president from 1972-74, and Mrs Hugh Anderson, president from 1964-66. 100-94-1

(Groomsport), Ulster Savings and Ferryhill Tours. Perhaps as a result of the income generated from the above, a new-look, larger magazine made its appearance in the early 1970s.

WI Festivals began bringing members together with a common interest to take part in the annual Music Festival, the Drama Festival, Quiz, Indoor Bowls and Golfer of the Year. Painting weekends also proved popular with aspiring artists. WI cookery books, produced every four or five years, were filled with a collection of recipes tasted and tried by members and were appreciated not only by members but also by the wider community. Two (the third and fourth) were published in the 1970s; the books still sell well at the Balmoral Show, where the WI organises a sales table to boost funds. During the late 1970s we also began serving teas and scones to Show visitors.

Mrs Evelyn McIvor, a founder member of Ballywalter Institute, was a well-known and outgoing personality of the 1970s. Small in stature, she was a bundle of energy and talented in many ways, as a raconteur, caterer, craftswoman and organiser; she was a superb cook who baked hundreds of scones over the years for Balmoral Show. She took a keen interest in the Arts and was passionate about her own community.

WI headquarters for Northern Ireland was located in the War Memorial Building at Waring Street, Belfast. During the early 1970s a need was shown to purchase a 'WI Home' as the staff had outgrown the rented offices. Through the magazine, a fundraising appeal was launched and Institutes around the province set about reaching the target of £28,000. Mrs Betty Lyttle (Portaferry) with her organising committee, and supported by all Institutes in the Area, held a successful WI Harvest Fair in the Queen's Hall. Through this effort 'the magnificent sum of £1,450 was raised' and a cheque for this amount was handed over to Dundonald WI stalwart Mrs Sally Cuthbertson, a former Federation chairman, at the 1975 Autumn Area meeting 'for the benefit of Federation House'. In 1978 Federation House opened at Finaghy following the presentation of a cheque for £23,000; the house was a former chemist's shop with the adjoining family premises at 209/211 Upper Lisburn Road.

Institutes were encouraged to start keeping an annual scrapbook in the 1970s to make a record of their meetings through photographs, press cuttings and illustrations – a page per meeting artistically presented and considered to be of interest to future generations. Competitions were held for the best page, best cover and best complete scrapbook.

Of course when a group of women meet, outings are inevitably discussed and they became an important feature of the 1970s in WI circles. Groups enjoyed trips by coach to places such as the Armagh Planetarium, the Lake District, Edinburgh, Chester, York, Harrogate and London. An Grianan, home of the ICA (Irish Countrywoman's Association) near Drogheda, was also a favourite venue for learning new crafts and enjoying good food and fellowship with our sister organisation.

WI is part of a much larger organisation of more than 8m women from around the world called ACWW (Associated Countrywomen of the World). Our collection of 'Pennies for Friendship' covers the administration and through further funding we seek to support women who are less fortunate than ourselves in developing countries – for example by sinking a village well in the 'Water for All' project, supplying help to those with nutrition deficiency blindness or giving support to a group of rural women attempting to start a small business to support their families in the 'Women feed the World' project. Northern Ireland has long been recognised for its generosity to ACWW. Through these projects several of our members have travelled to remote areas of the world such as Kenya and India to observe at firsthand the benefits to the women involved.

Today many WI members are proud to say they have attended their Institutes regularly for 30, 40, 50 years or more – and their mothers before them! All are agreed that through WI they have forged lasting friendships and brought enrichment to their lives.

1973

Making the News in the Chronicle

The three-year-old McKenna Community Centre, which was run by Ballycran GAA Club near Kircubbin, was targeted by bombers within the first hour of the New Year. An explosive device placed inside the building, previously targeted by firebombers, caused substantial damage. All the windows were smashed and a large hole was left in the expensive ballroom floor.

There was a British Empire Medal in the New Year Honours List for senior Newtownards fireman Robert Allen, of South Street. A plumber by trade, he held the position of Station Officer, having joined the Fire Brigade in 1938, when preparations were already under way for the outbreak of war.

Kearney Farm, covering 289 acres and located on the coast road between Cloughey and Portaferry, was sold for £150,000 to Dunleath Estates in early January.

Many shops and factories in Newtownards closed their doors on 7 February after calls were made for a province-wide strike by the United Loyalist Council. The new umbrella organisation had been angered by the internment without trial of two Protestants by the Direct Rule authorities.

Northern Ireland

THE BORDER POLL

VOTING BY POST

REMEMBER...

Completed Application Forms must reach your ELECTORAL REGISTRATION OFFICER on or before:

9th February 1973

Application Forms are available from local Council Offices and Post Offices

ISSUED BY THE NORTHERN IRELAND OFFICE, STORMONT CASTLE, BELFAST

Substantial damage was caused to the interior of St Mary's Primary School in Comber after a 10lb bomb exploded beside the front door on 7 February. Part of a wall was demolished by the force of the blast. Although no warning was given by those responsible, there were no injuries.

Anger was expressed by residents in the Belfast Road area of Newtownards in mid-February after plans were revealed by the Ministry of Home Affairs to use Kiltonga House as a temporary training school for young offenders, pending the completion of a permanent establishment at Rathgael, outside Bangor, later in the decade. Secretary of State William Whitelaw acceded to a call for a public enquiry from North Down MP Jim Kilfedder, on behalf of the residents.

Plans for a large shopping centre at Circular Road, Newtownards, including some 49 shops and parking spaces for 1,300 vehicles, were passed by the Borough Council on 5 March. The site was previously occupied by Dickson's Nurseries.

A second Town'n'Country opened its doors to the public in mid-March – the new entertainment venue being located in Cloughey and having the same parent company.

Millisle man Arthur Pack-Beresford refused to pay his colour television licence in March because he objected to the content of a BBC programme on the Troubles called Ulster Tribunal. He said it was "a matter of conscience" and started to list the programme's participants to RM Martin McBirney. His argument was dismissed by Mr McBirney who said it was a court of law and "not an arena for political or public protest." The defendant was fined £10.

The body of a Dundonald man was discovered on a grass verge along the coast road between Portavogie and Ballyhalbert, some 20 miles from his home, on 2 April. It was believed that 28-year-old David Thomas McQueen, from Craigleith Drive in the Ballybeen estate, was last seen alive on Belfast's Newtownards Road at 10.20pm; his body with a number of bullet injuries was found by a passer-by some 90 minutes later.

Mr McQueen, who was a Protestant and unmarried, had worked as a builder's labourer. There were suspicions of loyalist involvement in his murder.

Fire damage estimated at £100,000 was caused to the recently-opened Carnasure House Hotel at Comber on 24 April. The blaze, thought to have been caused by an electrical fault, destroyed two-thirds of the building. Owner Graham Wright said restoration work could take up to nine months but they would reopen the hotel. This was indeed the case, the premises reopening that November as The Highwayman.

A substantial extension to Ards Hospital was opened on 3 May and named the Calder Theatre Suite in honour of the late Alexander M. Calder, a key figure in the hospital's growth. He worked there for 33 years, serving as Consultant Surgeon until his death in 1965. A plaque was unveiled by his widow, Mrs N. M. Calder.

Strangford ferry engineer John Murray, from The Strand, Portaferry, fulfilled a life's ambition in May when he completed work on his own boat. It was constructed at Portaferry Technical School under the watchful eye of woodwork teacher Jim Mawhinney. Named *Roisin Dubh*, the boat was launched with the traditional champagne bottle by John's daughter Eileen.

Cllr John D. Beckett was re-elected in mid-May to serve as Mayor of Newtownards Borough for a fourth time – he would be the last Mayor of the old authority prior to the reorganisation of local government and its replacement by Ards District (later Borough) Council. Over in Donaghadee Cllr Henry Cosbey was re-elected as chairman of the local Urban District Council.

Although the new District Councils did not take over control until 1 October, the elections were held on 30 May (and also 20 June in Ards electoral area 'A' owing to the death of one of the candidates).

The 17 seats were filled by 11 Unionists (John Algie, Myrtle Cooke, David Hamilton, Hamilton McKeag, William Spratt, Henry Cosbey, John Scott, James Donnan, Thomas Pollock, Oliver Johnston and Jean McMordie), two Alliance (Charles Dorrian, Thomas McBriar), one Loyalist Coalition (Robert Brown), one Independent (James Caughey), one Labour (Edmond Gaw) and one SDLP (Brendan MacPolin). Mr Algie, a former Mayor of Newtownards Borough Council, was elected chairman of the new authority.

Newtownards bus driver Samuel Alexander Rush, from Windsor Avenue in the town, was killed on 10 June while driving his vehicle on a late journey between Belfast and Bangor. He was hit in the head by gunfire aimed at an Army vehicle checkpoint near Short Strand in East Belfast. The shots missed their intended target but struck the bus, which subsequently crashed into another checkpoint at Madrid Street. Soldiers and local residents comforted the shocked passengers until another bus was able to take them home.

Mr Rush's death was blamed on the Ulster Defence Association, which had been involved in a number of shooting incidents along the Newtownards Road. He became the 11th bus service employee to be killed during the four years of the

Troubles.

His father William, from Donaghadee Road, Newtownards, was also associated with local bus services for many years. The eldest of five children, Sam was survived by his wife, two sons and a daughter, as well as a wide family circle. He was a member of Newtownards Methodist Church, where the largely-attended funeral was held on 17 June. Interment followed at Movilla Cemetery.

A month after the Council elections voters returned to the polls (on 28 June) to return candidates to the new Northern Ireland Assembly. North Down returned eight members, including Unionist Major William Brownlow (Portaferry) and Lord Dunleath (Alliance). Easily topping the poll was sitting North Down MP Jim Kilfedder with 20,684 votes. He resided near Millisle.

Miss Clara Rigby retired from her position as Church of Ireland organist in Portaferry at the end of June, having played for a period of 63 years under a total of seven different rectors.

The Newtownards Chronicle hit the headlines in its own right on 19 July, when the paper celebrated its own centenary. Pride of place was given to a message from Secretary of State William Whitelaw, who stated:

> *"Any newspaper with such an outstanding record of service to the public as that which can be claimed by the Newtownards Chronicle, has every right to take pride in celebrating such a notable occasion."*

> *"As the paper moves into its second century and the challenges that must bring, my wish is that the news it will have to record will be in headlines that tell of steady continuous progress towards peace and prosperity for all the people of Northern Ireland."*

The longest-serving member of staff, Mrs Isabella Murphy, was accorded the honour of pressing the button to commence the printing of the centenary edition.

The first editor of the Chronicle was James W. McNinch; a century later the post was held by his grandson, Robert McNinch.

Among the 50 victims of the Summerland entertainment centre fire on the Isle of Man on 2 August was 30-year-old factory worker Wilbert Scott, from Scrabo Road, Newtownards. He was on holiday with his fiancée, who sustained severe burns to her back and legs. Eight members of the Boys' Brigade Company attached to the Methodist Church in Newtownards were in the centre when the fire broke out. All managed to escape without injury.

A new South Ards Community Association was formed in mid-August following a meeting in Kircubbin. The aim of the body, jointly chaired by Ernest Elliott (Portaferry) and James Smyth (Cloughey), was to seek better facilities for all the people of the South Ards area.

Ruth Patterson, from Lough Shore Road, Portaferry, became the town's first-ever female preacher in August when she spoke in the local Presbyterian Church, where her father, the Rev. Thomas Patterson, was the recently-installed minister.

The formation of a new company in Newtownards, B & J Jupiter Cruisers Ltd., was announced at the beginning of September with the promise that 130 jobs were in the pipeline. The company would manufacture fibre glass-hulled luxury cabin cruisers to an established Danish design.

Maurice Spence (25), from Dermott Park, Comber, was found shot dead in his car on a lonely road at Glenwherry, 10 miles from Ballymena, on 15 September. He was a self-employed road haulier and his wife was expecting a child. He had moved to Comber two years earlier. No motive could be established for the murder.

Plans for an 'ultra-modern' recreation centre for Donaghadee, costing in excess of £1m, were approved in principle at one of the last meetings of the town's Urban District Council. Councillors agreed to forward the plans to the Ministry of Education for funding approval when they met at the end of September.

The recreation centre – comprising a multi-purpose sports hall, swimming pools, function hall for concerts, lectures, etc., a minor hall, squash courts, viewing lounges and a restaurant – was envisaged for the site of the existing bus station (to the south-east of the harbour, between it and the quarry hole). It would be reached by a new road linking the seafront/ Lemon's Wharf to The Commons.

MOTORISTS!
Don't make it easy for **tragedies like this to happen**

Where YOUR car is concerned-

- Make sure it is securely locked at all times.
- If it doesn't have a steering column lock, fit an anti-theft device.
- If your house has a garage, use it, and keep it locked.

- Be careful where you park.
- Should your car be stolen, report it to the police immediately.

We must defeat the car bomber!

Mr and Mrs Albert McGimpsey, both natives of Newtownards (he was from East Street and she, born Martha Gunning, was from Greenwell Street), returned to the town from their home in New Jersey at the beginning of October to celebrate their golden wedding anniversary. It was also 50 years since they were last in Newtownards.

Twelve-year-old Gerard Delaney, from Circular Road, Newtownards, saved a young girl's life on 2 October after she fell into a water-filled hole at the former Dickson's Nursery site near his home. His prompt action in jumping into the water, which was 8ft. deep, prevented the child from drowning. Gerard subsequently received an Award of Merit from Newtownards Rotary Club.

The former Kiltonga House was renamed Lisnevin School and began operating as a temporary inter-denominational rehabilitation centre for young male offenders from 1 November. It comprised a 20-bed training school unit and a 20-bed remand/assessment unit, under the control of an independent board of management.

Five traffic wardens – four men and a woman – took up duties for the first time in Newtownards on 10 December. Their role was to assist the police and they were empowered to impose £2 fixed penalty fines for parking violations.

Plans were announced for the introduction of a nursery school from the beginning of the New Year, under the care of trained teacher Rosemary Armstrong, at the Debretta factory in Newtownards. The company already provided a similar service for the children of working mothers at their premises in Bangor.

The Town 'n' Country Inn at Cloughey was badly damaged in a firebomb attack on 21 December. Watchman James Palmer, who went into the building after hearing the sound of breaking glass, was greeted by a blast of flames and smoke. He was subsequently taken to hospital suffering from burns, while his guard dog Pax died from asphyxiation.

The premises were owned by Harry McGimpsey, who also ran the Town 'n' Country Inn in Newtownards. Many Christmas and New Year functions had to be cancelled or transferred to alternative venues, while the repair bill was estimated to run into "many thousands of pounds."

An architect's drawing of the new Town 'n' Country Inn to be erected at Main Road, Cloughey, by North Down Hotels Ltd. It is estimated to cost £100,000 and it is hoped to have it open by Easter, 1974. There will be accommodation of 12 double bedrooms with conference room, lounges and large dining and grill room facilities.

Pupils from Portavogie Primary School achieved great success at the Ulster Badminton Championships in January 1973. From left: Lorna Bell, Hester McCormick, Adelaide Rutherford and Karen McBride. 262-66-3

Described as Comber Road Primary School, Newtownards, in January 1973, their boys' team was the latest to enter the Newtownards and District Schools League. Unfortunately, at the time the picture was taken they had yet to record a victory. Described as "an unusual feature" of the team, one of the players was a girl – Susan O'Neill (front, right). The other players are (back, from left): Billy Lismore, Esmond Adair, Brian Johnston, Norman Wallace, Kenneth Butler, Victor Blain, Maurice Whitley. Front: Jim Patton, David Campbell, Billy Hamill and Samuel Quinn. 262-80-3

Portaferry Ploughing Society member William Johnston, from Kircubbin, took part in the world-style class at the annual Moneyrea Tractor and Horse Plough competitions in January 1973 at Unicarval, Comber

Ballywalter Junior BB won the Ards Battalion (Junior Section) 'Action Song Contest' with their rendition of 'Lily the Pink' in the Thomas McIlwrath Hall at Greenwell Street, Newtownards, in February 1973. Back (from left): Lt. J. Brian, A. Davidson, W. Monan, S. Orr, S. McKay, M. Neville. Front: E. Morrow, G. Shanks, C. Corry, S. Dempster, D. Eccles and D. Orr. Not included: S. Reid and D. Reid. 263-31-2

5th Ards BB's cross-country team won the Ards Battalion cross-country race at Comber in March 1973. From left: Alan Shaw, Francis McNulty, Colin Trueman and Frank Robinson. 263-41-1

First Comber Presbyterian Church Robins at their annual parents' night in March 1973. 263-75-1

Members of
1st Comber BB
at their annual
display in April
1973. 264-45-1

Some of the boys
and girls from St
Mary's Primary
School, Comber,
with Fr. McFerran
PP after receiving
their First Holy
Communion.
Included are Mrs
E. Falls (principal)
and Miss S. Devlin
(assistant teacher).
265-44-1

Teacher James
Miskimmin with
P6 pupils from
Londonderry
Primary School,
Newtownards, at
a farewell party
in May 1973 for
student teachers Mr
T. Shields and Mr A.
Stevenson. 265-64-2

Guests who attended the Lisbane and Lisbarnett Darts Club dinner dance at the Andrews Memorial Hall, Comber, in May 1973. 265-64-1

James Lemon, from Tower Road, Conlig, pictured in June 1973 with the model Ransome's threshing mill and Boyd baler he'd made over the previous five months. It went on show to the general public at the Balmoral Show. 265-39-2

Betty Byers (13), from Church Avenue, Kircubbin, with the Championship Cup she had won for the Double Reel at the Castlewellan Feis in June 1973. She was a member of the Ballycran School of Dancing. 266-32-3

Crowds watch as Kenneth Corken and Billy Kerr win the soap box derby at
Ballywalter Festival in June 1973. 35-1a-69

Competitors who took part in a sports day held in conjunction with the Millisle
Gala in July 1973. 5-13a-72

Sidney Spence, Worshipful Master of King David's RBP No. 175, with other officers and members of the band at his home in Stanwell Road, Greenwell Street, Newtownards, in August 1973. 30-10-73

Jack Savage, from Thomastown, Portaferry, leads his three-year-old donkey Suzie and five-week-old foal Thomas in August 1973. 25-11a-73

Students from Movilla Secondary School, Newtownards, were setting off on a trip to Switzerland in August 1973. 26-18a-73

Young people who were confirmed in St. Mark's Church, Newtownards, by the Bishop of Down and Dromore, the Rt. Rev. G. A. Quin, in September 1973. Included are the Rev. R. J. Chisholm, rector, the Rev. A. Morrow, curate assistant, and Mr Hamilton, organist.
267-76-3

Ards Gateway Club was presented with the Lawrie Trophy for swimming by Ards FC player/ manager Billy Humphries in October 1973. It was accepted on behalf of the successful swimmers by Errol McParland. Ards won the trophy in face of stiff competition from other Gateway Clubs around the British Isles. Coaches were Joyce Savage and Kay Trolan.
268-41-2

Members of the St. Patrick's (Portaferry) Ladies Committee at a dinner hosted by Portaferry GAC at the T'n'C in November 1973.
268-95-1

Regent House pupils before their annual prizegiving in
November 1973. 268-53-2

Mr E. McBlain, Millisle, gets a
helping hand from son Brice
in the tractor whole work
(open) section at Listooder
Ploughing Society's annual
competition in December
1973. 269-10-2

Brown Owl Mrs Ann Williamson received a surprise presentation of a stainless steel tea service to mark her 15 years' service with 1st Millisle Brownies in December 1973. The Rev. McAuley made the presentation, while Mrs Williamson also received a 15-year service ribbon from District Commissioner Mrs Sherrard. 269-7-1

Enoch Kirk, from Drumhirk Road, Comber, pictured in December 1973 with some of the trophies he had won in solo competitions in Ireland and Scotland during the previous season. The reigning All-Ireland solo champion, he was a member of the local Robert Armstrong Pipe Band. 269-31-1

Janette Lee (first) and Lorraine Burns (second), both pupils of Carrowreagh Primary School, with the certificates they received in the novice recorder class for under 12s at Bangor Musical Festival in December 1973. 269-6-2

Assistant teacher Mrs R. Willis with P1 and P3 from Ballystockart Primary School with infant Christmas murals depicting 'Follow the Star' and 'Santa Claus' in December 1973. 269-53-2

Section Leader Sam Parkinson, a member of the Portaferry Fire Service Unit for 26 years, was honoured at a retirement dinner in the local Scotsman licensed premises in late December 1973. He is pictured with Station Officer Jeff Jones, Sub Officer Robert Denvir (his successor), Leading Firemen and firemen. 269-63-3

Staff of Madge's Bar, the Corner House and the Abbey Arms at their Christmas dinner in the West Winds Roadhouse in late December 1973. 48-8-78

1973

Sport in the Chronicle

Following a string of successes both Margaret Dorrian and Cliff Thompson were called up for the Ireland table tennis team which would be competing in the World Championships in Yugoslavia that April. It was a first time trip for Margaret, while Cliff would be playing in his third and final World Championships.

Ards FC turned down an invitation in March – seemingly genuine – to play legendary Brazilian club Santos in a friendly fixture at Castlereagh Park after hearing it would cost them £5,000 plus £1,000 for expenses.

Ards Bowling Club officially opened their new pavilion off the Comber Road on 9 March. It had been constructed over a period of some five months on the site of the previous clubhouse.

Mr J. Lowry, president of Newtownards Bowling Club, watches as his wife officially opens the new season in April 1973. Club members look on. 264-40-2

The first all-girls rugby match involving pupils of Regent House took place on 5 April and raised funds for the school's Community Services Group. The game, between the Frilly Things and the Scarlet Pimpernels ended in a 4-4 draw. Tries were scored by Frilly Thing Catherine Lemon and by Scarlet Pimpernel Rosemary Harkness.

> **Frilly Things** – Ruby Keag, Evelyn Dobson, Linda Geddis, Alison McKelvey, Gina Smyth, Rosemary Morton, Marion Brown, Margaret Curry, Catherine Lemon, Hetty Gilmore, Lorraine Whyte, Dorothy Jardine, Margaret Groves, Anne Boyd and Carol Francis.
>
> **Scarlet Pimpernels** – Sally McKee, Rosalind Earnshaw, Ruby Johnston, Jean Selfridge, Olwyn Brown, Christine Stewart, Karen Burns, Fiona Carson, Barbara Neville, Barbara Gilliland, Rosemary Harkness, Cynthia Mitchell, Helen McKelvey, Alice Hanvey and Sharron Pinnons.

Ards Rugby Club, playing in the final of the Junior Cup for the first time in their 45-year history, lost out 20-12 at Ravenhill on 28 April to Ballymena, who were already holders of the Towns' Cup.

Newtownards Technical School won the Colts Cup (soccer) competition with a 2-1 victory over Dundonald High at the end of May. The goals were scored by Joe Long and David Bradley.

Colin Trueman of 5th Ards BB won the annual race from Conway Square to Scrabo Tower for the Columba Cup on 23 June. His time was 17 minutes and seven seconds (the record, set in 1968, stood at 15 minutes and 24.3 seconds).

Scrabo Golf Club won the Ulster Cup for the third time with an eight games to six aggregate victory over Fortwilliam. Team members were John Palmer, David Campbell, Johnny Rea, Jim Jordan, Ian Ross, Tom Davison and Jack Mawhinney. The non-playing captain was George Graham.

Enniskillen engineer Ted Keenan became the first Ulsterman to conquer the North Channel, between Donaghadee and Portpatrick, when he completed the marathon 32-mile swim on 11 August in 18 hours and 27 minutes.

Ards were defeated 3-0 by Crusaders in the early season final of the Carlsberg Cup. The consolation for Ards was a £500 runners-up prize but there were even better days in the offing!

North Down's cricketers won the Senior League's Section II following a single run victory over Donacloney at Comber on 25 August and a two-wicket win over Muckamore two days later.

Isobel Robson from Comber was a member of the squad for a fixture between the Northern Ireland women's soccer team and their English counterparts at Bath on 7 September.

Ards Bowling Club member Bill Curragh was acclaimed as All Ireland singles champion on 1 September when, as representative of the Private Greens League, he beat League of Ireland champion Don Mellor after staging an amazing comeback to win 21-18.

Ards made history on 12 September not only by hosting the first-ever European match at Castlereagh Park (previous fixtures having been held at Belfast grounds), but also by beating Belgian side Standard Liege 3-2 in the UEFA Cup first round encounter. Ronnie McAteer won with a penalty, the other Ards scorers being Dessie Cathcart and Billy McAvoy (also a penalty).

Standard Liege won the return leg a week later 6-1, giving them an 8-4 aggregate victory. Dennis Guy scored the Ards goal.

The Kiltonga Squash Club at Belfast Road, Newtownards, was officially opened on 8 September. The directors were Terence and Maureen Mack and Brian Hall. The opening was performed by Mr J. Copeland, president of the Irish Squash Rackets Associations and a former Irish international player.

Ards completed the first leg of what would become a trophy-laden season when they secured the Ulster Cup with a 1-1 draw against Crusaders on 13 October. They finished a single point ahead of Linfield and five points ahead of third-placed Bangor.

A second trophy, the Hennessey Gold Cup, joined the Ulster Cup in the club's trophy cabinet a little under three weeks later following a 4-1 victory over Bangor at the Oval on 1 November. Goalscorers were Guy (2), McAteer and Cathcart.

Ards Borough Council turned down a request from North Down Hockey Club on 11 December for permission to play matches against teams representing the Army on Sundays. The application related to the Council-owned all-weather hockey pitch at Parkway, Comber, as an alternative to their own pitch.

During a somewhat heated debate it was pointed out that the Council already opened its swimming pool in Newtownards on Sunday afternoon.

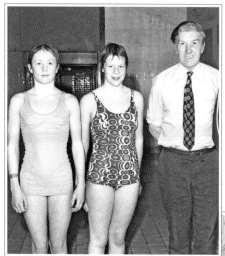

Diane Kirk (Movilla) and Sharon Boyd (Regent House), pictured with coach Gilbert McBride, were selected to represent Ireland in the Inter-Country Schools International event in Wales on 17 March 1973. 263-36-3

Mr R. A. Daniels, past chairman, and Mr W. McBride, past treasurer, hold an inscribed silver tankard presented in March 1973 by Mrs D. Murdoch on behalf of the Inler Angling Club, Comber, in appreciation of services given to the club. Both members were leaving for new lives in New Zealand. 264-28-3

Ards Battalion committee member Mr W. Hawkins presents the League Cup to B. Glenn, captain of the 1st Portavogie BB soccer team in May 1973. Back (from left): J. Beggs, Mr J. Mawhinney, D. Drysdale, B. Montgomery, B. Glenn, S. Mawhinney, Mr W. Drysdale, S. Cully, S. Thompson, Mr J. Miskimmin. Front: J. Palmer, W. Edmund, G. Mawhinney, M. McMaster and D. Clint. 265-44-3

Ballyblack Presbyterian Badminton Club won the Scrabo Badminton Cup in Section Six of the North Down League. Back (from left): N. Stewart (men's captain), W. J. Dalzell, M. Rankin, C. Rankin. Front: M. J. Lemon (ladies' captain), Miss B. Hanna, Miss H. Simpson and Mrs E. Rankin. 265-51-2

Terence Magowan, from Andrew Avenue in Comber, holds the rainbow trout weighing almost 6lb which he caught in Castlewellan Lake using a 4lb breaking strain line in September 1973. 267-78-1

The senior and juvenile badminton teams from St Mary's in Comber with chairman the Rev. H. Leckey in June 1973. The senior team had won Division 1 of the North Down Badminton League and the North Down Knock-Out Cup, while the juveniles (average age 12) had performed very well in their first competitive season. 265-87-3

Wendy Turkington

remembers ... Caravanning

In the late Sixties Wendy's father Tom and his father Alfred, both farmers all their lives, had identified an opportunity to diversify the business by developing some of their shorefront fields for people to pitch their caravans on for the summer months. .

By the Seventies when Wendy was born the business was rapidly expanding and thus Wendy's formative years were spent on the parks in and around holidaymakers and their caravans.

Today Wendy utilises many of the skills picked up in the family business to teach business, administration and retail studies.

My sister and I were born in the early 1970s when the caravan industry was entering an exciting period. Dad was working to secure the agencies of leading manufacturers Blue Anchor and Atlas, while at the same time local authorities and councils were beginning to appreciate caravanning's potential as a sustainable 'stay at home' boost to tourism and were gradually amending park licence rules.

One major licensing change involved allowing caravans to remain on caravan park pitches throughout the year. Every September, up until this time, Dad had to tow all of the caravans from Sandycove Park in Ballywalter across the road and store them in the main yard until the following Easter when the parks reopened. The operation involved lots of caravans, each with four jacks and usually wonky tyres, and with the help of only a Ferguson open-top tractor and Dad wonders why he has a bad back! The relaxation of that particular rule had a major impact on the evolution of the modern caravan, now more correctly known as a holiday home.

From memory, the stationary caravan model layout favoured in the 1970s was rectangular in shape, 10ft by 25ft, with a double end bedroom, a kitchen area and a front-cushioned seating area incorporating a fold-down dining table. The fold-down table was usually on the long side of the seating area and, of course, there was the all-important bunk bedroom. When meeting a new caravanning family for the first time it was not really important to find out who they were or where they were from; rather the priority was to find out who slept on the top bunk! Pemberton caravans had a fascinating 'pull down bed' but in most of the caravans a second bed was made up by folding down the dining table and rearranging the cushions.

Defining social hierarchy

In theory this sounds like a simple concept but making up the extra bed proved a perplexing challenge to some, with hilarious consequences. The curtains were generally yellow and orange with large flower patterns, which in someone's mind apparently matched the multi-coloured flowery upholstery of the cushioned seating area and the bright carpets.

Spot the bed!

The stationary model enabled local companies such as Whale to come up with innovative ways to pump water into the caravans. Super Ser and Valor developed safer systems and methods for cooking and heating, while Calor developed appropriate regulators and gas cylinder exchange sales.

From an early age I remember January being a very busy and exciting time as we had a constant stream of caravanners coming to the office to pay their annual caravan site rents and visit the accessory shop. All the administration was updated manually and the 'room with the locked door' housed what seemed to be hundreds of receipt pads, shelves and shelves of invoice books, and cabinets upon cabinets of bulging files. I was later to learn that Mum's extra-large desk diary was the centre of the administration hub. All, and I mean all, information had to be entered into the diary. Salesmen and others learned a salutary lesson – 'If an event was not recorded in the diary, it didn't happen!' My first important administration task was printing contact details for Sandycove on the back of the caravan brochures with a rubber stamp and ink pad.

DIY paradise at the Sandycove shop

Caravanners flocked to the accessory shop to buy items for both their homes and caravans. At that time there were no B&Q, Homebase or large supermarkets so Sandycove's accessory store was a real Aladdin's Cave for those needing packets of screws, hooks, torches, gas fittings, clothes pegs, batteries, etc. I was amazed at how the people seemed to get great satisfaction from bulk-buying items such as plastic sink basins, cutlery drainers, buckets, matches, glass mantles and gas globes. The luxury buy in the early 1970s was the latest model of Porta-Potti. It was also fascinating to watch people's excitement when the most up to date batch of Polywarm sleeping bags came into the shop. In fact at times the new ranges of sleeping bags seemed more important than the new ranges of caravans!

Although the caravan parks officially opened in the middle of March the first real buzz happened at the beginning of June. Caravanners took advantage of sunny 'exam time' weather and visited their caravans for the annual ritual of 'airing' them out for the summer. The parks would be adorned with makeshift drying lines with curtains, nets, sheets, etc. flapping in the sea breeze, while mattresses would be stacked in a variety of configurations to 'air'. I say 'ritual' as there was usually a tea or beer drinking ceremony associated with this task!

By the end of June there was a real hubbub around the caravan sites as caravanners started arriving for their summer break. It didn't matter if they arrived in a new Mercedes car, by bus or by taxi, or whether their holiday clothes were packed in leather suitcases or plastic bags, as once on site the first task everyone had to do was fill up their containers at one of the many water taps. Standing in the queues to fill those water containers was a great opportunity to meet people and make friends. People would work out rotas and 'buddy up' to fill containers. Of course, most people had a small spare container they would suddenly have to fill when certain individuals arrived at the tap to fill up their own container. I often asked Dad why people came out of their caravans and walked past two or three taps to fill their containers but I never really got a satisfactory explanation. Needless to say many romances were sparked waiting in the queue for the showers, water taps or at the payphone kiosk!

During the summer months as Dad's main helper I would sit alongside him in the caravan transporter, in the jeep or on the tractor happily watching everyone busily enjoying themselves. I think

Caravan transporter in the 1970s

I was about six when I decided it was time to help. While Dad was under a caravan painting the chassis with waste oil to prevent the salty air corroding it, I decided to speed up operations and paint the side of the caravan. When Mrs Miller saw my handiwork she screamed and fainted. It took Dad several weeks to repair and replace the panels of the caravan.

Those were some of the best weeks of my life and the start of my love for caravanning. With Mrs Miller as my adopted Nanny, I meet many friends when helping her fill the water containers and was introduced to many new exciting games, hobbies and pastimes. I still get excited when I hear an ice cream van's music and will never forget my first 'oyster shell' ice cream slider, the joy of catching my first lobster, and the horror I felt on seeing the poor creature being thrown into a pot of boiling water!

I even joined the elite group of aerial holders. When there were important football matches being screened some of the men used to wire televisions to batteries and hand us the aerials. The men would shout out instructions through an open window and we would dance about to try to get the best picture.

I spent many hours as part of the happy caravanning community in the 1970s. In the evenings, under flickering gas lamps, I listened to many stories about how important their caravans were to them and how safe and tranquil people felt staying at Sandycove and Ballyferris. I was too young to understand why Dad's caravan sites were described as a 'safe oasis' away from towns where emergency service sirens kept families awake at night, where soldiers with guns patrolled the streets and set up road blocks to search cars. It was an alien world to me.

Sandycove in the 70s

With the arrival of the beginning of July I remember a shroud of excited mystery surrounding the caravan parks. Trailers covered with tarpaulins arrived and piles of items were secretly covered at the sides of caravans. Basically, as some residents of Northern Ireland traditionally lit bonfires on the night of 11 July, so the caravanners in the parks used this date to light bonfires to mark the middle of the summer caravanning season. There was great competition between the caravanners along the stretch of beach, each competing to have the largest or most innovative fire, the fire that burnt the longest, the one who offered the best entertainment or served the best food, etc. My sister and I would go to bed really early on the 11th and then once the fires were lit Mum would wake us up and take us for a walk along the beach to join in the excitement. Sadly, now with environmental issues and health and safety legislation fires are not allowed to be lit on the beaches.

By August the parks were in full swing with a constant aroma of cut grass and barbecues lingering on the sea breeze. The tranquil buzz was often interrupted by the distant laughter of people playing on the beach or the occasional 'snore' from an outstretched body fast asleep on a sun lounger. I find it interesting to note that during the 1970s everyone seemed to be so busy enjoying the caravan life that the weather didn't seem to really matter. Nowadays, however, as portable battery-powered tellies have been replaced with plasma screens, rafts made from barrels and wooden crates have been replaced with jet skis and basic caravans have evolved into luxury holiday homes with all the modern conveniences, the weather, more than ever before, seems to play a major role in the overall caravanning experience.

But hey, anyone feeling nostalgic can always get a taste of the 1970s caravanning experience by immersing themselves in the latest glamping craze!

Frank Weir

remembers ... Kart Racing

The Ards Festival, which was held over a two-week period in the middle of June during the 1970s, always featured kart racing. Some would even say the kart racing was the highlight of the Festival, certainly if the huge crowd of spectators attending the races each year was anything to go on.

The races were held around the one-way system on closed roads and always on a Thursday evening. Thursday was chosen because it was half-day closing in Newtownards and the lesser footfall in the town centre greatly helped facilitate the setting up of the racing circuit. Practice runs usually started at 6.30pm, after the early evening buses had departed on their routes, and the racing got under way an hour later. By about 9.30pm it was time for the Mayor of the day to present the winners with their trophies and then the big job of cleaning up began.

During the early years of the event the paddock was that part of Regent Street adjacent to the Queen's

Frank Weir discovered kart racing in 1959 as a 12-year-old in an article in *The Motor*.

Eleven years later Frank graduated from the University of Strathclyde and for a graduation gift his parents bought him a kart. It soon became apparent that he would never be the quickest karter to grace the racing circuit.

However, he had an abundance of enthusiasm for the sport and in 1975 found a niche as an official of The County Down Kart Club.

In 1981, the 500 Motor Racing Club of Ireland, owners of Kirkistown Racing Circuit, took over The County Down Kart Club and Frank became the Competition Secretary for karting events held at Kirkistown.

Today in 2015, 34 years on, Frank still holds that position at Kirkistown.

Approaching the Start at the Post Office in Regent Street

Hall. The start/finish line was located at the light-controlled pedestrian crossing beside the Post Office. From the start the karts travelled along Frances Street behind the Town Hall before entering a speed-reducing chicane in front of what used to be the Ritz Cinema. Then the circuit continued along Frances Street before

Ken Graham negotiating the turn from Francis Street into The Doctor's Lane

making a right turn into The Doctor's Lane and heading down towards The Old Cross. Another right turn into High Street led the karts to Conway Square. The circuit turned right into the Square and a short distance further on it made a left to take a route across what was then the middle of the old Square car park, followed by a left turn onto a short straight towards a right turn into Mill Street.

In the early years of the races the circuit travelled a very short distance along Mill Street before making a right turn into Lower Mary Street, followed by a slight left and then a right turn back onto Regent Street to complete a lap at the front of the Post Office. Later the circuit was increased in length by continuing along Mill Street to Gibson's Lane, before entering Regent Street to head towards the start/finish area in front of the Post Office. This al-

Turning into Conway Square the late Bertie McIlwrath leads Bert Johnston, Ricky Smyth and George Weir

teration to the circuit necessitated moving the paddock to the area that stretched from the front of the bus station to the junction at Frederick Street.

The races always attracted large entries because they were qualifying rounds of the North of Ireland Karting Association Road Racing Championship. Competitors came from all over the island of Ireland and from further afield. On one occasion a group of Dubai karters participated under the guidance of Bert Johnston, a

Northern Irish gentleman who worked in the oil business in Dubai. He managed to persuade fellow members of the Dubai Kartwheelers Kart Club to make the trip to Newtownards to experience the thrill of racing karts on closed public roads. So taken was he by the area and the people, Bert would later return to Northern Ireland to set up a karting business in Newtownards known as Grange Karting. Other kart racing exponents from England and Scotland also participated, allowing them to sample the unique experience of racing on the closed public streets of Newtownards,

something that legislation would not allow at that time on mainland Britain.

The event was the idea of two dynamic members of what was then the Leisure Department of Ards Borough Council, namely John McKnight and David McVeigh. The racing was organised by the County Down Kart Club under the chairmanship of the late Hugh Lemon. Usually a week before the event a group of club volunteers would gather at Hugh's farm on the Ballycastle Road near

Pictured at the presentation of a cup from Ards Battery Service are (from left): T Wilkinson, H Lemon, Chairman of the County Down Kart Club, H Stanfield, N Blake and P Boyd (in Kart).

Newtownards. To a man they all had their socks stretched over their trouser bottoms to prevent the mice that lived amongst the loose straw in the barn travelling to places where they would not be welcome. The purpose of the assembly at Hugh's yard was to bale straw. Two large trailer loads of straw bales were used to mark out the course and to act as protection at corners should a racer lose control and collide with an immovable object. In charge of this part of the race operation was Hugh's son Brian, and in all the years he was responsible not one load of bales ever fell off a trailer during transportation to and from the circuit; quite an achievement considering the bales were built 10 rows high!

Just as the baling of the straw was a work-intensive activity, the provision of the public address was a job that took hours to erect and remove. The system was completely connected by wire – going wireless would be something for the future. This task was the responsibility of the then 'Voice of Karting', the late Derek Mason. Because all of the circuit could not be viewed at any one time, Derek and his fellow announcers, who were positioned at different locations around the circuit, kept the crowd fully informed about what was happening during the race.

In particular, Ards Borough Council, along with sponsorship sourced from local traders by the late Mary Lemon, wife of the organising club chairman, and donations received from the spectators attending the races, made the whole operation financially viable. Even then insurance cover and the costs associated with Road Closing Orders were substantial. The method of collecting donations from the spectators did not involve selling tickets as you would think; it was quite different and very low tech. Young ladies associated with the kart club walked around the circuit at the intervals during racing holding a large blanket at each corner – in such a way as to provide a cloth sump into which the coins thrown by the appreciative spectators could be collected!

Any form of motor sport is dangerous and in particular kart street racing. It was always a concern of the organisers that dogs and cats from nearby homes might encroach onto the racing circuit. There was also the possibility that inebriated patrons from local hostelries could evade the circuit marshals and be struck by a passing kart. Risk analysis in kart racing was still to be invented. In addition, a kart afforded little protection to its driver back then; crash-tested bodywork was also something for the future. However, in all the time the races were organised around the Newtownards town centre there were only ever a couple of broken ankles and one broken leg. Considering the speeds achieved and the nearness of such items as high kerbs relative to the size of small kart wheels, street furniture, trees, walls and shop windows, the kart racing safety record around the town centre circuit was better than good.

It may not have been the Ards TT races of the past, but competitors, officials and spectators enjoyed every minute of the kart racing. How could anyone possibly forget the colourful blossom at that time of year on the cherry trees around the town centre circuit, the sound of screeching tyres, the smell and the noise produced by rapidly racing two-stroke engines, and most of all the huge numbers of spectators who came to watch?

Donard McClean

remembers ... Ards Comhaltas Ceoltoiri Eireann

The first meeting of Ards Comhaltas Ceoltoiri Eireann (CCE) took place in Denis Calvert's home at Ballygrangee, Carrowdore, on 1 July 1976. For the next 36 years, until his untimely death in September 2012, Denis would be the driving force in promoting and fostering the love of traditional music, song and dance throughout the Ards area.

Denis was to be secretary and chairman for most of this period. It was no coincidence the first meeting was held in his own home, where many traditional musicians and friends would meet to enjoy the music and hospitality of Denis and his wife Anne. As the music sessions spread all over the Ards area, Denis would be at the forefront, always accompanied by his long tin whistle and a pint of Guinness, welcoming and encouraging friends and strangers alike.

Long before the setting up of Comhaltas there was a strong traditional scene in the Ards area. This is very well documented in Nigel Boullier's excellent book, *Handed Down: Country Fiddling and Dancing in East and Central Down* (Ulster Historical Foundation, 2013). The main sessions in the 1970s were held in Comber and Balloo, where the mainstay was a fiddler called Jackie Donnan. He enjoyed playing the local Co. Down tunes, not only in sessions but also at house parties and house dances. During the 1960s

Taking up a post in Bangor Technical College in 1971, Donard always had a keen interest in music having been taught to play the violin at a young age. As he could only play from sheet music he saw no sense going to a session where players were picking up tunes by ear.

This all changed when he wandered into a session in Newtownards and met the 6' 6" tall Denis Calvert, with his long beard and even longer tin whistle which he told Donard had been made in the Shipyard just as orders for ships were beginning to wane.

When Donard let it slip that he used to play the fiddle Denis demanded, as only Denis could do, that Donard turn up at the next session in the Saltwater Brig with fiddle in hand. And so started a journey which would take him all over Ireland, Europe and America.

The original Ards Comhaltas group (from left): Joe Mullan, Davy Simpson, Noel McQuoid, Jackie Boyce, Sean McGratton, Sam McAughey, Denis Calvert and Johnny Muir

Eddie McMullan from Newtownards regularly played the fiddle in the back room of Rice's Bar, accompanied by his wife Maud on the mouth organ. Eddie went on to form a ceili band, originally called the Tower Ceili Band and then the Shoresiders. This band included Jo Crilly on two row accordion, Joe Mullan, banjo, Johnny Muir, mouth organ and bones, Steve Egan, fiddle, Wee Eddie, piano, and Maud McMullan, who filled in on the piano when required. Nigel documents at least 40 musicians carrying on the tradition in the Ards Peninsula.

At the first Comhaltas AGM, held on Tuesday 30 November 1976, Joseph Mullan, another stalwart of the music scene, was appointed as chairman. The meeting got off to something of a 'sticky' start, the chairman-elect arriving late as he had fallen asleep by the fire! Joe, who was a banjo player and singer of considerable renown, was originally from Co. Tyrone but he had spent all his adult life in the Ards area, finally settling in Newtownards in the early 1960s with his wife Mary and family. Joe's love of traditional music was on a par with his passion for the GAA. He was among a group of dedicated Gaels who helped save Down hurling from possible extinction, being a member of Ballycran Hurling Club and secretary of the Down County Hurling Board.

Also present at that first AGM were Johnny Muir (Bangor), John Devlin (Portaferry), Sam McCaughey (Comber), Hugh and Marie Murphy (Kircubbin), Anne Calvert (Ballygrangee), Davy Simpson (Kircubbin), William White, George and Denise Russell (Bangor), Jackie Boyce (Comber), Joe Crilly (Newtownards), Dianna Skillen (now Boullier, Bangor), Noel McQuoid (Holywood) and Eddie McMullan (also Newtownards).

Ernie Swain (left) and Denis Calvert

The first session to be organised was the monthly one in Tom Finnegan's Bar at Kircubbin, while the first function was held on 25 March 1977 in Gilmore's Bar, Kircubbin, where the specially invited guests included Len Graham and the late Joe Holmes. The buffet supper for 100 people was in the very capable hands of Sheelagh Swain, Denis's sister, with Denis himself providing the free range chickens! The following year Sheelagh catered for 80 people at Portaferry Sailing Club, providing a meal for £1 per head, while at Christmastime Mavis Breen (Ardkeen) baked a cake which raised £40.

No sooner was the branch up and running than it had to plan for its first County Fleadh in 1978 and again in 1979, both in Portaferry. The first fleadh was organised with the support of the local gala committee and all agreed it was a huge success, with a profit of £100 being made. A further 10 fleadhanna would take place in Portaferry. They were always well organised events, welcoming musicians and visitors from all arts and parts.

A few years later Denis Calvert and his great friends Shirley, Tom and Ben Howard (Ballywalter) would revive the Ards Rhymers, who had last performed in the Ards area in the 1940s. The first meeting took place in The Tavern at Carrowdore, with the cast members travelling to the

The Rhymers

venue in Denis's cow trailer. Subsequently a TV crew came along to Finnegans Bar to film us in action. Presenter Sean Rafferty expressed his amazement at Miss Funny (Mavis Breen), who could say her lines, dance and smoke a cigarette all at the one time. RTE also spent a night with us. However, little did we know this would lead to a serious diplomatic row because all they showed was the fight scene, with the throwaway comment 'Sure they are always fighting in Northern Ireland.'

On a visit to a festival at Naul, to the north of Dublin, we were accompanied by Wilbur Magill playing the Lambeg drum. What a stir we caused that weekend! The Rhymers not only performed in the Ards area, but also throughout Ireland, Bulgaria, Sardinia and Washington, USA. In Bulgaria many people believed Denis Calvert was the real St Patrick.

The final year of the decade, 1979, saw the first of many All Ireland glories, with gold medals for Leon Agnew and Charlie Brown, both fine flute players. These days Ards CCE remains a strong force in the traditional music scene in the North Down and Ards area. From a small beginning of 16 members in 1976, today we have 120. For this we remain forever grateful for the foresight and courage of Denis Calvert, Joe Mullan and our other past members and musicians in the Ards area who kept the music tradition alive.

1974

Making the News in the Chronicle

Two members of long-established local families received Knighthoods in the New Year Honours List – Jack (J.L.O.) Andrews, from Comber, and Thomas Brown, from Portaferry. Mr Andrews was a former Deputy Premier of the Stormont Government (and also son of a former Prime Minister, Mr J. M. Andrews), while Mr Brown, a solicitor by profession, had given a lifetime of service to health-related matters. At that time he was chairman of the Eastern Health and Social Services Board.

Newtownards girl Maureen Redmond (19) was home for Christmas and the New Year from the Royal Academy of Music, where she was in her second year. While in Northern Ireland she took part in a recital in the Harty Room at Queen's University; it involved six individual young musicians aiming to make a career in music.

Speakers at a 'Save Ulster' rally in Newtownards Orange Hall on 9 January included the Rev. Ian Paisley, Harry West and Bill Craig. Opening and closing prayers were by the Rev. Robert Bradford.

> *"We have all had our differences in the past," declared Mr Paisley, "but tonight the loyalists are united and we are determined to lead the people of Ulster to victory and defeat the enemies of our beloved province."*

A new school for Comber, to be known as Andrews Memorial Primary School, was already operating in the Andrews Memorial Hall and in temporary classrooms

beside it. The existing Comber Primary School had become seriously overcrowded, hence the need for a second school. Plans were in hand to provide permanent premises on land adjacent to the hall, which had been formally taken over by the South Eastern Education and Library Board. The Board indicated its intention to make the hall available for community use upon completion of the new school.

> The body of a 41-year-old Dundonald man, Andrew Jordan of Kinross Avenue, Tullycarnet, was found in a field about a mile from Greyabbey on 14 January. Mr Jordan, father of five children, had been shot in the back of the head. He was reportedly abducted and murdered by the UVF.

Ards Borough Council granted the Glen Estate Tenants' Association permission in mid-February to use a house at William Street as a youth club until the area's new community centre was completed at the end of the year. The idea was that the club would open on three nights each week and would provide darts, snooker, draughts and other table games, as well as a coffee bar.

Members and friends of the Free Presbyterian Churches in Newtownards and Portavogie gathered outside the Regent Cinema in Newtownards on the evening of 4 March to protest against the screening of Jesus Christ Superstar. Some 40 or 50 people took part, with a number of them carrying placards. A short religious service was held after a letter of protest was handed to the management. It was signed by the Revs. A Chambers (Newtownards) and H. Cairns (Portavogie).

Portaferry town centre was devastated by a massive car bomb explosion on the night of 5 March, leaving many thousands of pounds worth of damage and a number of families homeless. The main targets for the bombers were two public houses at the Church Street entrance to the Square – the International Bar and Peter Tomelty's Inn – both of which were wrecked. Several adjoining houses were also severely damaged and rendered uninhabitable. There were no serious injuries but several people sustained cuts from flying glass.

Comber teenager Rory McKee, from Castle Espie Road, sustained serious injuries after he and a companion were caught up in an avalanche while climbing in the Cairngorms on 17 March. The 17-year-old Campbell College student suffered internal injuries which required several blood transfusions, while the other climber had a broken leg.

The Department of Agriculture advised North Down MP Jim Kilfedder in April that a feasibility study into enlarging and improving Portavogie Harbour was under way. Among the aims was to enlarge the harbour so it could accommodate 80 boats with an average registered length of 65ft.

The Ulster Workers' Council strike began just as the Newtownards Chronicle went to press and coverage in its 16 May edition was limited to the heading: 'Work comes to a halt' and an indication that a number of factory workers had found their way barred by 'strangers' and were turned away. Left with insufficient staff to maintain production remaining employees, who had reached their workplaces, were sent home.

By the second week the paper – itself beset by production problems – was reporting that industry in the area had "ground to a virtual halt", barricades that ringed Newtownards and Bangor had reduced traffic to the "barest minimum", electricity cuts were impacting on bread production, as well as coal and oil supplies, and there were numerous reports of businesses around the Ards being told to "close or else".

By the edition of 30 May the strike had been called off by the UWC following the resignation of Brian Faulkner and fellow Unionists from the Executive, the temporary (soon-to-be permanent) suspension of the Northern Ireland Assembly and the return of Direct Rule from Westminster.

The Catholic church in Kircubbin, along with the adjoining hall and parochial house were all extensively damaged when a 100lb bomb exploded on 7 June. The device had been placed at the side door of the church. Responsibility was claimed for the attack by the Ulster Freedom Fighters.

Scrabo Tower, by then in its 117th year, was becoming increasingly the target for vandals. Large lumps of the stonework had been hauled out of place, windows had been smashed and even the lock on the solid oak door had been broken. Other oak doors had been damaged beyond repair or stolen.

The death occurred of acclaimed Ulster comedian James Young after he suffered a heart attack while driving in Belfast on 5 July. The funeral took place from his home at Ballyhalbert to Roselawn Crematorium.

Rhonda Connell, who contributed notes about Conlig to the Newtownards Chronicle, was in the headlines herself when she recalled being evacuated to safety from strife-torn Cyprus in late July. She

had been on holidays in the resort of Famagusta when she became caught up in what she described upon her return home as "a raging war" which arose when the Greek Officer-led National Guard staged a coup on the island. Sleep proved impossible because of the incessant gunfire and shelling. Shortly after being evacuated to an RAF base four miles from Famagusta the town she had just escaped from was bombed by Turkish 'planes. Rhonda closed her report by saying it was "very nice to be back in friendly Northern Ireland."

Previously targeted twice for attack, the McKenna Community Centre at Kircubbin was completely destroyed by fire early on 15 August. North Down Assembly member Major William Brownlow said it "once again demonstrates that a handful of terrorists are trying to stir up community strife in the Ards."

The murder of Resident Magistrate Martin McBirney at his Belfast home on 16 September evoked considerable sympathy in The Ards as he had adjudicated at many local court sittings over a number of years. Solicitor Michael Bready, speaking at Newtownards Magistrate's Court the following day, said: "Never was a bench so faithfully served, never were the public of the area served as they were served by Martin McBirney, and never were they dealt with so fairly in their problems."

The parochial hall in Ballywalter was packed on 20 September for a farewell service to mark the retirement of Canon Cecil Jackson, rector of the local church for 37 years. Some 300 friends and parishioners attended, with parish patron Lord Dunleath taking charge of the proceedings. Canon Jackson's successor was the Rev. Cecil Mitchell – his brother, George, was rector of Bangor Parish.

Frank Cafolla and Sons of Conway Square, Newtownards, received a diploma in October from the Ice Cream Alliance for their ice cream. The Alliance, based in London, governed all of the United Kingdom.

Newtownards man John McLean (24), from Church Street, was murdered on 23 November by IRA gunmen as a reprisal for Catholic killings. He was shot in the back at the Edenderry Filling Station on the Crumlin Road where he was the newly-appointed manager, along with a female worker. A single man, he was the son of Mr and Mrs Thomas McLean, and had just returned home after a spell working in England.

A motorist who called for petrol at the station became suspicious when no one came out to serve him. When he looked into the small office at the back he saw the two murder victims. Both were Protestants.

The funeral service at St Mark's Parish Church on 26 November was followed by interment at Movilla Cemetery.

Portaferry man Patrick Vincent Cherry (36), from Steele Dickson Avenue, was murdered by UDA gunmen as he sat in his car in Newtownards on 25 November.

While on the night shift at the Rolls-Royce factory outside Dundonald he had been staying with his brother at North Street.

He parked in the vicinity of Castle Gardens School on the Portaferry Road waiting for workmates to join him. Instead, a gunman opened the door of his car and shot Mr Cherry, who was married and had two young daughters.

Requiem Mass at St Patrick's Church, Ballyphilip, on 28 November was followed by interment in the adjoining cemetery.

Lollypop lady Mrs M. Pollock of Queen's Square, Newtownards, won a place in the finals of the Nabisco 'Lollypop Man (or Lady) of the Year' competition in early December. She became the Ulster Television area representative after being nominated by Andrew Frater, a pupil at Victoria Primary School.

Weatherly Yachts Ltd., of Ballyfinragh, Portaferry, received an order in early December worth £27,000 for nine Ruffian 23 yachts, with an option for a further four, from the Royal Hong Kong Yacht Club. The company specialised in light displacement international racing yachts – the Ruffian 23 had achieved an excellent record for Weatherly.

Churches in the Newtownards area offered assistance to anyone who was disturbed after seeing the controversial Exorcist film at the local Regent Cinema. Pastor W. H. Holohan of the town's Elim Pentecostal Church told of encountering a girl who

> *"in a state of obvious shock (after seeing the film) collapsed on the footpath at my feet and had to receive medical attention."*

Mrs Anna Robson, of Castle Street, Newtownards, celebrated her 101st birthday on 22 December. She was predeceased by her husband John, who ran a grocery business in Castle Street. The couple had married in 1896. Mrs Robson lost two brothers during the First World War while a third was wounded helping to capture Al Capone. She passed away on 2 September 1976, aged 102.

North Down MP and local Assembly member Jim Kilfedder signs a petition outside Newtownards Town Hall rejecting the Council of Ireland, the Executive and the Sunningdale Agreement in late January 1974. Included are fellow Assembly member Charles Poots and United Ulster Unionist Council delegates. 270-16-3

Children from Magherascouse Primary School who took part in an Ulster Savings Movement concert and rally in Ballygowan in February 1974. 270-49-2

Picture from the Donaghadee branch UFU Cereal judging presentation includes Joan and Walter Brown, Frank Armstrong, Shirley Patterson, David McWha, Sally Humphries, Nelson Irwin, Lynn Semple and Harry Humphries.

Pupils from Alexander Dickson Primary School at an Ulster Savings Movement concert and rally in Ballygowan in February 1974. 270-49-3

Mr and Mrs William Mullan, of Shore Road, Portaferry, were joined by family and friends at the New Mount Royal Hotel, Donaghadee, to celebrate their golden wedding anniversary on 25 February 1974. The couple had eight children, 24 grandchildren and three great-grandchildren. 87-6-79

Re-elected North Down MP Jim Kilfedder and supporters travelled around Newtownards and district following his success in the late February 1974 General Election.

The Rev. T. A. McAuley partnered Mrs R. Kennedy and Mrs R. Colville in the Russian Ballet at a fundraising Irish Night in Carrowdore Parochial Hall in March 1974. 271-48-2

Boys from Portaferry Youth Club chopped blocks for local pensioners on Major William Brownlow's farm in March 1974. Included are Major Brownlow, Rev. Fr. P. McCollum and the Rev. J. Moore. 73-7-80

James Lemon, captain of 1st Ballygowan BB Company, was inspecting officer at the annual inspection and display of the 6th Ards Company. He is pictured presenting the Duke of Edinburgh Silver Award to Sgt. T. Millar. Sgt. Millar and Staff Sgt. D. Cunningham also received their President's Badges from their mothers. From left: Hugh W. J. Morrison, captain of 6th Ards BB, Mr J. Lemon, Mrs Lemon, Sgt. T. Millar, Mrs Millar, Staff Sgt. Cunningham and Mrs Cunningham. 271-70-1

Mr and Mrs W. Dodds, of Barnagh Grove, Donaghadee, enjoyed great success at the Ulster Golden Retriever Club's annual show in Lisburn in April 1974. Their two-year-old dog Royal Bleu Cavalier came second in the novice class, while their seven-month-old bitch Samara Pippa won first prize for the best bitch pup as well as a cup for the best pup in the show. 47-14a-82

Student nurses from Ards Hospital took part in a protest demonstration in April 1974 because of increased food prices in the hospital canteen and the failure of a promised pay rise to materialise. 68-6a-82

Mrs Mary Davison, from Victoria Road, Ballyhalbert, who celebrated her 100th birthday on 1 July 1974, holds the telegram she received from the Queen. 97-22-87

Three-year-old Samantha Prentice, from Tullynagardy Road, Newtownards, appeared on Ulster Television's Romper Room in April 1974. 54-7-81

Officers and members of Millisle BB at their annual display in the Presbyterian Church hall in April 1974. 76-19a-82

Pupils and teachers of the newly-formed Scrabo Tower School of Dancing who won major prizes in the open and confined classes at Bangor Music Festival in June 1974. 8-10a-85

Members of the Victoria Primary School PTA organised an end-of-term fancy dress parade for the children in June 1974. 1-7-87

Prizewinners from Carrowdore Show in June 1974. Back (from left): W. Ralston, Mrs E. Breadon, Robert McClurg, David McClurg, William McDonald. Front: J. McCracken, Lester Breadon and Bryan Hamilton. 15-24a-87

Aidan (11), Gerald (6) and Anne McGrattan (11), from John Thompson Park in Portaferry, with the trophies they won in an Irish Dancing festival at Movilla Secondary School, Newtownards, in July 1974. 27-37-88

Raymond Mitchell (Ballygarvan), Jackie Harris (Cloughey) and Ian Angus (Ballygarvan) at Greyabbey Horse and Pony Show in July 1974. 46-19a-88

Clergy and vestry members of St Mary's Parish Church in Comber with Mr D. F. Galbraith, who received a presentation in September 1974 to mark his 21 years of service as honorary secretary of the Select Vestry. 39-13a-91

Staff and management from Wardens of High Street, Newtownards, who enjoyed their first annual outing (to Portrush) in September 1974. Tom Fulton was the organiser. 59-28-91

1st Comber Presbyterian Church Young Wives during a break in the Beetle Drive they enjoyed in September 1974. 67-11-91

1st Newtownards Junior Christian Endeavour members at their installation service and presentation of prizes in September 1974. 13-9a-93

Sam Leckey, who had worked for Miskelly Bros. Quarries in Ballygowan for 45 years, received a retirement presentation in October 1974 from Mr A. Hanna on behalf of fellow workers. Included is manager Mr F. B. McKeown. 47-14-93

Star of Ards No 47, winners of the Junior Orange Women's Association of Ireland Sister Margaret Neill JP Memorial Perpetual Challenge Cup in October 1974. They received the trophy for introducing into their ranks the greatest number of new members in one year. 16-4-94

3rd Ards Scouts (St Mark's) took part in a 12-hour sponsored soccer marathon in the Scout Hall at Circular Road, Newtownards, in October 1974. 71-20-94

Officials and prizewinners of Millisle and District Pigeon Club in October 1974. 73-9-94

No fewer than 28 Post Office employees from Newtownards and district received safe-driving awards from the Royal Society for the Prevention of Accidents at the Town 'n' Country Inn in November 1974. Included with the men are Mr G. E. Templeton (RoSPA), Mr R. A. Drennan (Postmaster in Newtownards), Mr E. Mason (Head Postmaster, Belfast) and Chief Inspector D. McClinton (RUC). Among recipients were Alexander Eagleson (19 years), Robert Paden (18 years), Robert McBride (17 years), David Morrow (15 years), John Smyth (14 years), John Paden (12 years) and Wellesley Caughers (10 years). 49-18a-96

Pupils of Donaghadee Primary School received prizes in November 1974 following a very successful letter-writing competition organised by the Donaghadee Road Safety Committee. Sgt. Reynor from the RUC Traffic Branch handed over the prizes to Julianne Waugh, Janet Johnston, Ian Gourley, Russell Napier, Roger Moore, Kathy Sandford, Gary Girvan, Alan Mills, Ivan Moore, Karen Jayne Clegg, Fiona Ferguson, Joanne Robinson and Sonya George. Included in the photograph are Mrs Moore, secretary of the Donaghadee Road Safety Committee, Sgt. Reynor, the Rev. Gray and school principal Mr J. McKeag. 49-8-95

Mr A. F. Arnold, secretary of the North Down Savings Committee, is pictured with pupils of Victoria Primary School, Ballyhalbert, after handing over a certificate in December 1974 to mark 25 years of saving at the school. Included are Mr W. Thompson, organiser for County Down, Mrs K. E. McIvor, principal, and Miss H. E. McKee, assistant. 85-12-96

Roy Finlay, from Dromena Gardens, Newtownards, a member of the local camera club, was named Regional Photographer of the Year in December 1974. It was organised by the Northern Ireland Post Office Sports Association. 87-33a-96

1974

Sport in the Chronicle

Ray Mowat played his 400th game for Ards on 14 February in an Irish Cup first round replay against Ballyclare Comrades. He marked the occasion by scoring his 110th goal for the team in a 4-2 victory. Davy Graham was making his 100th appearance for Ards in the same fixture.

Regent House U14s won the Campbell College Invitation 'Sevens' Cup on 13 March, having defeated Belfast Royal Academy, holders Methodist College (twice) and hosts Campbell College.

Movilla Secondary School lost 4-1 to Dundonald Boys' High School in the final of the North Down Junior Cup. It was held at Castlereagh Park on 6 April. The home side's goal was scored by centre-forward David Campbell.

Ards secured their third trophy of the season with a 2-1 victory over Ballymena United in the Irish Cup final at Windsor Park on 27 April. The scorers were Dennis Guy and Billy McAvoy. They had previously won the Irish Cup in the 1926-27, 1951-52 and 1968-69 seasons.

An amazing fourth trophy was secured just 10 days later when Ards won the all-Ireland Blaxnit Trophy by beating Ballymena United 3-1 in the final at Windsor Park. The goals were scored by Dessie Cathcart, Ronnie McAteer and Syd Patterson.

Ards lost out to Instonians 2nd XV in the Junior Cup final at Ravenhill on 27 April. Instonians scored a try in the dying seconds of the game to secure a 10-9 victory.

Movilla Youth Club wound up the table tennis season in early May by winning the Belfast and District Senior League. It was the first time the title had been won by a local club since 1964 when the (subsequently) defunct Ards club was successful. Movilla team members were David Addy, Derek Weir and Stephen Tracey.

Newly promoted to the top section of the Senior League, North Down 1st XI began the season on 4 May with a 52-run defeat at the hands of old County Down rivals Downpatrick.

Ards bowler Bill Curragh failed in his bid to win the British Singles title in Edinburgh on 16 July after he lost by 21-10 to eventual winner David Bryant, already the English and World champion.

Regent House pupil Ken Campbell, from Ballyrainey Road, Newtownards, won the Ulster Schoolboys Golf Championships at Shandon Park in early August. He was a member of Donaghadee Golf Club and was also an Ulster and Ireland international schoolboy cricketer.

Ards met Dutch club PSV Eindhoven – including six World Cup internationals – away from home in the first round of the European Cup Winners' Cup on 18 September and suffered a long-to-be-remembered-for-all-the-wrong-reasons 10-0 defeat. The second leg, held at Castlereagh Park a fortnight later, was a little less painful, with Ards losing the fixture 4-1. The home side's goal was scored by Dennis Guy (equalising an early opener by the Dutch masters).

The Queen's Hall Billiards Club made history in October by winning the Belfast and District Senior Billiards League for the first time. There had been a billiards room in Newtownards Town Hall dating back to the late 1890s.

The North Down Table Tennis League was revived in mid-October with nine clubs taking part, including a number from the Ards area. An appeal went out for the return of competition trophies which were the property of the old North Down League.

Ards players Ronnie Cromie and Jackie Warren were both on the Northern Ireland Youth soccer team which defeated Iceland 3-1 at the Oval on 22 October.

Jason Forsythe, who learnt his rugby at Regent House and had been a member of the Ards side for a matter of months, was selected to play for Ulster Colts against Connaught in an inter-provincial game at Omagh on 30 November.

Newtownards postman Jack Cash (left) holds the Belfast County Singles Table Tennis Cup which he won in January 1974, some seven years after first hitting the headlines at the age of 16 following his successes at a provincial level as a member of the great Glenford team of the late 1960s. Also included is Clifford Thompson, another major name from the Ards table tennis scene. 269-90-2

The 1st Ballygowan and 2nd, 5th and 6th Ards BB teams who competed in cross-country races at Comber in February 1974. The event was organised by the Ards Battalion. 270-96-2

Richard Henderson and Sandra McCready, from Kircubbin Presbyterian Church Badminton Club, won the mixed doubles at the North Down Minor 'B' event in Bangor in March 1974. 271-22-3

Members of Ards Cricket Club were presented with their trophies by Mrs Ann Jones at their annual dinner and prize distribution in March 1974 at La Mon House, Gransha. From left: Robert Dunn, Anthony Payne, John McMillan and Geddis Dunn. 71-24-80

Members of Scrabo Rovers with trophies they won in the Ards Juvenile League in April 1974. 87-22-81

Bowlers from Carrowdore Parish Church show off their trophies at the annual dinner in May 1974. 18-10-83

Young table tennis players from Movilla Secondary School, Newtownards, returned home with three trophies from the Northern Ireland Championships at the Antrim Forum in April 1974, including league and cup winners. Back (from left): D. Law (PE teacher), G. Milliken, B. McMillan, C. Thompson (non-playing captain). Front: B. Haughian (junior captain), T. Boyce (senior captain) and T. Alexander. 86-12-82

The Newtownards Royal British Legion table tennis team won the H. Samuel Trophy in Portadown at the beginning of June 1974. It was their 22nd success in the competition out of 23. From left: A. Wright (junior), D. McClements, A. Wright (senior), R. Drain and J. Gaw. 9-17a-85

1st Donaghadee Junior BB beat 1st Comber in the final of the Ards Battalion Boys' Brigade Junior Section Knock-Out Cup in June 1974. 101-14a-84

Samuel Taylor delivers the first bowl at the opening of the new season for Cloughey Presbyteran Church Indoor Bowling Club in October 1974. 82-29a-93

The 2nd Comber Presbyterian Church BB team won the Ards Battalion League in June 1974. 91-91-85

Members and friends of Newtownards Sailing Club at their annual dinner and prize distribution, which was held at the Strangford Arms Hotel in October 1974. 32-3-93

Portavogie Gymkhana committee members and prizewinners at their annual dinner and presentation night in the New Mount Royal Hotel, Donaghadee, in October 1974. 272-44-1

Kieran McCarthy

remembers ... Kircubbin

Kieran McCarthy was born and reared at Ballycranmore near the Kirkistown racing circuit.

He attended St Joseph's Primary School and then Newtownards Technical College when it was located in South Street (where the Ards Arena is situated).

Kieran was first elected to Ards Borough Council in 1985, representing the Ards Peninsula and was returned at every subsequent election until he retired from Ards Council in 2013 after a total of 28 years as Councillor.

In 1990 Kieran took on more duties and responsibilities when he was appointed as a Justice of the Peace for the Ards Court District. In 1996, Kieran was elected to the Forum for Political Dialogue and participated in all of the talks leading to the Good Friday Agreement in 1998.

The late 1960s and early 1970 proved a very busy, exciting and happy time for me as I was married in July 1967 and we were expecting the birth of our second child at the beginning of 1970; Joanne McCarthy duly arrived on 27 February that year. At that time I was living in Church Avenue, Kircubbin, with my wife Kathleen and our one-year-old son Sean.

Before we were married, Kathleen and I opened a small drapery lock-up shop at Main Street, Kircubbin; at that time I was employed full-time, working in Cyril Lord's carpet factory, based at Rathgael just outside Bangor (where the Department of Education now has its headquarters).

We enjoyed living in the village although coming from a very isolated, rural setting of Ballycranmore, it took us some time to adjust to having neighbours all around us in the new housing estate. We made the decision to look for a suitable property on the Main Street of Kircubbin where we could live and have the shop all under one roof. The property at numbers 3, 5 and 7 came on the market and it seemed ideal for us, so we purchased it and were delighted that it also included the building which was the long-closed Picture House, called the Amethyst, at the back of the building on Main Street. We settled happily into our new home where we still live today and we also kept the drapery shop running for the next 40 years.

While the late 1970s may have been relatively uneventful in the local community, my own family was blessed with the arrival of another daughter who proved to be great company for her brother Sean and sister Joanne. Angela has always kept us 'on our toes' and added a lot of fun and love to the McCarthy household. Later, another son, Philip, would add even more joy to our family life.

My main interests in the 1970s concerned local football and hurling activities. Kircubbin has always had a great football team and indeed still does to this day. Of course, to have a successfully run football team, you need some really good administrators and I can recall William James Gilmore, Leslie Sinclair and their fellow helpers, yet I would have to admit my loyalties as a football supporter lay with teams from my rural homeland area, such as Road End Spurs and Cookstown. The hurling activities took place at Rubane, a few miles outside Kircubbin, and Rowreagh.

A brand new park had been opened in 1966 and this provided an excellent sporting facility for young people. The development of the park was the result of long hours of hard work by dedicated hurling enthusiasts over many years. Eventually it was opened and named McKenna Park after the headmaster of Ballycranbeg Primary School who always encouraged young pupils to get involved in outdoor sporting activities such as hurling as a means of getting some healthy exercise. This is how Ballycran GAC and Hurling Club came into being. By the end of 1970, the number of fixtures increased and the club was host to many well-known hurlers, so a brand new community centre and clubhouse was built at the McKenna Park grounds and was officially opened on 26 December 1970. During the 1970s, the successful Ballycran hurlers brought home many trophies and were highly regarded not only in Ulster but right across Ireland.

I recall the local football club in Kircubbin was not so fortunate as regards the standard of pitches and changing facilities. Their first home pitch was on a privately-owned field at Monaghan Bank in Kircubbin village, beside Strangford Lough. The managers and players were always

Later that same year he was again successful when he was elected to the new Northern Ireland Assembly at Stormont, becoming an Assembly Member for the constituency of Strangford.

He continues to serve as an MLA and is a Member of the Assembly's Agriculture and Fisheries Committee, as well as the Health Department's Statutory Committee. In addition he is the Alliance Party's Health spokesperson.

Kieran lives on the shores of Strangford Lough in Kircubbin, on the exact site of the former Amethyst Cinema, with his wife Kathleen and daughter Joanne. Kieran and Kathleen have been blessed with five wonderful grandchildren: Matthew, Laura, Cara, Shea and Michael.

Ballycran won the Ulster Club Hurling Championship in February 1977. 2-18a-19

grateful for the use of the field, even though we had to endure a stiff, cold breeze coming from the direction of the Lough. However, the teams always performed well at both junior and senior levels and on several occasions they brought back some silverware to the village, thereby instilling a sense of pride in the local community. When the Church Avenue estate was being developed in the late Sixties the local Council and others used to dump refuse into a landfill area between the new houses and Monaghan Bank. After it was filled up, the site was levelled by Council workmen who created a pitch and a pavilion to give Kircubbin Football Club a respectable place to host its home matches.

Of course, the 1970s could be a very dispiriting time as 'the Troubles' were raging across Northern Ireland and our own community was to become a target of terrorist activity when the McKenna Community Centre was destroyed by fire. Afterwards, the community rallied round and despite the setback caused by the fire, the hall was eventually rebuilt, even bigger and better than before and it continues to function as the most wonderful facility for everyone in the community to enjoy.

Another devastating incident happened in 1974 when our church, St Mary's Star of the Sea at Nunsquarter, was seriously damaged as a result of a terrorist bomb. The church was closed for nearly two years while the damage was repaired before it was re-opened in 1976.

The community centre offered all sorts of leisure pursuits and a cherished memory for me was my time with the Ballycran Amateur Dramatic Club, which was founded in 1978 at the McKenna Hall. I appeared in a few of the productions and can recall taking part in the play 'The Field', written by John B Keane, where my character was Dandy McCabe. I really enjoyed my acting scenes when I worked alongside so many talented people and we succeeded in giving local folks a good night out. We even took 'The Field' to the bright lights of Holywood (County Down, that is!) where we played to an audience in St. Patrick's Hall.

Another memory from my time spent at the Ballycran club was the formation in 1971 of a bowling club which competed in the league. The Ballycran bowlers, named Rowreagh Bowling Club, travelled to fixtures in places throughout the land and were, in turn, hosts for visiting clubs for return matches at the McKenna Centre, which created a great sporting fraternity.

Charles Bell, the most senior member of Rureagh Indoor Bowling Club, drives the jack at the first game to be played at the local McKenna Centre, in September 1971. Included are members of the Portaferry Presbyterian Church team. 246-79-2

During the height of the Troubles there was one particular event which brought me into public life. I attended a meeting in the Herron Hall in Kircubbin to consider what could be done to keep our community together. The outcome was the formation of a local community group to bring forward ideas and encourage people to improve the environment in and around the village. The new group became known as the South Ards Community Association and a committee was duly elected to bring forward plans to make Kircubbin a better place in which to live.

This proved to be my first experience of campaigning on behalf of the public. One of the first tasks facing the group was to find a suitable location for a car park for residents and visitors that would be close to Main Street in Kircubbin. Around 1973, we identified The Green, which had a square surrounded by derelict housing, and managed to secure an agreement to have the houses demolished and a car park formed, while still retaining a few green spaces. This was achieved with the help of the local Council in conjunction with other statutory agencies and the car park is still used to this day. The Council also engaged the services of Enterprise Ulster to construct a promenade along the seafront, provide a children's playground and complete the work at Kircubbin's football pitch, which all improved the general environment in and around the village.

It was around this time my employment at the carpet factory came to an end because the work I had been doing was transferred to a plant based in Lancashire. However, I found employment with Enterprise Ulster where I had the task of completing the work on the promenade in Kircubbin, so I really can claim to have had a hand in what we see today! Some of the work I did involved levelling the football pitch and removing stones using a tractor and rake and, after that was finished, I did the same thing for the pitches at Dairy Hall, behind the ambulance station in Newtownards. I stayed on with Enterprise Ulster for the remainder of the Kircubbin project before I returned to work at Donaghadee Carpets.

The South Ards Community Group continued to lobby for better facilities and we received great help from Cllr Billy Sheldon and Lord Dunleath, who at that time operated out of an Alliance constituency office on Kircubbin's Main Street. When these two Councillors decided to retire in 1985, they approached me about becoming a candidate in the election for Ards Borough Council. However, I declined a number of their requests as I was busy earn-

Kieran McCarthy and family in 1979

ing a living and rearing a family. They persisted and finally persuaded me to put my name forward and I was elected to the Council that same year – and was returned at each election until I stood down in 2013 after 28 years of service with Ards Borough Council.

I am glad I was persuaded to stand and was pleased to represent the constituents in the Ards Peninsula at the Council over those 28 years. I trust I have helped to make a difference for the better. The Councillors themselves honoured me with the title of Alderman which I was delighted to accept.

As the decade was drawing to a close, one of my most abiding memories was something I would never have expected to experience, namely the Pope's visit to

Drogheda in September 1979. This was a very special time for people throughout Ireland as it was the first time in history that a Pope had come to this part of the world. Many people from Kircubbin and around the Ards Peninsula made the trip to Drogheda, Dublin, Galway and other towns to witness this important visit.

I accompanied my daughter, Joanne, who was nine years old at that time and because of Joanne's rare medical disorder we were allocated two seats on a special coach trip to Drogheda. I remember both of us getting ready to leave the house at 3am, with Joanne's wheelchair packed into the back of my black Morris Minor car, and heading for the coach parked at Finaghy Road North in Belfast and we made the connection on time. When we arrived at Drogheda a huge crowd had gathered. I had difficulty pushing Joanne's wheelchair across the field but we reached our allocated space and waited for the Pope's helicopter to descend.

The excitement among the crowd was palpable which added to the momentous nature of the occasion and we were so fortunate to have a close-up view of Pope John Paul II when he gave his blessing as his 'Popemobile' passed by. It was a long day for both of us and Joanne slept on the coach all the way back to Belfast. By the time I had driven back to Kircubbin it was well after midnight but 29 September 1979 will be a day that Joanne and I will always cherish.

People living in Northern Ireland will have some troubling memories from the 1960s through to the 1990s but thankfully we now live in more settled times. It has been a pleasure for me to reminisce about some of the experiences that affected my life as well as the good people of Kircubbin and district during the 1970s.

Brian Ambrose

remembers ... Teenage Years in Portavogie

Brian's career, spanning 38 years in the aviation industry, has included senior management positions within Bombardier in Engineering, Business Development and Operations.

In 2004 he was appointed Chief Executive of Belfast City Airport and is responsible for a growing business with an annual passenger throughput in excess of 2.5 million. Employing 1,600 people to support 110 flights each day, the airport is a significant contributor to the NI economy.

Brian is also currently Chairman of Mencap Northern Ireland, Chairman of Tourism Ireland, Non-Executive Director of Phoenix Natural Gas, a Trustee of the Titanic Foundation and a Board Member of Business in the Community.

He was awarded an OBE in the New Year Honours in 2011.

What did The Ards look like in the 1970s through the lens of a teenager? Well it commenced with the daily 15-mile bus journey from Portavogie to school at Regent House. A number of big building projects were under way then, including the pioneering Ards Shopping Centre, better known as Woolco. The local tradesmen who shared the Ulsterbus journey enjoyed passing the time by lifting me and placing me in the luggage rack of the bus – life was certainly never dull.

The opening of Woolco changed shopping habits and over time we would no longer have the weekly visits to our home of the grocery van, the bread van, the butcher's van, the fruit and vegetable van, the lemonade man, the milkman and the chip van. The midweek visit of the latter was a highlight as the van arrived just before 'Sportsnight with Coleman' on the BBC. We only had three television channels then and colour sets, which most people rented, were a new arrival at the beginning of the decade.

To be cool in the 1970s involved wearing school trousers which were widely flared, Bay

The Lemonade Man. Photo courtesy of Miane Soft Drinks Ltd.

City Roller tartan stripes for the girls (not regulation uniform I should add), Noddy Holder sideburns for those with enough facial hair to grow them, kipper ties and platform shoes. I tended to fail the coolness test on most counts. A wrangler jacket was standard fare but they were not permitted as an outer garment at Regent House and so I had to wear a ridiculous navy overcoat. I probably set a world record for the number of times I arrived home without my coat, followed by my dad driving to Portaferry to retrieve it from the Ulsterbus lost property office.

The transition to Regent House from a small primary school was effortless, apart from the trauma of discovering that football was purely a lunchtime kick-around in the tennis courts, while 'rugger' and cricket were the sporting options. That said, I did play alongside Philip Matthews who went on to captain Ireland. However, my rugby career lasted only three weeks before it was decided my skills might be better suited to cross-country running – which appeared to be a mindless pursuit to this 11-year old. While the cross-country roll of honours was a tad limited, Regent nevertheless enjoyed some great success in the 1970s, thanks in no small measure to one particularly memorable games teacher.

Football at the turn of the decade wasn't so bad for a Manchester United supporter as nine of the 1968 European Cup-winning team were still playing and the Best, Law and Charlton triumvirate was still creating memorable matches. Several decades of Liverpool dominance hadn't quite arrived to leave emotional scars that would remain until the Alex Ferguson era put things back in proper order. In those days it was actually okay to acknowledge publicly to being a Leeds United, Wolves or Spurs supporter.

I still argue that the 1970s was a decade of pioneering technology, even if my kids don't buy the argument that the CB Radio was a 1970s equivalent to the iPhone 6. We did, however, progress through school without the aid of a PC, never mind mobile devices. With iTunes still decades away, I know of people who purchased LPs by Slade, Mud and Status Quo – and it says it all when the dreaded Bay City

Rollers were more popular than Bob Dylan.

A house alarm salesman would have had difficulty surviving during my teenage years as it wasn't actually customary to even lock the back door of your home at night or your car for that matter.

The fishing industry was thriving in Portavogie with perhaps 80 trawlers fishing mostly for cod and whiting in the Irish Sea. Among my peer group, a sizeable number of boys left school and 'joined the fishing', going on to demonstrate their superior earnings with the standard purchase being an RS2000, complete with additional Cibie spotlights.

My earnings as an apprentice in Shorts stretched to a second-hand Mini, which did receive the usual upgrade with a Man Utd stick-on sun visor. I did thankfully retain a degree of respectability and stopped short of a large set of dangling furry dice!

As part of my apprenticeship I did get to work in the local Hawlmark factory on the Crawfordsburn Road. I guess the pressures weren't quite the same back in the Government-owned era and so I put my time to good use, manufacturing a full set of tools using scrap metal. That tactic kept us apprentices out of trouble, well most of the time. We made components for the Shorts SD3 Series aircraft and

Shorts Skyvan taking off from the grass at Newtownards Airfield
Photo courtesy Shorts

its predecessor the Skyvan, affectionately known as the 'flying bread van' due to its square-shaped fuselage. There was a clear hierarchy with the hand adjusters, panel beaters and tool room operatives, but as apprentices we got to sample them all and then transfer back to Queen's Island with our newly acquired skills.

All those life experiences during the 1970s provided a platform which, looking back, had many positives to them. Whether it was school in Ards, work in Hawlmark, life in Portavogie or the blessings of home life, it all helped mould character, instil values and provide experiences for which I will always be extremely grateful.

Richard Young

remembers ... Racing at Kirkistown

While the Seventiess were traumatic years for Northern Ireland in general, it's fair to say that the Ards Peninsula was spared much of the pain which engulfed many other parts of the Province.

Fair, too, to say that motor sport on two wheels and four managed to remain largely untouched by the conflict going on elsewhere.

Kirkistown, therefore, managed to conduct business as usual throughout the decade, with full programmes of car and motorcycle races being run each year, and large crowds attending every one.

The owners, now as then, were/are the 500 Motor Racing Club of Ireland, which was formed to foster racing for the then-cheap 500cc Formula 3 cars of the 1940s and 50s.

Among the largest was an International Formula 3 event, held in conjunction with 'Ulster 71', a programme of events, sporting and cultural, with an exhibition centred on the Botanic Gardens in Belfast.

Formula 3 then was the recognised 'stepping stone' to Formula 1 and the 500 Club put together a truly international entry list with drivers from the USA, Germany, France and Sweden, in addition to a lot from the UK.

Among the latter was a young man by the name of James Hunt, who went on to dominate the headlines just a few years later with Grand Prix victories for the Hesketh and

Richard Young's passion for motor sport goes back to the time he was taken to the Ulster TT at Dundrod as a very small boy in 1953. And while he describes himself as 'essentially four-wheeled', his interest in motor cycle sport has grown too, helped by his current 'day job' as operations manager at Kirkistown Race Circuit. In between he has competed in numerous events, was Irish Hill Climb Champion three times and made occasional race and rally appearances.

Professionally he has contributed to many publications and enjoyed almost 20 years as part of the 'First Edition' breakfast show team on Downtown Radio. He is also motoring correspondent for Sunday World and an MSA-appointed car race instructor.

McLaren teams, culminating in the World Championship in 1976.

However, not for nothing was he known as 'Hunt the Shunt' during his formative years and his Kirkistown appearance was short-lived, lasting just two corners before he tangled with his team mate at Fishermen's Bend, ending up in a hedge!

For the record, the race was won by Londoner Colin Vandervell driving a Brabham.

Local interest centred on Norman Moffatt with the only F3 Crossle 17F ever built by the Holywood factory, but the Belfast man didn't feature in the results.

On the home front, motor racing was buoyant, with the newly-created Formula Atlantic topping the bill as often as not. After a short graduation period as competitors upgraded from the 'Twin Cam' machinery of the Sixties, 'Atlantics' became the top class of Irish racing, although the expense of running such a car kept overall numbers quite low.

There was talent aplenty though. Local stars like Patsy and Harold McGarrity, Jay Pollock, Joe Greenan, Mike Nugent and later, Gary Gibson, did battle regularly with Southern visitors like Des Donnelly, Vivian Candy and the man who went on to prominence as a Formula 1 team owner, Eddie Jordan. The fields may have been modest in size for most of the time, but the racing was very close indeed.

Eddie Jordan in pre-race lineup leaving the pits

It probably didn't help that some drivers preferred to run larger-engined Formula 2 and 'Libre' cars as and when opportunities arose.

However, it all added up to a considerable increase in speeds, the lap record being broken repeatedly during that period.

And then there was Formula Ford, which remains a mainstay of Kirkistown racing today.

Devised as a 'budget' category for budding racers, this involved a 1.6 litre Ford engine in standard trim fitted to a contemporary racing car chassis, and it was an immediate success when the first races were run in England in the late Sixties.

By 1970, Holywood's John Crossle Cars had devised a car to suit, and a number of them appeared at Kirkistown that year, to be followed by many more in the ensuing seasons.

Formula Fords lining up on the grid

Crossle went on to become one of Europe's most prolific and successful Formula Ford builders, with cars sold all over the world. Needless to say, the local machines were always close to the top of the Kirkistown results sheets, driven by a wide assortment of pilots, from so-called 'hobby racers' out for an enjoyable afternoon of sport, to serious competitors with their sights firmly set on Formula One.

Among the Kirkistown 'graduates' who used Formula Ford to follow in John Watson's wheel-tracks and make it to the top spot were Derek Daly (Ensign, Tyrrell and Williams) and David Kennedy (Shadow), Cookstown's Kenny Acheson, who became a factory Mercedes driver in sports car endurance racing, and Dublin's Michael Roe who went on to win the Can-Am Championship in the US. Belfast man Damien Magee, a regular Formula Ford winner during the early part of the decade, also made a brief F1 appearance, driving for Williams in the 1975 Swedish Grand Prix.

David Lindsay's highly modified Ford Anglia

But while these 'names' and a handful of others were focused on

Edmund Irvine (Eddie Irvine, Grand Prix driver's father) in his Chevron B17c. 38/14A-67

making it to the 'big time', most Kirkistown racers came to the Co. Down circuit to enjoy the sport and to do a bit of after-race socialising with like-minded people. Every race meeting – and at least six were held every year – also featured races for saloon cars, sports cars, and occasionally 'guest' events for Irish and (very occasionally) UK championships helping to add variety.

The 'Libre' cars were the fastest, and the outright lap record fell repeatedly as the decade went on.

John Watson was the first to average over 100 mph for a lap in 1975 on a rare home appearance at the wheel of Archie Phillips' Formula 2 Brabham, but before the decade was out the circuit had changed with the construction of a chicane on the back straight which, at a stroke, provided drivers with a new corner sequence to negotiate and also reduced speeds at the end of the back straight as these were beginning to cause concern. It would be several more years before anybody else lapped at the 'magic ton'.

Although primarily a car circuit, Kirkistown also played host to several motorcycle races each year, and while road racing was the main form of two-wheeled sport during the Seventies, the 'short circuit' events at Kirkistown were crowd favourites, where future megastars like the late, great Joey Dunlop and many others did battle over the often bumpy 1.5 miles of concrete and tarmac.

Kirkistown is, and always has been, unique. Not only is it today the only racing circuit in the UK owned and operated by a club, rather than a commercial company, it is also the only one which was, in the past, a ship – in name at least – having been named 'HMS Corncrake 2' during a period in the late 1940s when the Royal Navy had control of the airfield.

At the time or writing, the circuit is in its 64th year of operation and still providing a good grounding in motor racing for would-be professionals and amateurs alike.

1975

Making the News in the Chronicle

The headquarters for Newtownards Young Farmers' Club at Victoria Avenue was officially opened on New Year's Day by Ulster president John Scott, who travelled to the town from his home in Tyrone. Club president James McKee, who welcomed the large attendance of members and guests, said it was a day they had anticipated with enthusiasm and pride. Newtownards YFC had been in existence at that time for almost 40 years.

Comber company McKeown Plastics, of Killinchy Road, landed its first major overseas order in early January, when North American GP 14 champion John Wright ordered eight of the renowned sailing dinghies with the possibility of another three to follow.

'Opportunities for Industry in Newtownards', an initiative involving the Newtownards Development Council and the Borough Council, was launched in mid-January. Although news on the industrial front was generally good, with local unemployment standing at just 3.4 per cent and many companies actually finding it difficult to secure labour, the two bodies were mindful that the projected population of Newtownards by 1990 was 30,000.

Mayor John Algie said the town had a proud economic history but they had to prepare for the future. The initiative, he said, aimed to encourage more industries to move to the town with the result that Ards people would have plenty of work on their own doorstep.

Twice a week 60-year-old Albert White climbed a narrow vertical ladder-way in the 200-year-old Town Hall building at Conway Square to wind the clock mechanism. He recalled a time when the two faces of the clock were illuminated by gas lights.

'The Dead Cert,' a story by Newtownards playwright Jim McCallen, was broadcast as the Morning Story on the BBC radio network on 7 February. Educated at Movilla Secondary School, Jim's writing career had blossomed over the years since 'Flight of the Swallow' was broadcast, also by the BBC, in 1967. He was employed as an Education Welfare Officer by the South Eastern Education and Library Board.

Work began in February on a major facelift for a section of the Portaferry foreshore, with a number of old houses – many without a bathroom or indeed running water – being demolished. There was considerable regret among many residents that they were leaving homes they had grown up in, as indeed had their parents.

It was reported that the studios for Northern Ireland's first commercial radio station would be located in the major new shopping centre then under construction at Circular Road, Newtownards. The contract for the station was awarded to Community Radio Services, a consortium of Northern Ireland business people and assorted celebrities, including actor Colin Blakely, playwright Sam Cree and future Olympic Gold Medal winner Mary Peters.

The station, later named Downtown Radio, was in fact established at the Kiltonga Industrial Estate.

The Newtownards Youth Advisory Committee reported in late February that the district was experiencing a serious teenage drinking problem. Alcohol was being consumed in large quantities at supposedly safe teenage parties, parents were told, and there were assorted places around the town and district where young people gathered for drinking sessions. On one occasion police caught a group of 11-year-old boys with a half-bottle of vodka, while on another occasion children were found with a bottle of whiskey.

A new hall for Second Comber Presbyterian Church was opened and dedicated on 1 March by the Rt. Rev. Dr Temple Lundie, Moderator of the General Assembly. He received the invitation to open the hall from congregational secretary James Ritchie.

Sixty-year-old Comber man David Halliday died on 23 March in the Royal Victoria Hospital from gunshot wounds sustained in the course of a robbery, attributed to the Ulster Volunteer Force, the previous November.

Mr Halliday, from Castle Lodge, was the manager of an insurance company, which occupied the same building on Belfast's Crumlin Road as a branch of the Northern Bank.

Four men had entered the building on 18 November 1974, with one of them telling Mr Halliday, who had come out of his office, to 'freeze'. The Comber father-of-three took a step across the passage and was shot in the back by the robber, who was subsequently jailed for life for murder.

The judge said he was "guilty of a murder of a particularly savage and needless kind." He added: "You fired point blank at a man who was doing nothing to thwart you, but did not react promptly enough to your demand to keep still."

Ards Borough Council pulled the shutters down on the beach amusements at Millisle on 24 March, after voting against the renewal of the licence that had been held by operator Benny McAuley for the previous 15 years. Members had heard from Ballywalter Road residents who were annoyed that the best part of the beach was being monopolised by the amusements. They also complained it had been a major source of annoyance for years. In addition, they said the constant use of a generator was affecting local television reception.

Alderman Eddie Gaw produced a book containing 2,206 signatures, all in favour of the beach amusements. About one-tenth of the signatories, he said, were Millisle residents, while the remainder were people from all over Northern Ireland who visited the seaside village during the summer.

The subsequent vote went against Mr McAuley, who was advised to seek a more suitable site for his amusements.

There were fears that a cost-cutting measure by the South Eastern Education and Library Board would have a direct impact on Newtownards Swimming Pool. In a move to save £400,000 from its budget, the Board advised the Council it would no longer cover costs incurred by schools visiting the pool and other recreational facilities within its area.

Council officer Jim Ritchie warned that without schools using the pool it would be inadvisable to open it in the mornings. That, in turn, would lead to a reduction in staff numbers. Councillors sought a meeting with the Board and, if that proved unsatisfactory, then the Education Minister (Roland Moyle).

During the summer of 1975, when faced with a major fall in attendance numbers by swimmers and spectators, the Council increased admission charges at the pool, reduced opening hours and laid off a number of part-time and full-time workers. Councillors placed the blame for the measures on the "present economic situation."

Officials and guests at the Ulster Flying Club's annual dinner in the new clubhouse in April 1975. 29-14a-105

Group Captain Douglas Bader, accompanied by his wife Joan, returned to Newtownards to open the Ulster Flying Club's new clubhouse at the Portaferry Road aerodrome on 5 April. He had first visited the town back in 1961 to open the original clubhouse. In the intervening time the Ulster Flying Club had become the largest flying club anywhere in the United Kingdom with approximately 500 members, including flying and ground members, and about 25 aeroplanes.

Donaghadee Young Farmers' Club president Billy Martin was the unanimous choice of delegates as the new president of Young Farmers' Clubs of Ulster at their annual meeting in Portrush on 10 May.

The 100th anniversary of the opening of Comber Orange Hall was marked by a special parade and service on 24 May, which was attended by Most Worshipful Grand Master Bro. the Rev. Martin Smyth. While little had changed at the hall over the years, a major refurbishment programme was carried out in the months leading up to the centenary.

The opening of the new Glen Estate Community Centre on 27 May was heralded by Mayor John Algie as the "realisation of a dream" for the people of the area. The centre had its origins in local anger over a rent increase three years earlier, when many residents agreed the newly-formed Community Association could be more than just a protest organisation. Rather, it could work for the betterment of the estate, which it achieved largely thanks to the endeavours of chairman Jack Sharkey and the management committee.

Twelve people were injured but mercifully no one was killed when a bomb exploded outside the International Bar at Frances Street, Newtownards, late at night on Friday 5 June. The cylinder device, containing between 10 and 20lbs of explosives, had been left at the door of the licensed premises. However, it toppled over and rolled to the edge of the footpath before exploding.

The resulting blast shattered the windows of almost every building in the immediate vicinity, while a fragment of the bomb went through the ceiling of the International Bar. Fortunately no one was in that part of the building at the time. Damage to the bar was estimated at £10,000. Mrs Margaret Rice, speaking on behalf of the owners, said it was their intention to reopen within two or three weeks. "We are very grateful no one was killed," she said. "Money can replace everything else, but not life."

The South Eastern Education and Library Board notified Ards Borough Council of its intention to close Ballyphilip Boys' Primary School and St Mary's Girls' Primary School at Portaferry and to replace them with a co-educational maintained primary school (St. Mary's). It was also proposed to replace St Joseph's Primary School, Ballycranbeg, and St. Mary's Primary School, Kircubbin, with a new school in Kircubbin.

A 6ft Russian bear, on tour with Fossetts Circus around the Ards Peninsula, had to be destroyed on 22 July after attacking its mother. When sufficient tranquilisers and drugs to kill around 40 men failed to have any effect on the bear, it had to be shot and killed by a lance-corporal in the Ulster Defence Regiment. The soldier ended up requiring hospital treatment when his second shot ricocheted off the bear's cage, sending a splinter into his leg.

Eighteen-year-old Ian McGreechan, from Upper Movilla Street in Newtownards, had gained first place in the All Ireland Senior Drum Major Championships at Tralee in July 1974, when he was a member of the Dr Wright Memorial Pipe Band. In 1975 he won the English and World Junior Drum Major titles at the World Pipe Band Championships, which were held in Corby at the beginning of August. By then he was a member of Ballycoan Pipe Band.

Ian McGreechan. 7-9-89

Samuel Gunning (55), who was reared in the Ards Peninsula, was shot dead while standing at the corner of Aberdeen Street and the Shankill Road in Belfast on 13 August. Also killed in the attack, which preceded the bombing of the Bayardo Bar, was Mr Gunning's brother-in-law, William Gracey, doorman at the licensed premises.

Mr Gunning, formerly of Tubber Road, Kircubbin, had worked at the Mackie's factory in Belfast for 22 years. He was survived by a wide family circle, many still residing in the Ards area.

Comber boy Mark White (11), from Glen Road, was hailed a hero after saving the life of an eight-year-old boy who had fallen into the sea while fishing off the pier in Bangor on 31 August. Mark pulled the child into the hired rowing boat he was in and brought him safely to shore.

A young police constable, who was shot by accident by a colleague while on guard duty at the Donaghmore (Co Tyrone) home of SDLP politician Austin Currie, was a native of Comber. Twenty-year-old Adrian Johnston, who died on 11 September, the day after the incident, was a son of Mr and Mrs Noel Johnston, who ran a bakery at Castle Street, where the young man had worked while waiting to join the RUC.

Ards Hospital Radio Service volunteers (from left) Billy Caughey, Tony McMullan, Blair Mayne and DJ George Morris in September 1975. 66-5-116

The Ards Hospital Radio Service, run on a voluntary basis in conjunction with the RUC Community Relations Branch, began broadcasting in mid-September. It became the first in Northern Ireland to join the National Association of Hospital Broadcasting Organisations.

Ards Borough Council indicated in early November it was interested in acquiring the lead mines at Whitespots, near Conlig, for amenity purposes. Users, it was suggested, could include local archery, model aeroplane and clay pigeon clubs. It was agreed in the first instance to seek a valuation of the land in question.

The opening of a new £450,000 telephone exchange in Newtownards on 4 December also required the addition of '81' to the old four-figure numbers. The facility catered for 2,800 customers, replacing the former exchange which had opened in 1959 with just 600 lines available for local residents and businesses.

Officials and prizewinners at Kircubbin Homing Pigeon Society's annual dinner in the New Mount Royal Hotel, Donaghadee, in January 1975. 18-7-99

The Rt. Rev. G. A. Quin (right), Bishop of Down and Dromore, and the Rev. G. P. Ridgway took part in a confirmation service in St Saviour's Parish Church, Greyabbey, in February 1975. Back (from left): Mrs Pritchard, Rector's Church Warden, Alan Coffey, Elizabeth Carson, Audrey Atcheson, Miss Norah Fisher, People's Church Warden. Front: Shirleen Dickson, Jacqueline McCutcheon, Elizabeth Whittaker and Jennifer Taggart. 67-2a-100

Officials and guests at a social event organised by Brian Gibson of the North Down Vegetable Growers' Association in February 1975. It was held in the Old Crow, Comber. 64-4-101

Mrs M. Morgan, representing co-sponsor Morgan's of Cloughey (along with BP Gas and Container Gases), is pictured with prizewinners from Rureagh Indoor Bowling Club's triples tournament in February 1975. 72-6-101

Heather McConnell, of 4th Newtownards (West Winds) Girl Guide Company, presents cheques totalling £83, representing the proceeds of a shoe-shine fundraiser, to Miss M. P. Irwin, regional organiser for the Save the Children Fund, in March 1975. Included are Mrs S. Ferran, Captain, and Miss A. Jardine, Brown Owl. 89-6a-101

Thomas Brown and James McDonnell, from Portaferry Presbyterian Church Indoor Bowling Club, won the club's pairs tournament, sponsored by the Milk Marketing Board, in March 1975. Included are organisers and some of those who provided refreshments for the competitors. 52-15-102

The Rev. W. R. Brown (chaplain) with leaders and boys of 1st Comber Presbyterian Church Robins at their annual inspection and display in March 1975. 50-0-102

Staff Nurse Betty Harkness (left) presents a bouquet to Alva Morrow after she organised a fashion show in the Mawhinney Hall at Ards Hospital in March 1975. The show raised valuable funds towards patient comforts. Also included is Mrs McCandless, Senior Nursing Officer. 15-19-103

Principal John Merrick with staff and senior pupils from St Columba's Secondary School, Portaferry, who organised a sponsored walk in March 1975 to help raise funds towards a new school bus. 19-19-103

Millisle
Presbyterian
Church Girls'
Brigade members
at their annual
display in March
1975. 89-8a-103

Members of Ards
Gateway Club
who took part
in a fundraising
variety concert
at Regent House
in March 1975.
272-75-1

A section of the crowd attending the opening of Comber Orange Hall in May 1975. 10-16-108

2nd Newtownards Presbyterian Church GB Explorers in fancy dress at their parents' morning in the Palmer Hall in May 1975. 39-16-108

Pupils from Killard House School, Newtownards, before setting off on a trip to Morecambe and the Lake District in June 1975. 61-4-109

Pupils from Victoria Primary School, Newtownards, feed Greylag and Canada Goslings during a visit to the Strangford Lough Wildfowlers Association's conservation area at Glenvale, Crawfordsburn Road, in June 1975. Included is Tom Cardy, a member of the Association's education sub-committee. 24-16-109

Fancy dress prizewinners at the Andrews Memorial Primary School, Comber, sports day in June 1975. 272-85-1

Mill Street Heroes LOL 1908 and Junior LOL 141 on parade in Holywood on 12 July 1975. 22-3-112

Angela Graham, Norman Graham and Lynda Patton took part in a fancy dress competition at Ballyhalbert Fair in July 1975. 57-2-112

Members of the Donaghadee lifeboat crew with members of the Ladies Lifeboat Guild at a fundraising supper dance in the Imperial Hotel, Donaghadee, in October 1975. 34-8-118

Members of Millisle and District Pigeon Club at their annual dinner in October 1975 at the Strangford Arms Hotel, Newtownards. 33-2-118

Sixth Formers from Regent House, Newtownards, who decorated the school canteen for a Hallowe'en dance in October 1975. 93-19-118

The Donaghadee Primary School Senior Choir appeared on Hughie Green's Opportunity Knocks on Ulster Television on Monday 15 December 1975. 34-1-121

P5 pupils from West Winds Primary School, Newtownards, visited the nearby farm of Mr H. Patton, Comber Road, in December 1975 as part of a farming project. Picture includes Mr Patton and members of staff. 76-10-121

Mr and Mrs James Nixon, of Ravara Road, Ballygowan, were joined by family and friends at a party in Moneyrea Orange Hall on 23 December 1975 to celebrate their 50th wedding anniversary. The couple, who were married in Comber Non-Subscribing Presbyterian Church in 1925, had two sons and five daughters, 32 grandchildren and 19 great grandchildren. 74-11-123

1975

Sport in the Chronicle

Lorna Bell, badminton captain at Portavogie Primary School, came home victorious from a Champion of Champions knock-out competition on 21 February after defeating her opponent from Hillsborough PS 11-3, 11-5.

David Carson, a member of the Scrabo Secondary School soccer team, was selected to play for Northern Ireland Schoolboys against England, Scotland, Wales and Dublin in forthcoming fixtures. He became the third pupil from the school to play for his country.

Ards FC trainer Jimmy Tucker, whose long association with the club dated back to his playing days two decades earlier, when he was a member of the 1952 Irish Cup-winning side, announced he would be retiring at the end of the season. He had worked with four managers (Eastham, Graham, Neilson and Humphries) and even had a short spell in the role himself.

Comber driver Craig Canmore, from Copeland Drive, was one of 49 competitors who completed the Circuit of Ireland Rally, which started in Ballymena and finished in Larne. He was driving a Mini Cooper S in his first international rally and it was the only Mini Cooper to complete the 1,300-mile circuit.

Two Newtownards table tennis players, Brian Haughan (15) and Pamela Graham (16), were selected for the Irish Junior team to play in the European Junior Championships in Yugoslavia from 1 to 10 August that year. Brian was a pupil at Movilla Secondary School, while Pamela attended Regent House. Both already had a number of successes under their respective belts.

For the second time in four years Ards won the Junior League Championship (the Past Players Cup), following a 13-9 victory over Division 3 winners Dungannon II at Ravenhill on 26 April. The club also secured the Karl Mullen seven-a-side trophy at Arklow, giving it one of the most successful seasons in its history.

The Ards Rangers side that played against Downpatrick Rec. in the Clarence Cup final in May 1975. 79-11-106

Ards Rangers were defeated 2-0 by Downpatrick Rec. in the Clarence Cup final. The match was played in atrocious weather conditions at Solitude on 9 May.

Kart-racing drew a 3,000-strong crowd to the streets of Newtownards for a three-hour spectacle promoted on 19 June by Newtownards Lions' Club and the County Down Kart Club. Presented as part of a festival week organised by the Newtownards Youth Advisory Council, the event was in fact the third round of the prestigious Northern Ireland Championships and attracted many competitors from around the district.

Regent House pupil Clark Millar, of Frances Street in Newtownards, was selected in July by the Irish Schools Athletic Association to represent Ireland in the 100m and 200m sprints, as well as the 4 x 100m relay intermediate event of the forthcoming British Schools Championships.

Kirkistown Castle won golf's Ulster Cup on 4 July after a monumental battle with neighbours Scrabo. The latter had won the first leg 5-2 but the second leg witnessed an identical turn-around score for Kirkistown, which meant the result had to be determined on the number of holes won by each club. There was no doubt in the end, with Kirkistown well ahead at 18 holes up.

Regent House secured cricket's Graham Cup with a three-wicket victory over Lisburn at Wallace Park in early July. The Newtownards team was competing in the competition for only the fourth year and had previously secured the runners-up spot (in 1972).

North Down fell to old rivals Waringstown by 131 runs in the two-day final of cricket's Senior Cup at Ormeau on 2 August. Lawrence Hunter was adjudged to be North Down's best player. He bowled 56 overs for 122 runs and took six wickets.

Former Ards and Ards Rangers player Michael Rooney was awarded the Rothman's Soccer Gold Medal in Queensland, Australia, for the 'best and fairest player,' as judged by Brisbane First Division referees. The diminutive centre-forward and midfield player, who had joined the Annerley club at the beginning of the season, received the award in October from Sir Colin Hannah, Governor of Queensland.

Ards Rugby Club's 1st XV lost out to rivals Bangor 20-12 in the floodlit final of the Bass Boston Cup at Upritchard Park on 16 December.

The Donaghadee Primary School 'A' team was competing in the Bangor Schools Football League ('A' Section) in January 1975. 84-7-96

The 1st Donaghadee Boys' Brigade volleyball team represented Northern Ireland in the National Boys' Brigade volleyball competition in Glasgow in March 1975. Back (from left): Terry McBratney, Paul Gillespie, Martin Strain, Billy Fraser (lieutenant-in-charge). Front: Foster Gaw, Samuel Hunter and David Cleland. 35-1-102

North Down Hockey Club's 1st XI in March 1975 before a League fixture against Annadale in Comber. 22-2-102

Portavogie Rangers FC, who competed in the Lower Ards Summer League, received a new strip in May 1975. 86-6-107

The Bridge Ladies Darts team won the Bangor and District Knock-Out Cup in May 1975. Back (from left): E. Ritchie, E. Patterson, S. Stevenson, T. Boyce, R. Bennett, E. Ross, K. Watson. Front: N. Thompson, E. Massey, M. Munn (captain), S. Malcolm and L. Watson. 79-8a-107

Richard McCaughey (front, second from right), Kirkistown Castle's Ulster Cup-winning captain, holds the trophy with Billy Miscampbell and George Cardy in July 1975 after the team upset the odds by defeating Scrabo in the final. Included are Seamus Dorrian, Sam Alexander, Sidney Caruth, Maurice McKinley, Thompson Magennis and Harry Irwin. 75-9-111

Officials, guests and prizewinners at Donaghadee Cricket Club's annual dinner in the New Mount Royal Hotel, Donaghadee, in October 1975. The dinner followed a very successful season for the club. Included are Mrs A. Topping, D. S. Jones (British Airways sales manager for Northern Ireland), John Scott (chairman), W. Beard, I. Reid, T. Hamilton, R. Elliott, B. Duffy and G. Elliott. 80-8-118

Members of the Movilla Youth Club table tennis team pictured before departing for the Limerick Open Championships in November 1975. Back (from left): Harold Burch, Kerry Doherty, Gillian Murphy, Pamela Graham, David Montgomery, Derek Harkness, Joe Smith, Gordon Milliken, Brian Haughian, Margaret Dorrian. Front: Trevor Alexander, Roland Magill and Zander Dorrian. 45-15-120

1st Millisle Junior BB footballers won the Donaghadee and District Junior League Cup in December 1975, beating Groomsport Wanderers 4-2 in the final. 50-7-123

Ivan Coffey

remembers ... Ards Rugby

Ivan Coffey has been centrally involved with Ards Rugby Club for nearly 60 years and has taken a prominent part in all the advances and developments the club has made. He has held every major position in the Ards club, in most cases for lengthy periods. As a player, he was captain of a highly successful I[st] XV in 1965/66. Thirty years later he occupied the position of President.

Ivan's services to rugby at local and provincial level were acknowledged with the award of the Ulster Branch's Dorrington B. Faulkner award in 2003. Through his general interest in amateur sport in Ards, he has been a committed member of the Ards Borough Sports Development Committee, of which he was Chairman in 2013/14.

We departed the Sixties with rugby at Ards – as David Coffey noted in this book's predecessor – continuing to grow. And what a surge in growth occurred in the Seventies. By the end of the decade a homely little entity of modest proportions was on the cusp of producing one of the leading Senior sides in Ulster.

The old grounds at the bottom end of South Street, Newtownards, where the club had resided for some 40 years (and which, by the way, were never given a name), were manifestly not capable of supporting the burgeoning playing membership. In light of this, the momentous decision was made in 1970 to move to new pastures. And it was literally new pastures that Ards moved to – nine acres of prime land in the countryside on the Comber Road side of the town.

Work on the ambitious relocation project was carried out in the first half of 1971, culminating in three full-sized playing pitches, a floodlit training area, premises containing six changing rooms, spacious shower facilities, a kitchen and central hall. By early 1973 further improvements included conversion of the hall into a members' lounge and an extension incorporating a committee room, bringing the total cost of the project to £45,000.

At the annual general meeting held on 3 May 1971, it was unanimously determined to name the new headquar-

The Ards 1st XV and the President's XV before the start of the match in September 1971 to commemorate the opening of Hamilton Park. Included is referee Mr A. Sturgeon (Malone), 245-97-1

ters Hamilton Park, after the celebrated John P., on the proposal of S. L. Orme and A. W. Moore. Hamilton Park was officially commissioned on Friday evening 10 September 1971. The opening ceremony was followed by the first ever match played at the venue between Ulster Branch President Sam Edgar's select team and the Ards Ist XV. The latter comprised Ian Stead, Will Barker, Ivan Coffey, Jimmy Mahon, Bobby Bishop, Wesley Campbell, Derrick Nash, Jim McFerran (captain), Roy Cromie, Brian Hutchinson, Barry Calvert, George Ferguson, Terry Finlay, Crosby Cleland and Denis Calvert. Coach to the team was David Heron and team attendant was John Dalzell.

On the Saturday a collection of Old Hands, marshalled and captained by David Coffey, played against Davy Wright's 3B XV. The teams featured a host of personalities evocative of Ards rugby – the likes of Will Brown, Robin Davidson, Eddie Devlin, Bill Ferguson, Don Hanley, Bert Jordan, Ronnie McBratney, Barney McCaughey, Tom McCullough, Denny McKee, Jim Millin, Archie Moore, Dennis S. Nash, Graham Savage, Jim Scott and Billy Shaw, with the vociferous presence of Dougie Harley on the touchline. The majority of them had given committed service to Ards in the years before 1971 and many continued to do so for years after, and some continue until the present

Ards Rugby Club secretary Sam Orme hands over a gold watch to chairman John P. Hamilton at the opening ceremony for the club's new grounds in September 1971. The presentation was made on behalf of club members to mark the naming of the new facilities as 'Hamilton Park.' 245-98-1

day. It is heartening to report that all the aforementioned are regular attendees, well over 40 years on, at the now well-established monthly gatherings of the FARLS (Friends of Ards Rugby Lunch Society).

At about the same time, developments were taking place across the way at the Donaghadee grounds. The Dee had availed for some 35 years of two Nissen huts, one devoted to changing and showering, the other to welcome post-match hospitality. The Ulster fries served up by the Ladies Committee were the stuff of legend. The facilities, while basic enough by present day standards, afforded comparative luxury when compared to what the Ards rugby fraternity had had to put up with. The old huts were removed to be replaced by a modern pavilion, in time to be extended and enhanced. Comprehensive refurbishment works were also carried out on the playing surfaces. As a result Dee home matches had to be played at another venue. That was provided by the supportive Kennedy family who made fields available at their Ballyhay farm.

Donaghadee chairman Jimmy Donaldson (back right) with the players of the President's XV and the Donaghadee XV, who played a match to celebrate the opening of the new clubhouse on 25 September 1976. 93-21-14

Any disruptive effects arising from the relocation arrangements, which entailed changing in the new pavilion and travelling out to the Kennedy property by car, were dissipated by the 1972/73 season. That ended with the Dee gaining promotion to Section 2 of the Junior League by way of a play-off win over Cooke.

While competing at that level proved hard enough, by the mid-1970s Donaghadee had established and consolidated a firm place in the middle level of Junior rugby, with Jimmy Donaldson continuing to provide a steady guiding hand.

Over in Newtownards, residency at Hamilton Park had given a mammoth impetus to the local club. By the mid-1970s, seven teams were being fielded, with the

The Ards squad which won the Junior Championship in 1974/75. Back (from left): D. Heron (coach), B. Calvert, T. Lyttle, E. Gordon, R Haddock, D. Calvert, D. Taylor, N. Edgar, J. Kyle, W. Campbell. Middle: R. Hedley, C. Anderson, R. Cromie, J. Hamilton (chairman), D. Nash (captain), S. Orme (secretary), I. Fraser, C. Cleland, J. Mahon. Front: W. Thompson. T. Finlay.

Ards 1st XV developing as the top team in Junior rugby. Indeed, the overall Junior Championship was won the very first year. The next year, with that giant of a man, stature and personality-wise, Denis Calvert leading the team, the runners-up place was achieved. Two years on (1974/75), Ards were champions again with a rejuvenated Derrick Nash as captain.

Cup success was proving harder to come by. Notwithstanding regular appearances in finals, it wasn't until 1976/77 (with Denis Calvert again at the helm) that the first major success since the 1961/62 Towns' Cup campaign was achieved with the winning of the Junior Cup.

The headway being made was no real surprise since Ards had recourse to players of the calibre of Teddy Sloan, Jimmy Mahon, Wesley Campbell, Trevor Haslett and, shortly after, Ian Moles, Freddy Wishart and Garston Mowat in the backline. In the pack there were Ian Wallace, Reggie Haddock, Crosby Cleland and, later, John Horner, Leslie Cunningham, Mervyn Lappin and a very youthful Nigel Carr. And to cap it all, the Calvert brothers, Denis and Barry, and the formidable Neville Edgar. Ards' opponents must have experienced no little awe as they took the field of play against this hirsute trio.

Strength in depth was also being experienced. By 1973/74 a second team was featuring in Junior level competition. Below that, Ken Hoey's 2A XV gained promotion in successive seasons. Danny McKee's 3A side in 1973/74 and John Jamison's and Billy Menagh's 3As and 3Bs in 1974/75 and Barry Kerr's 3Bs in 1975/76 also moved to the higher grades. In that latter year, Garry McCreery's 3As contested the McCambley Cup final, the first time for an Ards team to do so at that particular level.

By the mid-decade, seven teams were participating in leagues and cups with an eighth playing occasional friendlies. An U-18 Colts side, formed under the mentorship of David Coffey, included the three Davidson brothers, John, Paul and Stephen, Jason Forsythe and David Rainey, along with 17-year-old Alistair Wilson who in due course graduated to the club Presidency and who still performs a central role in the management of the club.

Like Ards, the Donaghadee club experienced a healthy growth in playing numbers. In late October 1976, four League teams were being fielded. The 1st XV contained the likes of Garth McCartney, Sam Holley, George Torrence and Wesley Martin. The 4th XV selected to play Malone opposition comprised J. Erskine, J. Laverty, Bill Boomer, Alistair Kyle, R. Fitzsimmons (captain), Jackie McKeag, S. Moore, Stephen Donaldson, A. Sherrard, P. Conaty, A. Hakin, S Clemo, R. Kirk, Ken Ross and B. Mawhinney.

Bill Boomer, of course, later on rendered sterling service in a variety of administrative capacities, including the onerous one of fixture secretary and until recently he was the longstanding and respected President of Donaghadee.

Not without some justification, Ards had ambitions for Senior status which accordingly crystallised into a carefully prepared submission to the IRFU Ulster Branch in October 1974. The 1st XV reinforced that claim by, as noted, coming out top again in Junior rugby. In preparation for that, the transformative season, 1976/77 was one of the most successful ever enjoyed by Ards. Bangor's prestigious Boston Cup floodlit cup, played midweek, was to all intent and purpose a Senior competition to which Ards were invariably invited.

Lo and behold, Ards shocked the rugby world by recording a memorable victory in a stirring final on Tuesday evening, 21 December 1976, by virtue of two Tom McCombe penalties. The opposition? None other than home club Bangor, then the leading Senior club in Ulster, if not Ireland. What a night for Ards rugby!

That 1976/77 club year was notable on two other counts. The reconstituted Presidency was occupied by John Hamilton, with David Coffey and Bobby Bishop nominated as his deputies. Sam Orme, the club's indefatigable secretary, relinquished his onerous position after 17 years' stalwart service.

The local sporting calendar for 1977 records two other notable highlights, namely Regent House School appearances in Provincial finals. Under the tutelage of the incomparable D. A. McMaster, later to be a hugely successful Ards and Ulster coach, Regent progressed to its first ever Schools' Cup final. Captained by Clarke Millar, in the absence of Nigel Carr through injury, and containing future Irish interna-

Members of the Regent House Ulster Schools' Cup Final squad: Back (from left): L. Stead, B. McLaughlin, B. Iveston, C. Campbell, R Johnston, P. Matthews, C. Whyte, M. Steel, T. Johnston. Middle: J Boucher, D. Wallace, D. Baird, C. Millar (capt), A. Moles, J. Wishart, N. Gordon. Front: S. Lennox, G. Scott.

tional Philip Matthews and Ulster coach Brian McLaughlin, the team suffered an agonising injury time reverse at the hands of Armagh Royal. Some compensation was obtained with the girls' hockey team's victory in their Provincial final.

Of that 1976/77 cup final rugby team, 13 went on to pursue their rugby careers at Ards, some with outstanding success.

On to the 1977/78 season and to glory.

Senior rugby seemed to be beyond the reach of Ards as the 1st XV suffered a few lapses in the League campaign. Providence, however, decreed a play-off and, almost unbelievingly, the tantalising prospect of promotion to the top level. It was a chance which was never going to be missed by an Ards team, now coached by former captain Billy Dickson who has given a lifetime of service and who still is deeply involved in the club's day to day affairs, and led on the field by Denis Calvert. A try by Clarke Millar and a conversion and two penalties from the educated boot of Wes Campbell gave Ards a 12 points to nil win over opponents Ballymena 2nds. Senior rugby had been achieved. The developing strength in depth was confirmed by the performances of Jacko Kyle's 2nd XV – winners of their League section and thereby gaining promotion, and contestants in no fewer than three Junior level cup finals.

Every other Ards side won their League section or gained promotion, including John Jamison's 7th XV which used 73 players in all over the course of the season. We do not propose to enumerate all that number but the team that did duty on a typical Saturday epitomises what rugby at Ards was all about at that time: T. Breen,

A host of trophies for Ards in the 1976/77 season! Back (from left): R. Hamilton (touch judge), S.L. Orme (Hon. Sec.), W. Dickson (coach), I. Wallace, D. Kyle, B. Calvert, N. Edgar, D. McKinstry, B. Marshall, W. Campbell, T. Smith, J. Campbell (hon. treas.) J. Millin (chairman of selectors). Front: T. Sloan, C. Cleland, T. Haslett, T. McCombe, J. Hamilton (president), D. Calvert (captain) D. Coffey (sen vice president), J. Armstrong, T. Finlay, I. Fraser, S Martin

W. McGrath, M. Mateer, J. McKee, L. Shaw, G. Thompson, C. Bennett, E. Bisset, W. Menagh, N. Hughes, J. Jamison (captain), D. McCullough, E. Devlin, J. Devlin and B. Kelly.

The 2A XV – and you wouldn't have been selected unless you were a regular attender at training sessions – comprised B. McCreight, P. Davidson, D. Paul, P. Gray, S. Wilson, M. Andrews, G Mowat, D. Mackey, A. Cheater, J. Miskimmin, H. Quayle, H. Ming, L Sinclair, G. Wylie, D. Porter (captain) and M. Rankin.

The opening 1978/79 season Senior league game was narrowly lost. The second game saw Ards claim their first Senior points with a Hamilton Park victory over Academy on Saturday 30 September 1978. The team on that historic day was Mike Hodgens, Clarke Millar, Teddy Sloan, Ian Fraser, Will Barker, Wes Campbell (captain), Garston Mowat, Barry Calvert, Terry Finlay, Bill Brundle, Reggie Haddock, Mervyn Lappin, Crosby Cleland, Denis Calvert and Nigel Carr. Clarke Millar, Nigel Carr and Barry Calvert gained Ulster trials, with Nigel, who had gone onto the Ards 1st XV team straight from school, winning an Ulster cap, the first Ards Senior League level player to be selected for the province.

That first Senior season was challenging enough, but Ards had entered a new dimension and manfully stood up to the challenge. It was a harbinger of things to come. But that takes us into the glorious Eighties.

Elizabeth Rea

remembers ... The Young Farmers' Clubs

If you were a young person living in the countryside in the 1970s, leisure time was either spent in Church-based youth activities such as the GB or BB, or you were a member of the local Young Farmers' Club. Ballywalter Club was one of the earliest, set up in 1930, and by the time I joined it in the Seventies it had a thriving Junior Club. It was for 12-16 year-olds and was set up in 1956 by Jack McCracken and May Little.

Ballywalter Juniors met fortnightly in what was then the Presbyterian Church Lecture Hall on the Main Street. Forty to fifty young people faithfully attended on Friday nights, not only from the Ballywalter area but also from as far away as Portaferry. I can still remember the clattering of eager noisy feet on the wooden stairs as members rushed up into the hall! It was the ideal place to meet up with school friends and neighbours for a night of fun. Senior Leader Margaret Patton and President Isobel Kennedy worked hard with the Junior Club's committee members to organise the meetings.

Like the Seniors, the Juniors had their own Club Leader, Minutes Secretary, Correspondence Secretary and Public Relations Officer. The members were always encouraged by Isobel and Margaret to run the meetings and work to-gether to plan the year's programme and outings. Even at this early age, the Club was very much run by the young

Elizabeth Rea (née Orr) was brought up with her four brothers on her parents' farm outside Greyabbey.

After attending the village Primary School, she went to Regent House Grammar School. She then studied at Stranmillis College, Belfast, where she completed a teaching degree in English and Education.

Elizabeth currently works in Loughries Primary School, near Newtownards. She, her husband Ronald and their three children live on the family's dairy farm outside Donaghadee.

Members of Donaghadee Young Farmers' Club who took part in a fancy dress competition in late January 1972. 250-61-2

members themselves.

As is still the case today, a wide range of activities was on offer at the regular meetings. Different speakers came along to entertain the members on topics such as First Aid, various crafts and working as a fireman or vet. Parties and games nights were the most popular, especially as Senior Club members would come along to help with games such as Forfeits, the Winking Game, Set the Fashion and Balloon Football, which were always noisy and great fun!

The priority at the first night of each new session was to get members signed up to take part in the competitions. Margaret and Isobel were very persuasive and before they knew it, even the newest members had put their names down for most of them. Everyone was encouraged to at least have a go, and after the first nerve-wracking experience most people were hooked. There was always plenty of help and enthusiasm from coaches like May and Fred McAdam, Isobel, John and Jim Goudy and many others, and members were very competitive and keen to do their best for the Club.

To this day the Public Speaking Competition remains an important part of the Young Farmers' programme. In the 12-14 age group competitors were given a picture and, following 30 or 40 minutes' preparation time, they had to write a two-minute story which they then retold to the judges. This was an enjoyable task for people like me who enjoyed reading and had a good imagination, but there were many moans and groans as some others struggled to come up with a good storyline!

I vividly remember nervously standing on the old wooden platform at the far end of the hall, giving my very first speech in front of the judges. Despite the nerves, I quickly began to enjoy this competition. I also recall Isobel Kennedy taking a group of Junior members to compete at the Northern Ireland finals at Greenmount. However, there was really thick fog on the way there and we just made it in the nick of time.

Group Debating was also extremely popular with even the most reluctant speakers being encouraged to take part thanks to the expert help of coaches like May McAdam, Isobel Kennedy, John

Teams from Millisle Young Farmers' Club took part in YFCU area debating competition at Movilla Secondary School in January 1974. 270-14-2

and Jim Goudy and James Brown. I remember teams from different age groups travelling to Magherafelt High School on a Saturday to spend all day there competing in the Northern Ireland finals. We soon got to know some of the staff from Headquarters at these events, and I especially remember Dulcie Proctor, Pam Robinson and, of course, Arthur McAlister, who kept things running smoothly.

There was also a very strong emphasis on crafts thanks to the enthusiasm and skill of Evelyn McIvor. All members, in both the Junior and Senior Clubs, were welcomed into her home, where she showed a variety of different crafts covering such a wide range that there was always something to suit everyone. With Evelyn's help, my cousin Jean McCollam (Orr) became an expert in making soft toys, while others learnt to do tapestry work and embroidery. I was

Ballywalter Young Farmers' Club members who took part in a YFCU debating competition at Regent House, Newtownards, in January 1978. 61-8-51

Mavis Breadon, from Ashgrove Farm, Ballyhay, Donaghadee, won the 14 to 16 age group for sheep judging at Greenmount Agricultural College's sheep and pig judging finals in August 1971. She was a member of Donaghadee YFC. 244-88-1

shown how to do macramé, using different-coloured string and special knots to make items such as table-mats, handbags and wall-hangings. Many a time before the Club competitions, Evelyn would help members late into the night to make sure they got finished in time. She was such a perfectionist and was only happy to accept the highest standard of craftwork.

Stock judging was, and remains, an important part of the programme and we were lucky to have many willing farmers and coaches who were happy to pass on their knowledge to members. George Patton, Jim and John Goudy, John and Henry McCracken and Hubert Walker were just a few of the talented stockmen who helped prepare members, both Junior and Senior, for the competitions. All that coaching and practising usually paid off as members always did well at Area, County and Northern Ireland level. There was keen friendly rivalry between Ballywalter and the other local Clubs – Newtownards, Donaghadee, Millisle, Ballygrainey and Ballymiscaw – and it was always rewarding to come out on top against other members from all over the six counties.

It was as a Junior member that I attended my first County Dinner to receive a cup for public speaking. It was held at the Drumkeen Hotel in Belfast and, as was the custom in those days, Margaret Patton and Isobel Kennedy took us to get our awards. My mother made me a long purple and pink flower-patterned dress especially for the occasion. I remember the chef slipped and fell, with a whole tureen of soup spilling over him and a couple of the young waitresses! County Dinners were the entertainment highlight of the year, with many of the Club's Junior and Senior members among the 400 young people there to receive their awards and enjoy a great night's music and dancing.

Back in 1975 members in my age group, including Jean McCollam (Orr), Michael Warnock, Karen Dunn and Kenneth Hamilton, joined me in moving up to the Senior Club which catered for 16 to 25-year-olds. Meetings now moved to Wednesday nights in Ballywalter Masonic Hall but the overall format of Club nights and competitions was still quite similar. Now, however, the social aspect really took off! There were numerous Inter-Club events such as sports nights, quizzes and discos so every weekend there was somewhere to go. The older members were always willing to act as chauffeur but we really got our freedom as those in our own age group passed their driving test. Michael Warnock was one of the first who got

James McKee, president of Newtownards Young Farmers' Club, and YFC members who helped to entertain local children at a Christmas party in December 1975. 100-7-122

his own car – a green Morris Minor – and he was happy to let as many of us as possible squeeze into it for trips to weekend discos, dances, treasure hunts, quizzes and sports nights across the province.

Another annual event that stands out in my memory from those years is the County Down Rally, which was held, as now, on the first Saturday in July. Back in the Seventies it was a big family day out, often held on a farm such as Billy Martin's at Greyabbey, and well supported not only by members of the Clubs around the county, but also by parents and people living near the venue.

There was always a theme for the day and in 1977, for example, it was the Queen's Silver Jubilee. Instead of today's sideshow, each Club had to decorate a float relevant to the year's theme and there was then a float parade around the field so they could all be judged. Up to six Seniors took part in the Farm Tasks, while two younger members did the Junior Jobs. In 1977 this included activities such as making paper flowers, judging lambs and making a scarecrow, and just like today there was 'It's a Knockout' – team games that involved plenty of water!

The grand finale to each year's Club programme was Parents' Night and the members always put on a great effort to entertain family and special guests. In those days the evening started with a sit-down salad tea for everyone. The hall was an amazing sight with lines of tables draped with white tablecloths, pretty flower arrangements and the best china set out for parents and supporters of the Club. Each girl acted as hostess for the

MILLISLE YOUNG FARMERS' CLUB
ANNUAL DINNER DANCE
in THE CULLODEN HOTEL
on FRIDAY, 16th JANUARY, at 8 p.m.
Dress Informal
Music by THE LINESMEN
Tickets available from : Paddy McAvoy, Portavo (phone Donaghadee 3352); Joyce Lemon, Ballyblack (phone Newtownards 812362); or any Committee Member.

Harry and Richard Hamilton of Trench Farm, Comber, with the trophies they won in October 1975 at the Newtownards Young Farmers' Club show. 31-6-118

eight or 10 people at her table and was responsible for making sure they had plenty to eat and enjoyed their meal. If you had just joined the Seniors you had a table at the very back of the hall but then each year you moved further up towards the front as you went up through the age groups! The highlight was, of course, the presentation of proficiency certificates and the many cups which over the years had been generously donated by past members and their families to encourage and reward members for their skill and dedication to the Club. Then followed the entertainment which was usually singing and, of course, the one-act play.

We were lucky to have the help of Tommy Hall, who for many years was producer of the one-act plays the Club performed at Parents' Night and the one-act play competition. Members such as George Angus, Leonard Brown, Rosemary Angus (Warnock), Careen Bailie (McCracken), James Hamilton, Alec Boyle, Violet Brown, Dianne Patterson (Foster), Michael Warnock, Jean McCollam, myself, and many others rehearsed faithfully for weeks leading up to the big night, and when Tommy could not find a script to please him, he even wrote a few plays himself!

The fortnightly meetings stopped over the summer but there was still plenty to do with the stock judging practices and competitions, games and sports nights, car slaloms and the day trip away to Newcastle or Portrush.

Young Farmers' Clubs offered so many great opportunities in the Seventies. I continued to be a member at Ballywalter into the Eighties and then had the privilege of being Senior Leader of the Juniors for two years. I have such happy memories of my time in Ballywalter Club and the friendships made and the skills learnt then still benefit me today.

After marrying Ronald, I became involved with Donaghadee YFC, which my children now belong to, and I am glad to see the organisation is still going strong, having celebrated its 85th anniversary. It still has a vital role to play in supporting and encouraging today's young people to become 'better farmers, better countrymen and better citizens', developing the skills and talents they need to be the leaders of the future.

1976

Making the News in the Chronicle

Ruth Patterson, daughter of the Rev. T. A. Patterson, minister of Portaferry Presbyterian Church, and Dr Ruth Patterson, had the distinction on 2 January of becoming the first woman ever to be ordained to any Church in Ireland.

A graduate of Queen's University, she was ordained by the Presbytery of Carrickfergus in Gardenmore Presbyterian Church, Larne. During 1975 she had served as assistant to the Rev. Victor Lynas at Gardenmore, where, for the time being, she was remaining.

The well-known newsagency shop of Hampshires was completely destroyed by a fire during the early hours of 9 January. The blaze, described as one of the biggest witnessed in Newtownards for many years, was tackled by firemen from the town itself, as well as Bangor and Donaghadee.

Newtownards postman Robert McBride made his last delivery run on 21 January, bringing to an end a 49-year career that started when he was employed as a telegram boy at Belfast Post Office. Recipient of the Imperial Service Medal for his work on behalf of the Post Office, he lived with his wife Esther at Whitespots.

Benny's
VARIETY
MARKET
WEST STREET
Every Saturday
Convenient to Car Park
"Visit Our Stalls"

Plans were revealed for the recommencement of the traditional Saturday market in Newtownards following a break going back a number of years (during which the site at Conway Square had become a car park). Ards Borough Council received representations on behalf of 14 potential traders in early February, with members agreeing that a feasibility study into the proposal should be prepared.

A Probus Club for retired professional and business men was formed in Donaghadee in mid-February, under the sponsorship of Newtownards Rotary Club and with James O'Hara serving as chairman, Ken Lynn as vice-chairman and Ken Andrews as secretary/ treasurer. It was anticipated that membership would be around 30.

Ballyhalbert man Desmond Wilson, then living in England, was one of 14 oil rig workers rescued after the helicopter they were travelling in plunged into the North Sea during a snow storm on 15 March. The men boarded a life raft, only to discover it was punctured. Fortunately the rig's support vessel picked them up and they were transferred to a Royal Navy tug and taken safely to Hull.

Northern Ireland's first commercial radio station, Downtown Radio, began broadcasting on 16 March, from its new Kiltonga Industrial Estate base. Programme controller was renowned BBC broadcaster Don Anderson (33), while head of news and sport was former freelance broadcaster and newspaper journalist Louis Kelly (28).

Speed Show '76

QUEENS HALL, NEWTOWNARDS,
SATURDAY, 6th MARCH 1976

Open 10.00 a.m. – 9.00 p.m.
Admission: – Adults 50p; Children 20p

★ SPECIAL ATTRACTION
A charity football match at Londonderry
Park, Newtownards with the stars of SPEED
SPORT and ULSTER TELEVISION personalities
Kick-off at 11.00 a.m. ★

Promoted by N.I. Junior Motor Cycle Club

Before it was decided to name the new station Downtown Radio, other suggestions had included Radio Belfast, Radio Ards, Radio Rainbow and Radio Atlantic. Downtown was the brainchild of Belfast Telegraph advertising manager Paul Jellett, who was rewarded with two one-gallon bottles of Old Bushmills Whiskey.

Comber teenager Mervyn Jess, of De Wind Drive, was selected in April by Lions International as one of two representatives from Ireland for a trip to Holland. He was nominated by Newtownards Lions Club.

The Ava Arms in Kircubbin was targeted on 15 April by a lone bomber who walked into the public house with what appeared to be a lunch box under his arm. He ordered a drink but then complained of feeling unwell and went outside "for some air." However, moments later he was seen running along the street to a waiting car. Realising the lunch box was very likely a bomb, a brave customer picked it up and carried it to a safe area some distance away. When the device exploded it caused a few broken windows but damage was otherwise minimal.

Ards Borough Councillors were warned in mid-April by works manager Paul Wright it would cost between £2,000 and £2,500 to repair the outdoor swimming pool in Donaghadee if they were proposing to open it during the summer months. The pool was leaking badly and at times was "quite dangerous." Local Councillor

John Scott said "mountains are being made out of mole hills" and there was never a year the pool did not open.

It was subsequently agreed to carry out adequate repairs to "put the pool in a reasonably satisfactory condition." In addition, the springboard would not be erected as a safety precaution.

Newtownards Chamber of Trade urged the Borough Council in early May to support charging motorists who used the South Street car park. Chamber member Eric Glasgow, claiming it would reduce the number of all-day parkers, pointed out that free parking existed at the South Street car park "on the proposal of a Donaghadee Councillor seconded by a

Comber representative." Shoppers, he warned, would go elsewhere if they could not find a parking space. The Council subsequently supported the Chamber and recommended to the Roads Service (the responsible authority) that charging be introduced – but with the first hour free.

Twenty-year-old David Spratt, from Dickson Park in Ballygowan, was shot dead at the home of his sister at Darragh Road, Comber, on 2 June. It was a case of mistaken identity. The killing was later attributed to the UDA, whose intended target was stated to have been a Catholic relative. A full-time member of the Ulster Defence Regiment from Comber was subsequent jailed after admitting a conspiracy to murder charge.

Local man Christopher Byers (24) was killed and several others were injured, some seriously, when bombers struck at the International Bar in Portaferry on 5 June. A device containing up to 15lb of commercial explosives had been left in a stairway leading to an upstairs toilet when the premises were crowded for a Saturday night sing-song. Mr Byers, one of a family of nine from Cloughey Road, Portaferry, was struck by a door that was blown off by the blast. The funeral service for the Donaghadee carpet factory worker was held at St Patrick's Church, Ballyphilip.

In 1985 a self-confessed UVF member was jailed for life after acting as a lookout during the attack.

TV personality Derek Hobson (fourth from left) attended a reception in the Strangford Arms Hotel to mark the opening of the nearby Woolco store in June 1976. Included (from left) are: Tom Turner, manager of the Ards Shopping Centre, John Kelly, Belfast Progressive Advertising, cabaret star Tina Marlowe, Alan Mawhinney, Woolco divisional manager, and DJ Michael 'Hendi' Henderson from Downtown Radio.
96-14-7

The official opening of the Ards Shopping Centre on 15 June, including an appearance by TV personality Derek Hobson, prompted a massive advertising campaign in the Newtownards Chronicle by town centre businesses, many fearing for their own future livelihoods.

Billed as "Ireland's first regional shopping centre," it offered 5.5 acres of shops, some 50 different businesses in all and parking for 1,350 vehicles on a site at Circular Road which occupied 18.5 acres. Woolco, the 78,000 sq. ft. main anchor store, was described as "Ireland's first hypermarket."

The centre also featured two banks and three restaurants, including a late-opening Skandia. Penneys and Stewarts opened their doors to the public in October. Plans to also include a public house were opposed by the Borough Council.

It was announced on 11 June that Black & Co. (Newtownards) Ltd. and Berkshire International (UK) Ltd. were in negotiations with a view to integrating the former's sock business into the latter's hosiery division. The aim of the takeover, the companies stated, was to ensure the Blaxnit and Pathfinder sock ranges, with their high reputation for quality, continued to be manufactured in Newtownards.

Four local men were among a party of veterans from Northern Ireland preparing to visit the Ulster Memorial at Thiepval on 1 July to mark the 60th anniversary of the Battle of the Somme. Participating in the poignant pilgrimage were Messrs. James A. O'Neill, Edith Helen Road, and Robert McMillan, Greenwell Place, both Newtownards, G. N. Hackney, Old Dundonald Road, Belfast, and Robert Millar, Main Road, Cloughey.

Despite being retained for three weeks at the Tonic in Bangor, members of Ards Borough Council refused to permit the adult film Emmanuel to be screened at cinemas in Newtownards and Comber. Six members voted in favour of the ban, four were against and a further six abstained.

Councillors called in early July for the immediate reopening of the night casualty service at Ards Hospital. It had remained closed for a number of months with casualties being transferred to the Ulster Hospital at Dundonald. They were told that from 29 March until 30 April, between the hours of 11pm and 9am, no fewer than 102 people from the Ards and North Down area received treatment at the Ulster Hospital, with 24 requiring admission.

Newtownards man Ted Griffith, chairman of both the Federation for Ulster Local Studies and Ards Historical Society, called on the public to support the former's campaign against the Post Office's policy of dropping townland names from rural addresses. The Federation, which won the backing of the Borough Council, feared the names, which were an important part of the area's heritage, would fall into disuse.

Conservative MP Marcus Kimball called in late July for a sparsely populated area like the Ards Peninsula to be developed into a new city to house British passport holders arriving in the United Kingdom from Africa and the Far East. He envisaged a "vigorous and colourful colony like Hong Kong" which offered sanctuary to refugees, as well as providing a new stimulus to the prosperity of Northern Ireland.

Killinchy couple Andrew and May McMaster, of Ballymorran Road, celebrated their 70th wedding anniversary on 28 July. The couple, aged 96 and 90 respectively, were married in Bolton, Lancashire, and lived there until moving to Killinchy in 1932. Andrew was a native of the village and during the First World War was captured by the Germans and held as a prisoner of war.

Greyabbey milkman Samuel Brown, of Main Street, boasted a proud record of service going back 55 years to 1921, when he assisted his father, also Samuel. The present day milkman's assistant was Alan Caughey, of Islandview Road.

Local women joined together to stage Newtownards' first Peace Rally in Conway Square on 11 September. There was a sizeable attendance of men, women and children.

Valerie Wright, younger daughter of Mr and Mrs James Wright, of Belvedere Road, Newtownards, was appointed a medical missionary with the Methodist Missionary Society in early September. The former Victoria PS and Regent House pupil was preparing to take up a position as Nursing Sister at Mwandi Hospital in Zambia.

Donaghadee's new RNLI lifeboat, named *The Nelsons of Donaghadee* in honour of the long-serving local family, commenced service at the end of October. Self-righting and costing £150,000, it replaced the *Sir Samuel Kelly*.

The opening on 30 October of Avondale, a purpose-built centre for the Ards branch of the National Society for Mentally Handicapped Children at South Street, Newtownards, was described as "the dawn of a new era" by George W. Lee, the charity's secretary general. The building, completed at a cost of £100,000, was the first of its kind in Northern Ireland.

Newtownards man Kenneth Cardy, son of Mrs Elizabeth Cardy and the late Mr Alexander Cardy, was appointed in early November to a high-ranking position in the United Kingdom Delegation to the United Nations Educational, Scientific and Cultural Organisation in Paris. He was educated at Castle Gardens PS and Regent House, moving to London in 1964 to join the Ministry of Overseas Development, which was responsible for the development of Britain's programme of aid to developing countries.

Plans were revealed for a regular hovercraft service between Donaghadee and the Scottish port of Portpatrick. The aim was to convey 254 passengers and 30 cars across the North Channel, a distance of some 20 miles, in about half an hour.

Investment consultant Neil Oliver believed that after an initial outlay of £10m for the hovercraft, ideally a Mountbatten-class vessel, and a further £3m to develop appropriate port facilities, the service could become viable. Five such hovercraft, he said, were already in regular service with English Channel operators.

Two hundred factory workers from the former Blaxnit firm, which by then had been taken over by Berkshire International, went on strike over a claim for disruption money. Following the takeover, Berkshire had been making arrangements for the transfer of the Blaxnit workers to their Donaghadee Road factory or else to Dundonald.

The Portaferry Hotel, which was under new management, was offering a seven-course Christmas Day lunch for £6.50 (£4.25 for children), while the charge for the standard four-course lunch on other days was £1.50, except on Sundays when the price rose to £1.75. For some reason there wasn't a VAT supplement on the Christmas Day meal, but one was applied to all other charges.

Entrants in a comical 'Miss Ards' contest, held as part of the Ferry Minstrels Concert in Nunsquarter Hall, Kircubbin, in January 1976. Included are James Fitzsimmons (Miss Balligan), Paud Branagh (Miss Knocknagow), Joe Watson (Miss Slans), Hugh John Kelly (Miss Bird Island), Paddy Smith (Miss Lisbane), and Michael Doherty (compere). Not included in the picture were Patsy Ritchie (Miss Ballyfindra) and Patsy Clarke (Miss Ballycran). 4-10-124

Comber Ploughing Society member Denis McBride with some of the spectators who attended the Moneyrea Tractor and Horse Ploughing Society's annual competition in January 1976. 25-17a-124

Principal Mrs K. E. McIvor, assistant teacher Mrs M. C. Irwin and pupils from Victoria Primary School, Ballyhalbert, who presented a cheque for £48 to Mrs M. Hutchinson, appeals organiser for Dr Barnardo's Homes, in January 1976. 36-13-125

County Down Grand Treasurer John Ellison (third from right) presents a long service medal to Greyabbey LOL 1592 member Albert Patton in February 1976 in recognition of his 52 years as an Orangeman. Included are James Crockard, District Secretary, Hugh Shields, Worshipful Master, David Coffey, Secretary, William Davidson, Treasurer, and Herbert Higginson, Chaplain. 34-1-125

Frank Cafolla Jun. (left) with Junior World Champion Drum Major Ian McGreechan in March 1976 after presenting him with his new drum major's outfit, a gift from Frank Cafolla Sen. The latter was sponsoring Ian in the World Championship, to be held that August at Hawick in Scotland. 95-14-127

Pupils from Andrews Memorial Primary School in Comber who visited Edinburgh in April 1976. 7-18-2

Explorers from Greenwell Street Presbyterian Church GB won the Newtownards District PE competition at Strean Presbyterian Church hall in March 1976. Included are Julie Wright, Sharon Finlay, Alison Woods, Gillian Mawhinney, Mandy McKittrick, Helen Anderson, Fiona Smylie, Joanne Boal, Sub-Officer Lesley McCracken and helper Beverley Wallace. 16-1-1

Elizabeth Brown presents a cheque for £125 on behalf of P6 and P7 pupils at Ballywalter Primary School to Oxfam regional organiser Russell Thompson in April 1976. The money went to the charity's Guatemala Earthquake Fund. 3-1-2

The Rev. T. A. Houston with the boys and girls of Portavogie Presbyterian Church Junior Christian Endeavour at their 12th anniversary party in April 1976. 17-10-1

To mark his retirement in May 1976 as superintendent of 2nd Newtownards Presbyterian Sabbath School after 45 years' service, John Algie was presented with a gold watch by Thomas Galway, Clerk of Session, on behalf of the congregation, and with an inscribed Bible by the minister, the Rev. W. J. McIlfatrick, on behalf of the Sabbath School Society for Ireland. Mrs Algie received a bouquet of flowers from Mrs Harry Beale, wife of the former Session Clerk. Included are Mrs Galway and Mr Beale. 76-11-3

Explorers from Carrowdore Presbyterian Church at the Company's annual display in May 1976. 29-14-4

Gillian Booth presents a cheque for £119 on behalf of the senior pupils of Portavogie Primary School to Mrs M. Hutchinson, appeals organiser for Dr Barnardo's Homes, in May 1976. 20-25-4

Young people from Ballyblack Presbyterian Church Sunday School before their children's day and prize distribution service in June 1976. 77-22-6

Members of 4th Newtownards Girl Guides Company pictured in June 1976 at their annual parents night in West Winds Primary School. 26-20a-7

Senior citizens from Newtownards and Comber who enjoyed a week's holiday in Newcastle thanks to the fundraising efforts of Newtownards Round Table. Included are Round Tablers, chairman Ross Workman and young helpers. 80-14a-7

A farewell evening was held in June 1976 at the Queen's Hall, Newtownards, to mark the retirement of curate Fr. McAuley from the Parish. He received a cheque from Parish Priest Fr. McFerran on behalf of parishioners in Newtownards, Comber and Donaghadee. Also included are his successor, Fr. McPolin, the St. Patrick's Choir and guests. 73-14-8

Pupils from West Winds Primary School, Newtownards, who made a farewell presentation to principal Mr D. Cartlidge in June 1976. 79-2-8

Robert Savage and John Millar, both members of Kircubbin Volunteers LOL 1900, received 50-year long service medals prior to the Twelfth celebrations in Millisle in July 1976. 72-6-9

Members of Kircubbin Clay Pigeon Club at their monthly shoot in July 1976. From left: Leslie McKee, Mervyn Savage, Eric Johnston, Bill Carter, Tom Gilmore and B. Anderson. 23-6a-11

Members of Londonderry Park Bowling Club after receiving the Ards Jewellers Cup (pairs) and the John Gilmore Cup (men's singles) in August 1976. 3-7-12

Girls from the Wetherdair factory in Ballywalter who took part in a beauty competition in September 1976. The joint winners, Mildred Adair and Margaret Mahood, both aged 16 and from Portavogie, qualified for the Miss Textile contest in the London Hilton the following month. 13-14a-15

Tutor Elizabeth Graham presents a gold necklace to Sister E. M. McComb on the occasion of her retirement from Ards Hospital in September 1976. Included are Senior Nursing Officer Mrs McCandless and some of her nursing colleagues. 20-6-13

Officers and members of Star of Ards Junior LOL No 47 with the trophy they received in October 1976 for being the most progressive Lodge in County Down. 93-12-15

Members and guests who attended Cottown Pipe Band's annual dinner dance at the Imperial Hotel, Donaghadee, in October 1976.
66-13a-15

Alan Graham, president of Ards Bowling Club, and Mrs Graham who presented the awards in November 1976 at the club's annual dinner. Prizewinners are included.
60-12-17

Just before Christmas 1976 members and friends of Newtownards Lions Club distributed bags of logs to senior citizens around the district. Included (from left): Jackie Hillis, Charles Hutton, Julie Hutton, Hugh Brown, Warden Dick, Joe Hetherington, Mike Leonard and club president Joe Bannon.
66-10-20

1976

Sport in the Chronicle

Newtownards man Reggie Bell scored a hole-in-one at Scrabo Golf Club's 292-yard par 4 ninth hole on Sunday 29 February. It was believed to be the first time the feat had been achieved at Scrabo. Reggie, whose handicap was nine, was playing with Tom McCullough, Chad Bailie and Andy Davidson.

Ards Rugby Club broke new ground over the weekend of 6/7 March when the 1st XV played – and won – their first ever fixture outside Ireland. They were playing the famous London Irish Club's 2nd XV and defeated them 20-10 at their equally famous Sunbury grounds. Star player for Ards was Derrick Nash.

Peter Orr, son of Tom and Doreen Orr from Greyabbey, was selected in March to captain the Ireland U-21 hockey team. He played for YMCA.

Regent House won the Medallion Shield for the first time in the school's history, beating Bangor Grammar School 6-3 at Ravenhill on 2 April. The winning try and conversion, courtesy of Rodney Jess and David Baird respectively, came after just six minutes of play. Bangor Grammar pulled back three points thanks to a penalty scored well into injury time in the first half. The final whistle blew with Regent firmly encamped in the Bangor 25 and the scoreline still in their favour.

Team – S. Gregg, R. Jess, G. Heron, A. Foster, J. Keag, D. Baird, J. Boucher (captain), I. Shanks, G. Conroy, P. Andrews, J. Barclay, N. Keenan, B. McGimpsey, J. Park, A. McCartney. Subs: M. Matthews, J. Horner, P. Chalmers.

The Cafolla Snooker Trophy final on 7 April saw holder George Maxwell (Scrabo Golf Club) defeating Jim McLaughlin (St Patrick's) by four games to one at the Queen's Hall. The encounter was a repeat of the previous year's final.

Ards Rugby Club's 3As fell short in the McCamley Cup final at Ravenhill on 26 April, losing by 12-7 to Ballymena. Teddy Sloan scored an unconverted try and Fred Wishart made no mistake with a penalty kick but Ballymena proved the stronger side, particularly in defence.

The Ards Ladies 2nd XI won the Intermediate Plate on 8 May, defeating Coleraine Ladies 1-0 at Malone. The winning goal was scored by Gillian Murphy, a student at Regent House. The trophy was retained in 1977 (30 April) thanks to a 2-0 victory over Kilkeel. Scorers on that occasion were Pamela Foster and Joan Bishop.

Movilla High School student Len Kirk (15) won the Northern Ireland Junior 10-mile cycling championship on 21 August, along the difficult Coleraine / Kilrea road. His time was 24 minutes and 41 seconds.

Donaghadee Ladies' Bowling Club finished their season in a blaze of glory, winning the Senior League title in Dublin on 22 September, earning acclamation as All Ireland Champions.

A new pavilion and playing pitches for Donaghadee Rugby Club, costing a total of £65,000, were officially opened on 25 September by the Mayor of Ards, Cllr H. S. Cosbey. The programme for the day included a mini rugby match between Donaghadee PS and Bloomfield Road PS (Bangor), a tough encounter between the Donaghadee 1st XV and the President's XV (the latter winning 42-0), and a supper dance at the Old Forge Hotel.

Newtownards thrower Dawson Harris (Westmount) defeated a competitor from County Tyrone by two games to nil (both in 18 darts) to win the Carreras £200 Individual Challenge at Ards Sports Club on 14 December.

Ards beat Bangor 6-3 on 21 December to secure the Bass Boston Cup, reversing the outcome of the previous year's encounter between the same two teams. Bangor had previously been undefeated in all Northern Ireland Senior rugby fixtures that season. Two penalties by Tom McComb secured the winning points for Ards.

It proved third time unlucky for Ards Seconds when they lost out 2-0 to Brantwood in the Steel and Sons Cup final at Seaview on Christmas Day. Despite playing very well they succumbed to a double strike from Brantwood in the final four minutes of the game.

North Down Hockey Club's 2nd XI, winners in April 1976 of Junior League II in the Ulster Hockey Union. 98-14a-2

Karen McBride (left) and Lorna Bell, from Portavogie Primary School, who competed in the Ulster Under-12 Badminton Championships at the McCallum Hall in Belfast on 1 January 1976, came home victorious as doubles champions. In addition, Karen beat Lorna to secure the singles title, while Lorna won the mixed doubles with partner John Evans. 98-5-123

Ards Blues, winners of the North Down League in May 1976. Back (from left): P. Cooling, R. Milligan, W. Cummings, T. McKay, W. Rollins, J. Angus. Seated: R. McKechnie, C. Trueman, S. Clements (captain), J. Vennard, K. Montgomery. Front: G. Black and J. Carville. 93-7a-4

Millisle United and Portaferry Celtic met in the final of the Bunting Shield in the North Down League at Ards Rangers' ground in May 1976. 77-17-3

Deputy Mayor James Caughey and Brian McSharry from Downtown Radio presented the awards at Ards Swimming Club's annual gala in May 1976. Included are prizewinners and club officials. 10-10-6

The St Finian's Primary School football team which won the Newtownards Primary Schools League in May 1976. Back (from left): Mr McDonald (coach), T. Byers, B. Farren, B. Reid, M. Cafolla, M. McMullan, R. Loyer, Mr Leopold. Front: B. McKeown, P. McKeown, A. Monaghan, P. Murray (captain), J. Smyth, S. Murray and H. McCall. 10-15-5

Members of the Ballyphilip Boys Gaelic football team from Portaferry, winners of the Lecale Primary League, the Lecale Primary 7-a-side competition and the first-ever East Down Primary Championship in July 1976. Back (from left): G. Fitzsimmons, J. Denvir, P. Moreland, G. Mallon (captain), J. Murray, B. McGrattan. Front: J. Bailie, P. McGrattan, P. Sands, M. Curran and P. Donaldson. 22-15-9

Comber Tennis Club Ladies 'A' team, winners of the Belfast and District Ladies Junior Knock-Out Cup in August 1976. They defeated Knockbreda Ladies in the final at CIYMS. Team members were Jean Bowers, Karen McGreeghan, Fiona Wolseley, Anne Blackstock and Elaine Gibson. 80-6a-11

Some of the children who took part in Donaghadee Golf Club Juvenile Captain's Day in August 1976. 45-5a-12

Newtownards businessman Derek Harkness, who donated skips and trophies to Drome Olympic FC, presents the player of the year trophy to Jack Leckey In November 1976. Included are players and manager Jim Allen, along with the Ards Summer League Cup and Manor Cup, which the club won during a very successful season. 91-11-16

Jim Palmer

remembers ... The Scene

It was the first Coke bottle (the glass variety) over his shoulder that convinced Prince Jim that all might not be well at the end of his dee-jaying stint in the Freakeasy at the Queen's Hall in Newtownards back in 1970.

The drink-fuelled loyal patrons were awaiting the National Anthem – as was the Hall's policy – but neither the Prince nor the caretaker could find the appropriate record. Thinking quickly, the Prince (tone deaf!) informed the riotous-looking mob that he would lead the singing of the Anthem himself. It did not turn out well!

The out of tune rendition had only got as far as "God save our gracious Queen", when the Coke bottle opener whistled past his ear and when others followed the Prince was to be found cowering under his dee-jay deck.

Three bouncers plus the assorted chair legs they produced from under their jackets quelled the riot and the Prince was despatched off down West Street against the one-way system.

Prince Jim was yours truly!

But it wasn't always that exciting on the Ards entertainment scene all those years ago. In Newtownards itself the Freakeasy with a mix of groups and discos was the only show in town for the young folk, though there was plenty to choose from in the pub entertainment market.

The Freakeasy had a poll to find the top-rated groups

Jim Palmer has recently retired after writing for the *Newtownards Chronicle, County Down Spectator* and various other local and national papers during a career stretching back over 45 years.

Retirement still finds him living in Ards with his wife Elizabeth, whilst daughters Gillian and Ruth live just up the road this side of Dundonald.

A book on the local entertainment scene over the 30-odd years he wrote the 'Scene' column has been ruled out.

"No one would believe some of the things that happened," says Jim, "... Come to think of it, I can hardly believe them myself!!"

Members look on as Comber PACE (Protestant and Catholic Encounter) representative Mrs Iris Peacock presents cheques to Mrs P. Cloherty, on behalf of the Comber Coal Fund, and Mr Jim Palmer, for the Enler Youth Club. The money was raised at a PACE social event in December 1974. 88-2-96

with locals Gumm at the top followed by Jargon Junction, Chips, Blood and the Few, but the venue didn't survive the early Seventies.

Among the pubs in Newtownards we had Tria and Peter Whitlock directing the Steeplechase at South Street with stars like Marjorie Rea and *Opportunity Knocks* winner Brian McCann on offer.

Pat and Ian Falls opened a new cabaret spot in their bar called Jellicos with Belfast names such as Kenny Eden starring. Meanwhile Paddy Hyndes and David Magill had Safari as residents in their Jubilee Bar at North Street and the Devonshire Arms in High Street had weekend music from groups such as the Traceys.

Out of town you could have caught Eileen Donaghy in Finnegans at Kircubbin, while the Grand Prix in Ballywalter ran groups like The Sons of the Sod. The dance on Friday at the Andrews Hall in Comber had closed its doors but Crossgar's War Memorial Hall continued successfully playing bands such as the Gaylords and Chad. The latter was fronted by Milton Godfrey, who was described in the Chronicle ad as the "coloured singing sensation"... no complaints from readers on that one, though it was in pre-PC days!

The Sundowners also had their picture in the paper (a bit of a rarity as our Editor wasn't exactly a 'Scene' fan!). Colm and the boys were everywhere, re-opening the Locarno in Portaferry, appearing at the Sunday night St Pat's Ballygalget dance and later in the McKenna Community Centre, which opened in late 1970.

There was a Drive-In Disco at Roden Street in Kircubbin, and discos too at weekends in the White Horse Inn, Carrowdore. Back to the Locarno, though, for a little yarn. One night Brian Coll and his Buckaroos were playing there and I happened upon the band (who I knew well) across the road in Hinds' Bar.

Now Brian was teetotal and the Buckaroos were warned that anyone drinking spirits would be sacked. It was not a sensible decree! While the lads were indeed not drinking spirits they were getting thoroughly stuck into Carlsberg Specials and after leaving a table heaving with empties they staggered across to take the stage!

By the mid-Seventies the Troubles in Northern Ireland were hitting hard but being for the most part a safe area there was a big expansion of entertainment venues led by the Town 'n' Country at Regent Street in Newtownards. Owner Harry McGimpsey had spotted the potential of customers coming in from Belfast as well as the whole Ards area and he was spot on.

He provided country nights, pop nights, cabaret and discos using his Scrabo Lounge and the main ballroom. That meant everything from Dickie Rock to the California Brakemen, the Fast Ed disco to Big Bad John, Fred Hanna and Lomax. Scene follower Blair Mayne was my main man in the T n' C, keeping me up to date with all the local gossip.

The Strangford Arms had a supper dance where Candy Devine could have been singing, while La Mon at Gransha was also in the cabaret business with Denis McBride and his Countrybeats often onstage with guests like the Alexander Brothers and Andy Stewart.

The Old Crow in Comber ran supper dances as well, while the Stormont Hotel opened its Hillbilly Club, the Highwayman at Comber had a Saturday buffet dance and the Quarry Inn at Dundonald followed suit.

There were many new pub venues in the Seventies with Donaghadee, for example, boasting the Imperial Hotel, Dunallen Hotel, New Mount Royal Hotel, Central Bar and Drift Inn. Ballywalter had the New Lenador Lounge and Portaferry contributed to the entertainment scene with the Leprechaun and International Bars. Greyabbey was well served by the Abbey Arms, run by George Smith, and also the Rosemount Arms.

The calm of the area was somewhat shattered by the 1975 bomb at the International Bar in Regent Street, as well as the despicable murders that same year of three members of the Miami Showband. It meant most of the Southern bands refused to play north of the border and who could blame them?

The big news as that year ended was the opening of the Coachman at Rathgael with shows six nights a week, featuring everyone from PJ Proby and Sandy Shaw to the very top cabaret names around... many arriving from Belfast where the Troubles had really closed things down.

On then to the end of the decade and most of the singing pubs had remained in business, with the addition of great night spots such as the Squires Inn at Ballygowan with Barry Brent and Sweeney in residence. By then the T'n' C had closed its doors as had those super dancehalls Milanos and Caproni's, amongst others, mainly because the dancehalls were denied drink licences and hotels, plus premises pretending to be proper hotels, opened their own licensed dance venues.

Discos had mushroomed for the simple reason they were far cheaper to run than hiring bands. The days of pop showbands were numbered but at least the resurgence of country music meant plenty of country bands were on the road (as indeed there are now some 35 years on).

So ended a decade where the *Chronicle* cost just 12p, a bottle of vodka was £3.59 and my 'Scene' column photograph suggested I would soon be returned to the Maze!!

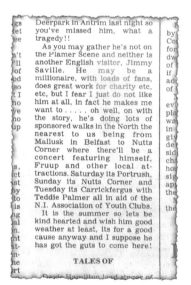

Deerpark in Antrim last night so you've missed him, what a tragedy!!

As you may gather he's not on the Plamer Scene and neither is another English visitor, Jimmy Saville. He may be a millionaire, with loads of fans, does great work for charity etc, etc but I fear I just do not like him at all, in fact he makes me want to ..... oh well, on with the story, he's doing lots of sponsored walks in the North the nearest to us being from Mallusk in Belfast to Nutts Corner where there'll be a concert featuring himself, Fruup and other local attractions. Saturday its Portrush, Sunday its Nutts Corner and Tuesday its Carrickfergus with Teddie Palmer all in aid of the N.I. Association of Youth Clubs. It is the summer so lets be kind hearted and wish him good weather at least, its for a good cause anyway and I suppose he has got the guts to come here!

TALES OF

can book . . . . .

Interesting visit next Wednesday to our shores of one of the best known dee jays of all time Emperor Rosko — he's at a Disco Exhibition in the Drumkeen Hotel from three till nine and everyones welcome . . . . .

Let's finish on a controversial note folks — Jimmy Saville is the worst bore on Tee Vee, only rivalled by Rolf Harris . . . .

Jim may not have been happy with his column's masthead but it was obviously the place to go if you wanted sound advice about the 'scene' as these two clippings from 1974 (left) and 1979 (above) show ... remember you read it first in the Chronicle!!

Ismay Woods

remembers ... Teenage Pop Idols

As the new decade started I was approaching adolescence. By 1972 I was attending Regent House School and other than being a junior in the Girls' Brigade at Strean Presbyterian Church, my only interest in life was music – the variety which featured on Radio One and Radio Luxembourg.

Along with millions of pre-teen and teenage girls across the world, I was madly in love with David Cassidy, he of the silky dark hair; the American singer and actor who had achieved worldwide fame playing the part of Keith in The Partridge Family. He was my idol, my life and all pocket money was spent on magazines which featured pictures and stories about David Bruce Cassidy, born 12 April 1950, son of Jack and Evelyn, stepson to Shirley Jones, who played his mother, conveniently also called Shirley, in the TV show. Oh yes I knew everything there was to know about the lovely David – well, everything the publicists of the time would allow his fans to know...

My fascination for Mr Cassidy did not mean I was not aware of other artists in the pop charts of the time. As with previous and future teenage generations, I was obsessed with popular music, having been influenced initially by the tastes of my older sister and brother. I was a bit of an anomaly amongst my peers, however; while they were getting into Bowie, T. Rex or whoever, I was still listen-

Ismay Woods was born at Adair House in Newtownards Hospital, the youngest of four children to father Harry – it was his 50th birthday – and mother, also Ismay.

She attended Castle Gardens Primary School and Regent House Grammar School, before embarking on the pre-entry newspaper journalism course at the College of Business Studies in Belfast.

She joined the Newtownards Chronicle as a junior reporter in March 1980, without finishing the course, though she managed to complete her shorthand exam, attaining 100 wpm.

She is still employed by Spectator Newspapers, owners of the Newtownards Chronicle, holding the position of Deputy Editor.

The Alma Mater, Castle Gardens Primary School

ing to my sister's Tamla Motown and soul records, and acquiring a collection of my own in the same genre.

Of the artists of that time whose music would have been categorised in a similar vein, there was one stand-out act, the Jackson 5, and more particularly their lead singer, a young chap called Michael. In fact, and in an ironic twist, the first single I ever bought with my own money was not a David Cassidy tune but Michael's first solo release, *Got To Be There.*

School, of course, got in the way of everything. Having been a pupil in the relatively small, cosy environment of Castle Gardens Primary (sadly no longer at its original site, having been razed to the ground by idiots), I was now a small fish in a huge ocean. For the first two years I floundered (unintentional piscatorial theme continuing there); academically, I was a fairly average student. My overriding memories are of the people I met, one of whom was to become a friend for life.

By Third Form – Year 10 as it is referred to nowadays – our class had the dubious reputation of being the worst in that year. It could be argued we did have the most disinterested, and possibly the most disruptive, group of young men in our class. About half a dozen of them seemed intent on entertaining themselves and others in the class, though not everyone (especially the teaching staff) always got the joke. One incident comes to mind, and I have enjoyed recalling it over the years. We were in a Biology classroom and, in a rare moment, all was quiet. That was until someone (one of the boys) piped up: "Are you ready, Steve?" The reply came from another part of the room: "Uh uh." The first voice: "Andy?" Response: "Yeah." First voice: "Mick?" Third responder: "Okay." The Brian Connolly of this dialogue: "All right, fellas, let's go!" Then silence fell once more.

The teacher was stunned; we all fell about laughing. If the references have you stumped, let me explain. These lads were re-imagining their version of the opening lines of a hit record of the time – *Ballroom Blitz* by the Sweet. That was how we rolled...

Meanwhile, there were political machinations and violent episodes occurring in the world outside this teenager's spectrum. Naturally, I was aware of the ramifications of it all; while thankfully the horrors of murder and destruction did not have a direct, personal impact on me, the situation of the time affected my life as it did everyone in Northern Ireland. A trip to Belfast was a rarity; staying out of the city became the norm. When you did 'go up to town', it was something of a shock to be confronted by manned security turnstiles, being searched going into shops, and seeing soldiers patrolling the streets while everyone appeared to be going about their normal business. A journey into Belfast was unnerving and I was always glad to be on the bus back home.

In typical selfish teenage mode it was the Ulster Workers' Council (UWC) strike of 1974 which caused me the most upset; no electricity meant no television and no television meant no Top of the Pops. It seemed to go on for an eternity; it was in reality a fortnight. But two weeks is a long time when you're 13. Roads may have been blocked, people were having to cook dinner on bricks set in the fireplace (well, that's what my mum and dad did) and there was no bread, but all I was concerned about was missing my weekly fix of the only chart show on the telly.

It was the 1970s that witnessed the erection of security barriers, sand-filled barrels at street entrances and Newtownards closed off at night. When I watched The Simpsons Movie a few years ago, and laughed when Springfield was cut off from the rest of the world and contained in a huge impenetrable dome, I was reminded of how my town (and of course others) had the life sucked out of it after the permanent barriers were placed across the road and locked, preventing traffic from entering or leaving the main streets of the town centre.

Back then there was little in the way of entertainment for anyone. I was too young for the T'n'C, there wasn't always something on at the pictures I wanted to watch, and the Blue Lamp discos, organised by the RUC's community relations unit and held

From teenybopper pop to Irish rock - an evolution of a teenager from the seventies musical tastes

in the Orange Hall, while welcome, were infrequent and unfortunately at times a bit intimidating; being grammar school girls often set me and my friends apart from those who attended the other secondary schools. We were looked on as snobs, wrongly it had to be said; we faced prejudice not because of which church we were perceived to belong to, but simply because of the school we attended.

The Troubles also meant few bands or singers would contemplate adding Northern Ireland to their tour itinerary; I did manage to see the Bay City Rollers in Belfast and Bangor, but it would be the 1980s before concert-going became a regular event.

Monday nights were GB nights; I loved my years as a member of Strean Girls' Brigade. It was a small company and we all got on brilliantly. There was none of the favouritism I had observed in the previous GB company I had been more or less forced to attend during my primary school years. I left when the time came for A-Levels; I was so disorganised that combining GB commitments and school work was well beyond my capabilities. Still, I managed to stay on long enough to obtain my Silver Duke of Edinburgh Award, which I worked on with my best friend and others who were members of Regent Methodist GB Company. The expedition section of the award necessitated a trip up the Mournes, all the way from Castlewellan. An overnighter in Slievenaman Youth Hostel; for some reason when I hear the late Demis Roussos sing *Forever and Ever*, I am reminded of thee...

In 1979 I was no longer in love with David Cassidy; he had been usurped by Leslie McKeown of the Bay City Rollers, who in turn was supplanted by Rick Parfitt of Status Quo. There have been others, too numerous to mention. I was also in my last year at school; the highlight of my Sixth Form years at Regent House was my involvement in the school's dramatic society, taking on the role of Elaine Harper in Arsenic and Old Lace and Ishmaelia, leader of the gypsies, in Maria Marten: or the Murder in the Red Barn. The latter was a particular triumph, as initially the character was called Ishamael; thanks to a stroke of genius by the wonderful Sophie Morrison, the drama teacher at Regent at the time, she decided the part should have a sex change, gave me the role and I had a wonderful time prancing about the stage, flinging my cloak about and projecting for all I was worth while affecting a Romany accent!

By the end of the last year of the 1970s, I was halfway through the journalism course at what was then the College of Business Studies in Belfast; my favourite album of 1979 was Michael Jackson's *Off the Wall*. It still sounds good today...

Oliver McGuigan

remembers ... Billiards and Snooker

I was one of the many who made the rapid change away from billiards to snooker, largely thanks to the high profile the game was enjoying on television with the likes of 'Pot Black' following the introduction of colour in the early 1970s. Those televised matches were keenly watched for tactics and shot routines, which then sent us all back to the practice tables. Intense discussions often ensued as to how Alex Higgins or Steve Davis had managed to do this or that; many hours were then spent trying to emulate those particularly difficult shots.

In billiards team play I was fortunate enough to win league and cup titles over the years in the Downpatrick League. I also played snooker for the Queen's Hall for a few years in the Bangor and District League. Moving from one club to the other was acceptable practice in those early years. During the decade I played golf at Scrabo, where for many years I also represented the club playing snooker.

My personal highlight occurred in the inaugural year of the Bangor and District League when I battled my way through the scratch individual competition, reaching the final, only to go down to quality local player Wilbur Walker, from Holywood. I also represented St. Patrick's teams and won the Senior League snooker title on a few occasions.

During the Seventies two major billiards and snooker

After leaving school Oliver McGuigan began work in the construction industry and from there he progressed to the role of Building Control Officer with North Down Borough Council, and then, for the longest part of his working career, 26 years in all, he was on the teaching staff at North Down and Ards Institute, lecturing in CAD and many aspects of construction.

During the late Seventies as a mature person he put the cue down in favour of night school for a number of years at Belfast Institute, completing his education at the University of Ulster with a Bachelor of Education (Hons).

Members of the St. Patrick's Billiards Club from Newtownards at their annual dinner and prize distribution in June 1974 at the Strangford Arms Hotel. 2-14-87

clubs existed in Newtownards, the Queen's Hall and St. Patrick's. In addition, Scrabo Golf Club had two tables and competed in their own golf club snooker leagues. Thanks to the boost snooker was receiving from television every lad had his own cue, which was a marked difference from previous generations when you just lifted a cue from the rack and hoped to get a straight one!

Such enthusiasm among the younger players for snooker forced club committees to make the big shift away from billiards to snooker. It was the fastest change imaginable, driving billiards virtually out of existence within the decade. Northern Ireland champion Dessie Anderson and Jimmy McLaughlin (sports writer 'Baulkline') were the men behind the new Bangor and District League structure. It was thanks to their hard work and Jimmy's organisational skills that the league came into existence. Initially it provided for snooker and billiards on an equal footing. The two main clubs from Newtownards entered teams, joining others mainly from Bangor. This provided a tremendous level of competition as most teams had their quality players.

St Patrick's, formed in 1915, played out of the old National School building in Ann Street; this was modified many times, with ongoing maintenance over the 70 years the club used it. Despite the fact it was limited to a two table set-up, it was home to many of the finest cue men who ever graced the local billiards and snooker scene. Among these were Hugh Quinn, Nario Cafolla, Joe Campbell, Jimmy Victor McLaughlin (one of the leading lights in the move to snooker), a list of McGuigans from Seamus, Leo, wee Joe, Oliver and Dessie, Peter Leonard and Bernard and Paddy Mulvenna, young guns Eugene Rogan, Colin Ritchie, Dessie O'Reilly, Joe Crilly and John McLaughlin.

Members of the Queen's Hall Billiards Club, Newtownards, with the Belfast and District Senior Billiards League Trophy which they won (for the first time) in October 1974. Back (from left): J. McKnight (secretary to the trustees), D. Catney (chairman), R. Hully (treasurer), W. Mayne, J. Cochrane, R. McClements. Front: William McBride (captain), R. Thompson, G. Duignan and W. Moore. 22-9a-89

It is said the common thread within very good sportsmen is the will to win. These players had that in abundance and their level of commitment transmitted through the club teams, making our teams and players very hard to beat.

The Queen's Hall club opened in 1959 as a successor to the old Town Hall club which was originally formed in 1897, remaining in existence until its relocation to Regent Street. In fact, one of the billiards trophies still being competed for originated from 1904.

The new club enjoyed beautiful purpose-built surroundings with five tables on a highly polished parquet floor; this was the very best setting in which to play. The large Queen's Hall membership was very proud of this club and its facilities. Initially a public utility, the local Council employed a person as marker, where anyone wishing to play could pay a daily fee. However, this idea of being able to walk in off the street was from a different era and led to poor players bashing balls around and damaging expensive-to-repair tables. All clubs recognised that a fully vetted membership, made up of able players, was the way forward. This has carried forward to the present time.

The big players from that period included John Thompson, who was excellent at both billiards and snooker. He reached the Northern Ireland snooker semi-final, earning himself the nickname 'Flying John'. Yes, before Hurricane Higgins we had our very own speedy player! Among those who excelled at billiards were Billy Moore, Billy McBride and Gabriel Duignan – just watching them in action was

The St Patrick's A billiards team from Newtownards won the Downpatrick and District Senior Billiards League in March 1973. Back (from left): Leo McGuigan (captain), Hugh Quinn, Jim McLaughlin, Seamus McGuigan. Front: Eugene Rogan and George Quinn. 263-39-3

an education in the game's finer points. Adding to the talent pool in a club awash with talented players were regular team players John Cochrane, Jim McNeilly, Blakley Anderson, Edgar Wallace, Peter Foers, and George Stannage.

At the beginning of Seventies both Queen's Hall and St Patrick's played their competitive matches in the Belfast leagues. The former fielded teams in the Belfast and District League, while the latter competed in the Down and Connor League. However, given the worsening nature of the Troubles, travel in and out of various areas of Belfast became more dangerous. As a result the committees of both clubs decided in the early Seventies to cease playing in Belfast for the safety of their travelling players. This had a massive impact on how all the snooker and billiards players around Northern Ireland engaged with each other for more than two decades – much longer than anyone could ever have envisaged.

In the interim, St. Pat's entered four billiards teams, each with four members, in the Downpatrick and District League in 1970. The years 1970-77 provided a very rich harvest for our little club as we won all the cups and the league many times. If it wasn't the A squad it was the B squad bringing home the trophies! There was a bit more travel involved as many a night we had to journey as far as Newcastle, Downpatrick, Crossgar, Ballynahinch, Drumaness or Killyleagh.

The St. Pat's A squad of Hugh Quinn, Nario Cafolla, J. V. McLaughlin, Leo McGuigan and M Trolan were league champions many times. Hugh Quinn was the billiards player of the decade within Newtownards District – in this squad he was very ably supported by J. V. McLaughlin. The B squad of Peter Leonard, Oliver McGuigan, Bernard Mulvenna and Dessie McGuigan also secured the title a few times with their entertaining style of play. The various league cups were won frequently by both squads. We had an abundance of players at this time and the squads changed when other equally talented lads came along, including Paddy Mulvenna, Colin Ritchie, Dessie O'Reilly and Joe McGuigan, not forgetting our long serving chairman Seamus McGuigan and Francis McLaughlin, who played in both squads over the years.

SCRABO SNOOKER SCENE

It was not widely known within the town that a vibrant snooker section existed at Scrabo Golf Club, which was better known then for its Ulster Cup-winning golf teams. Nevertheless, with a man of George Maxwell's ability playing, a new snooker culture developed within the club, which a lot of members bought into and enjoyed immensely.

The club entered a team in the golf league and we won the B division at the first time of entry. Of course I was lucky once again to be surrounded by quality players like George who was a seriously good player, former Town Hall players Jack Reilly and Wilbur McNeilly, ex-Ards footballer Ivan Patterson and the others who made up a very competitive team ably captained by Tommy Taylor.

We competed valiantly in the A division for many years but just could not win the title, finishing runners-up on two occasions in the Seventies. George did, however, prove his pedigree by reaching the Northern Ireland final, only to lose out to Donal McVeigh who was already one of the finest in the country. He did, however, win the Cafolla Cup on numerous occasions, his first victory being against favourite J. V. McLaughlin (St. Pat's). In a packed St. Pat's clubroom J. V. missed a sitter pink ball for a 4-2 victory, thereby allowing George back to the table to take that frame and the next to win the title. The following year, I too battled with George, taking a 3-0 lead from the home leg in St. Pat's, but I lost the first frame on a black ball at Scrabo. After that the class player took over and dominated the game.

THE MAKING OF A PROFESSIONAL

Right from the outset young Tommy Murphy could handle a cue, playing shots he was just not entitled to make. Attitude, polish and class were evident within a very short time. Indeed, Tommy was in the club less than a year when he was selected for a team and he took to this like a veteran. I remember driving the team to that first match and our starlet got the usual 'don't do this and don't do that' from the rest

Tommy Murphy

of us. His name came out against Dessie Anderson – what a baptism to have! We needn't have worried as he romped home, leaving Dessie to state with good grace: "What a find you've got in that lad."

The quality and style of Tommy's play had a major impact on the local game. The men who had switched away from billiards played a cautious game snookering and waiting for mistakes. Tommy's method of play was attacking snooker and all the young players followed him, which was great for the game. He was hitting breaks of over 100 before he was 17. Nothing seemed too difficult to him and his progress from being very good to becoming the best was rapid.

Along the way he won everything he entered, including British age group titles and the Northern Ireland snooker title in the Maple Leaf Club in Belfast, where he beat Billy Mills on a memorable night. This led to many big matches to test Tommy's mettle, including professional Doug Mountjoy at Scrabo Golf Club. It was only a short time later, in 1981, he turned professional. A lad from a provincial town with a touch of class made it onto the world stage.

Finals night at St. Pat's

These were memorable occasions for the members, not only because of the high standard of play but also because of the entertainment afterwards. At St Pat's we were graced with many talented singers and stage entertainers from the Patrician Players, who were also playing members of the club. We had Hugh Quinn, a group lead singer who would do the latest hits and a few Roy Orbison numbers, while J. V. McLaughlin could be relied on for Country and Western standards and Elvis Presley's *Blue Suede Shoes*. Not forgetting the unique barbershop quartet routine involving Seamus McGuigan, Luke Murray and Owen Dorrian who acted the patsy under Leo McGuigan's tutelage, with polished performances every time.

Seamus McGuigan would recite his own monologues which had us all in stitches. Then on would come Harry McMullan with his top hat and cane doing a stage version of *The Man Who Broke the Bank in Monte Carlo*. Tommy Murphy was another fine singer and I can still remember big Basil Clarke and Seamus Murray duetting with songs from South Pacific. It was a real touch of class.

We did not fully appreciate it at the time but looking back to the Seventies we can all recall fun times, great games and inter-club matches. I hope this reminiscence reminds us all of our young life in the game and the spirit for sport within Newtownards at that time. The game and the clubs continue...

1977

Making the News in the Chronicle

Ards FC president and secretary Harry Cavan, by then a major figure in world football, was awarded an OBE in the New Year Honours List. An Ulster doubles table tennis champion in his younger days, Mr Cavan's connections to Ards FC dated back to the 1930s. His qualities as a legislator were recognised beyond Newtownards, with Mr Cavan being elected president of the Irish Football Association in 1958.

By the time he received the OBE for his services to sport, Mr Cavan was vice-president of FIFA, football's governing body. The award was presented to him by the Queen Mother the following month.

Amanda Reid, from Ballyrogan Road, Newtownards, travelled to London in mid-January to appear on the BBC children's television programme Crackerjack. She was representing Northern Ireland in a competition to find the nation's top junior entertainer. Amanda was accompanied by her mother Rosemary and ballet teacher Audrey Sloan, whose school she attended.

In a report delivered to Ards Borough Council on 24 January by Recreations Officer Jim Ritchie, several major projects were proposed for the area over the following five years, including separate sports centres for Newtownards (£740,000), Comber (£240,000) and the Ards Peninsula (£240,000), a reclaimed recreational area at Whitespots (£175,000) and an indoor swimming pool for Donaghadee (£250,000).

Full planning permission was granted to Ards Borough Council in early February to build an abattoir at Portaferry Road, Newtownards. Councillors decided to write to the Department of Agriculture, the controlling authority, to put on record their wish that first priority to slaughtering should be given to local people, with the abattoir's availability to those from outside the Borough being dependent on its capabilities.

Local Councillors decided in mid-February not to sign a declaration of principle and intent to operate the Fair Employment (NI) Act of 1976. Members reasoned that as they had always abided by Acts of Parliament, to sign such a declaration could be interpreted as an admission this had in fact not been the case.

A trawler from Portavogie, fishing off the Isle of Man on 17 February, hauled on board a 500lb World War Two mine. The 'catch with a difference' was made by the new £200,000 vessel Sparkling Wave, with part-owner and skipper Edward Mawhinney, part-owner Joseph C. Mawhinney, Sam Thompson and Hugh Coffey, all of Portavogie, and Sam McMaster from Ballywalter, all on board.

Portavogie Harbour was sealed off by police once Sparkling Wave had docked and Army personnel spent the night on board the boat. The mine, thought to have been anti-German defence dating from 1940, was later neutralised in Ballyhalbert Bay.

Kircubbin Presbyterian Church celebrated its 200th anniversary with a series of special services in March, which coincided with the redecoration of the main building and assorted extension work. Moderator of the General Assembly the Rt. Rev. Dr. A. J. Weir visited the church on 11 March and dedicated a new organ. The minister of the congregation was the Rev. C. McCurdy.

Mothers carrying placards protested outside St Patrick's Church at North Street in Newtownards on 21 March against the alleged decision by Dr William Philbin, Bishop of Down and Connor, to refuse the Sacrament of Confirmation to some local children because they did not attend Catholic schools. Members of the All Children Together group, including chairman Cecilia Linehan, stood with the protestors during the service.

A province-wide strike – announced by the United Unionist Action Council because of the deteriorating security situation – began at midnight on Monday/ Tuesday

2/3 May after a meeting between Secretary of State Roy Mason and political leaders Ian Paisley and Ernest Baird failed to bring about an agreement.

Most shops in Newtownards remained open and many people went to work, but it was a different story in other parts of the Ards Peninsula with reports of strangers patrolling in cars to ensure businesses remained closed. There were tractor cavalcades around the district and some barricades appeared across roads, but the latter were quickly removed with a general feeling abroad that the strike was not well supported.

The Copelands Hotel in Donaghadee was destroyed by fire on 11 May. The blaze was spotted by a passing police patrol, with two officers helping to rescue several members of staff who were trapped by the advancing flames. Another person was rescued from an upper floor ledge by members of the Fire Service.

A total of 37 candidates stood for election on 18 May to the 17 seats that comprised Ards Borough Council. Twelve sitting Councillors were seeking re-election, with Area C (Comber, Ballygowan and Killinchy) attracting the greatest interest with 11 candidates in pursuit of just four seats.

No fewer than 11 first-time members were elected to office, with the Mayor and Deputy Mayor (Messrs. H. S. Cosbey and J. B. Caughey) among the casualties. There was a 100% success rate for the DUP, with all three candidates (J. Thompson, H. D. Boyd, T. Gourley) elected to office despite fears the recent strike might count against them.

Other party strengths were – Official Unionists, six (J. Scott, W. J. Caughey, R. C. Ambrose, J. Algie, W. Boal, H. McKeag); Alliance, five (Lord Dunleath, W. Sheldon, O. Dorrian, H. Gallagher, J. McBriar); Independent, one (J. Shields), NI Labour Party, one (E. Gaw), and SDLP, one (P. Doherty).

The new Mayor, selected without dissent at the annual meeting on 1 June, was Donaghadee Official Unionist John Scott, while Comber party colleague Hamilton McKeag was elected as Deputy Mayor over long-serving NILP representative Eddie Gaw on the Mayor's casting vote. Exactly the same thing happened the following year – in what was Alderman Gaw's fourth unsuccessful nomination for the position. However, success finally beckoned in 1979, with Alderman Gaw serving as Deputy Mayor to Cllr McKeag.

Stephen Boyd, of Ben Hur fame, died at his home in Los Angeles, California, on 2 June, aged just 45. Although he was a native of Glengormley, his sister, Mrs Maisie

Lindsay, lived with husband George at Circular Road, Newtownards. The actor had visited the town on a number of occasions, most recently in 1972.

A glider crashed at Newtownards airfield on 19 June but fortunately the pilot, from Bangor, sustained only cuts and bruises. The Queen's University glider, valued at between £3,000 and £4,000, was extensively damaged.

The Portaferry Cinema closed its doors for the final time in June, having served the town and district for some 54 years. It was opened by John K. Hinds in 1923 and the Hinds name remained synonymous with the cinema all down the years. Among the last films to be screened were Deadly Strangers (Hayley Mills and Simon Ward) and Race for the Devil (Peter Fonda and Warren Oates).

Due to reorganisation within the company the 50-year-old butchery business of R & A Morrison Ltd., 37 High Street, Newtownards, closed its doors on 30 July. The firm's bakery business continued to operate.

Newtownards man Ronnie McBride, drum major with Cottown Pipe Band, won the Champion of Champions title in early August at Portrush, venue for the final Royal Scottish Pipe Band Association (NI Branch) competition of the season.

Colin Coffey, from Boyd Avenue, Kircubbin, was one of a number of local Duke of Edinburgh Gold Award recipients who met Prince Philip on board the Royal Yacht Britannia during August's Silver Jubilee visit to Northern Ireland by the Queen and the Duke of Edinburgh.

Portavogie fishermen suffered a major blow in mid-August when the Isle of Man government decided to issue just 100 herring fishing licences to the whole of the United Kingdom, with 36 of those licences being earmarked for Northern Ireland boats. Of that number, just 10 applied to the 50-vessel Portavogie fleet. The European Economic Community and the British Government at Westminster had previously delegated the licensing power to the Isle of Man government, which indicated it would not be changing its mind.

Ballyhalbert residents launched a petition in early September urging Ray Carter, the Minister with responsibility for planning matters, to refuse permission for any new caravan sites or the expansion of any existing ones in the area. The resident population of Ballyhalbert was around 250 and the local community association was of the firm belief that, notwithstanding the problems created by all the extra traffic, no single site should be permitted to outnumber the village itself.

A new hall for Newtownards Free Presbyterian Church was opened on 24 September in the presence of a capacity congregation. The service was conducted by Senior Minister the Rev. Fred Greenfield, while the opening address was delivered by the Moderator, the Rev. Ian Paisley.

Comber man George Morris, a key figure behind the highly successful Ards Hospital Radio Service, was named Hospital Broadcasting Disc Jockey of the Year in the British Isles at the end of September. He received a £100 prize and a spot on Downtown Radio.

An incendiary bomb attack on the Regent Cinema on 8/9 October left Newtownards without a picture house. The devices, which ignited early in the morning, created a blaze of such intensity that the building on Regent Street was completely gutted. Only the projection room escaped the attack, which was claimed by the Provisional IRA.

Fire tenders from Newtownards, Bangor and Knock attended the scene within a short time of the fire being spotted by a Borough Council employee, who raised the alarm. It was understood the firebombs were placed in at least two locations, the stalls and the balcony area.

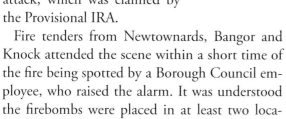

The Regent Cinema opened on Christmas Eve 1938 with a screening of the Mickey Rooney film Thoroughbred. In the intervening years it provided a mix of films and live performances, building up a faithful clientele whose loyalty had kept it open in the darkest days of the Troubles. On the same night there was a failed attempt to destroy the Borough's only other surviving picture house, the Comber Cinema. A cassette device burned out in the seat where it had been concealed.

Newtownards Chamber of Trade urged Ards Borough Council in October to provide additional car parks in the town, including the reopening of Conway Square to attended vehicles. Chamber members believed the lack of adequate parking facilities was having a detrimental impact on trade in Newtownards. The Council rejected the Conway Square call, saying it would not be used as a car park.

Keith Chegwin introduced his 'Swaporama' segment of BBC TV's Multi-Coloured Swap Shop live from the Kirkistown racetrack on 15 October. Resplendent in red and white racing leathers plus helmet, he had arrived at great speed in the sidecar of a racing bike, watched by an audience estimated at between seven and eight million. Programme host Noel Edmonds was back in the main studio in London, from where he helped to conduct a series of swaps. Gloria Hunniford joined 'Cheggers' on the stage and swapped a guitar for a pocket xylophone.

Ards Borough Council lent its support on 17 October to a notice of motion, forwarded by neighbouring Down District Council, calling on the Northern Ireland Housing Executive to sell off existing houses to sitting tenants, subject to appropriate safeguards being in force. The motion was supported by 11 votes to four.

Terrorists returned to Newtownards for the second time in three weeks, this time destroying the popular Town 'n' Country hotel and nightspot on 22 October. Once again they left incendiary devices which led to the outbreak of a fierce fire which completely gutted the building. Firemen from Newtownards, Bangor and Belfast fought for 10 hours to control the blaze but

it proved impossible to save the building, given the number of separate outbreaks around the hotel.

Thankfully, due to a last-minute change of wind direction the halls of St Mark's Church, which had been cleared of their contents in a major operation, survived the flames.

Town 'n' Country owner Harry McGimpsey indicated the hotel would be rebuilt and reopened within a year.

An appearance by the group Manasseh (billed as "seven young people firmly committed to Jesus Christ") at Greenwell Street Presbyterian Church Hall in late October was described as "the church's answer to punk rock."

Further firebomb attacks on business premises in Newtownards on 5 November, specifically the Regency Restaurant in Regent Street and the Co-Op in Frances Street, resulted in little or no damage but once again placed the town in a state of high alert.

Fears were expressed for the future of Newtownards Technical College after a proposal for the expansion of Bangor Technical College was announced in mid-November. Alderman John Algie said there a strong likelihood that building and mechanical engineering classes would be transferred from Newtownards to Bangor once the work was completed. He was greatly concerned that Newtownards would end up with a college catering largely for evening classes.

In the run-up to Christmas, Fosters Electrical Discount Stores in the Ards Shopping Centre was promoting Rank Arena Teletext televisions with all the usual programmes, as well as an up-to-the minute news and information service via the remote control. Previously, said the company, the service (Oracle on ITV and Ceefax on BBC) was only available to a small number of sets fitted with a special decoder. Now, however, it was available to everyone at the touch of a button.

Former Newtownards man Hugh Thompson (25), who was serving with the Royal Irish Rangers in England, was killed in an accident in Manchester on 6 December while on fire-fighting duties as the result of a firemen's strike. Ranger Thompson, formerly of Rathmullan Drive, had served in Cyprus, Germany and England and was due for a posting to Canada.

The Green Goddess fire engine he was travelling in to a call-out crashed at Newton Heath, killing two Rangers, including the Newtownards man, and leaving another four seriously injured. The call later proved to have been a false alarm.

Millisle farmer David Stanley Shannon (54) was called to the Bar at the Royal Courts of Justice in Belfast on 20 December, having pursued a legal career late in life, following spells as a garage proprietor, a civil servant and, most recently, a farmer. His change of direction began with a one-year course at the College of Business Studies in Belfast where he achieved three A-Levels. He then undertook a four-year course at Queen's University, graduating in 1975 with an LL.B Honours degree. Following completion of his Bar examinations he gained his Barrister-at-Law degree.

In common with colleagues around Northern Ireland, Ards Borough Councillors were given an allowance increase just in time for Christmas – entitling them to a £5.50 payment for meetings that lasted under four hours, rising to £11 for meetings that exceeded that length of time. There followed quite a few long nights!

Doctor Who (William Hawkins), Muddles (Alan Miller), Dame Trot (George Mayne), Gretel (Paula Sandford) and Hansel (Peter Vance) rehearse a scene from the pantomime The Babes in the Wood, which was presented by 5th Ards BB Company in January 1977.
15-8-22

County Commissioner Mrs Eves with members and officers of 1st Greyabbey Girls' Brigade in January 1977, following their enrolment service in the local parish hall.
1-3-23

Members of the First and Last Ladies Darts Social Club, Millisle, who attended their annual dinner in the Dunallen Hotel, Donaghadee, in April 1977.
63-3a-27

Members of the John Street Good News Club at a rally in Newtownards in May 1977. 43-14-30

Leaders and members of the Scrabo Hall Every Girls Rally, Newtownards, at their annual display in May 1977. 4-9a-31

8th Down Scouts and Cub Scouts who formed a guard of honour for Dr William Philbin, the Bishop of Down and Connor, at a confirmation service in St Patrick's Church, Ballyphilip (Portaferry), in May 1977. 27-15-31

Scrabo Tower School of Dancing, Newtownards, won the confined and open classes in Irish Dancing at Bangor Music Festival in May 1977. Included are teachers Jane O'Reilly and Sylvia Smith, winners of the senior championships. 67-10-31

Children from Circular Road, Newtownards, at their Queen's Silver Jubilee party in the local Scout Hall in June 1977. 77-3-33

The Queen's Silver Jubilee children's party at Shackleton Walk, Newtownards, in June 1977. 77-8-33

The children's party for the Queen's Silver Jubilee at Valetta Park, Newtownards, in June 1977. 77-6-33

Pupils from Victoria PS, Ballyhalbert, who gained the school's first ever cycling proficiency certificates in June 1977. Included are John Palmer, Janet Neville, Laura Bennett, Diane Hall, Helen Gunning, Hazel McClements, Joyce Bailie, Ruth Hammond, Mary Bailie, David Smith, Mrs M. C. Irwin (assistant teacher) and Mrs K. E. McIvor, principal. 25-5-36

Portaferry residents who attended a First Aid class run by the St John Ambulance Brigade in June 1977, receiving certificates for their endeavours from Mr K. Elliott (seated centre). Included are Mr W. Ellis (area superintendent), Mrs Ellis (area secretary) and members of the St John Ambulance's Newtownards Division, who gave a First Aid demonstration. 98-18-36

Retiring Carrowdore Primary School vice-principal Mrs A. J. Pollock with children who received cycling proficiency certificates at the end of term in June 1977. 5-14-36

The Rev. Trevor Williamson (centre) was joined by the Commission of the Ards Presbytery after being installed as minister of Glastry Presbyterian Church in August 1977. From left: the Rev. C. McCurdy, Kircubbin Presbyterian Church; the Rev. R. N. Cameron, minister of Millisle and Ballycopeland Presbyterian Churches; the Rev. D. J. McKelvey, Moderator of the Ards Presbytery and minister of Ballygilbert Presbyterian Church, and the Rev. H. C. Spence, Clerk of the Ards Presbytery. 20-1a-41

Members of the 1st Newtownards Liverpool Supporters Club before setting off from the town's Tudor Inn to attend the First Division fixture between Liverpool and Chelsea at Anfield. The match, played on 8 October 1977, saw the home side winning 2-0 thanks to goals from Kenny Dalglish and David Fairclough. 12-3a-45

The Rev. R. H. G. Gamble, founder chaplain, and Mrs May Armstrong, founder captain, cut a cake to mark the silver jubilee of 1st Donaghadee Girls' Brigade Company in November 1977. 79-17a-48

Leading Fireman John Kisby from Newtownards lays a wreath at the Ballywalter War Memorial in November 1977. 66-16a-47

A retirement presentation was made at Ards Hospital in December 1977 to domestic assistant Miss Frances Hughes, who had commenced work there in 1953. She received a hostess trolley, sherry glasses and a silver stand from domestic services manager James Pauley as former colleagues looked on. Nursing staff presented Miss Hughes with a cut-glass vase. 82-15a-49

Cast members from The Boy Friend, a musical play by Sandy Wilson, which was presented by the Movilla High School Dramatic Society in November 1977. 43-3-48

Beavers and Cub Scouts from the newly formed 1st Greyabbey Pack in December 1977. Included are leaders Mrs A. Carson, Mrs M. Pritchard, Mrs D. Long and Alistair Morrison. 19-3-49

Some of the lucky children who saw Santa and his helpers at Mawhinney's toy shop in Bridge Street. Comber, in December 1977. 55-11a-49

Members of the organising committee responsible for the Portavogie senior citizens' Christmas party in December 1977 at the local Orange Hall. 75-11-49

1977

Sport in the Chronicle

Ards Rangers crashed to a 6-0 defeat at the hands of Downpatrick Rec in the New Year's Day Border Regiment Cup final at Monkstown.

David Dunn, from the Meadowbank Snooker Club in Donaghadee, was selected in February to represent Northern Ireland in the final stages of the British Boys' Snooker Championships in England later in the year. He was also the youngest-ever player to take part in the Northern Ireland Championships.

Regent House 1st XI girls' hockey team defeated Rainey Endowed 1-0 on 16 March to bring the Schools Cup back to Newtownards for the first time. The goal was scored by Gillian Murphy, the other team members being Elaine Smyth (captain), Elaine Gibson, Norma McMullan, Marian Mateer, Pamela Bell, Linda Donnan, Linda Davidson, Carolyn Weir, Samantha Livingston and Beverley Heaney. Additional panel members were Caroline Agnew, Wendy Crosby and Fiona Marshall.

The success, however, was not repeated by the Regent House 1st XV rugby team, playing its first ever Schools Cup final at Ravenhill. Without skipper Nigel Carr, who had sustained a chipped bone early in the competition, they were gallant 12-9 losers to Armagh Royal School on St Patrick's Day. The winning score that broke Newtownards hearts in the 15,000-strong crowd came in injury time.

Ards Rugby Club secured the Junior Cup for the first time in its history, defeating Malone 7-0 at Ravenhill on 23 April. The sole try of the game was scored by Neville Edgar.

Jim Hayes, a member of the Ballydrain Harriers from Comber, knocked five minutes off the record for completing the gruelling Mourne Wall Walk. He set a new best time of four hours and eleven and a half minutes on 5 June.

Backdeed Man, owned and trained by Newtownards greyhound enthusiast David McClenaghan, of Lislean Place, won the Guinness-sponsored Ulster Derby and Trigo Cup by seven lengths at Celtic Park on 1 July. The attractive odds were 7/2. Mr McClenaghan subsequently rejected a "commanding offer of four figures" for the dog.

Carrowdore man Roy Magowan was a member of the Ireland team that won the 43rd International Four Home Countries clay pigeon-shooting competition at the end of July. It was their first-ever victory in the contest. Roy was the reigning Ulster doubles champion as well as Irish Gold Cup winner for 1977.

Northern Ireland Minister of State Lord Melchett visited Newtownards on 5 December to officially open the new Ards FC Sports and Social Club at Castlereagh Park. He was welcomed by Ards president and secretary Harry Cavan OBE.

Ards FC scored six times in a 10-goal thriller against Linfield at Windsor Park on 10 December; unfortunately two of the six were own goals and Ards lost the encounter 6-4. The own goals were scored by Roy Walker and Dave McCoy, with the 'real' ones coming from Allen, Cromie, Kennedy and McCoy (penalty).

Some of the players who competed in the quarter-finals of the Newtownards Vintners Darts League Individual Championship at the local Royal British Legion in February 1977. Back (from left): R. Bailie, W. Quail, J. Graham. Front: F. McCallum (runner-up), T. Dalzell (winner), D. McQuilken and R. Meharg. 95-19a-24

Children from Portavogie Primary School who reached the finals of the Under 10 and Under 12 sections of the North Down badminton tournament at the Ards Arena in February 1977. Back (from left): Julie Mawhinney, Joanne McVea, Sarella Lawson. Front: Patrick Hunter, Alan Carson and Mark Cully. 56-5-25

Members of the Ards Arena team who won the Blue Lamp table tennis competition at the Antrim Forum in April 1977. Included is RUC Community Relations Officer Mervyn Cassells. 60-18-29

West Winds United wearing the new skip they received from the local Tenants Association and Social Club in May 1977. 58-3a-30

William Armstrong, captain of West Winds United FC, accepts a new skip from West Winds Tenants Association and Social Club chairman John McClelland in May 1977. Included is secretary Alan Butler. 58-2a-30

Children from schools in Ballywalter, Millisle and Kircubbin who competed in a mini rugby competition at Donaghadee Primary School in June 1977. 33-8a-34

Alderman John Scott in July 1977 with members of Donaghadee Ladies hockey team who played Ballynahinch in the final of the Donaghadee Festival Shield. The home side lost on penalties after extra time. 33-7-39

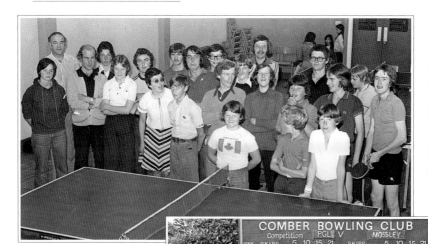

Competitors in a table tennis tournament run in July 1977 by Donaghadee Table Tennis Club in conjunction with the local festival week. 30-17-39

Comber Bowling Club members after a Senior League match against Mossley in August 1977. 85-6a-40

Members of the Newtownards Manchester United Supporters Club team who were beaten Scrabo Shield finalists in August 1977. 70-16-41

Five pioneer members of Ards Rugby Club, Norman McNeilly, Stanley Ditty, John Reynolds, Alexander Orr and Ted Griffiths, with the present day team's trophies at an exhibition of club mementoes in September 1977. 41-13-42

Brothers Derek and Bob Gilmore, of Kircubbin Sailing Club, were winners in September 1977 of the Lipton Cup, an annual open event at Carrickfergus for Flying Fifteens. 16-19-44

Geoffrey Bowman

remembers ... Gliding at Ards

Geoffrey Bowman is the older brother of the compiler of this book. Born in November 1954, in Bangor, where he was raised and educated, Geoffrey came to appreciate the road to Newtownards when he discovered gliding at Ards airfield as a Queen's University student in 1973.

The gliders flown by Geoffrey were light and streamlined for soaring in thermals. Over 30 years earlier, Geoffrey's late uncle, the original Geoffrey Bowman, was an RAF pilot during the Second World War and on one training exercise landed a Bristol Beaufort twin-engined bomber at Ards.

Geoffrey now lives in Belfast with his wife Sandra and is a partner in a leading Belfast firm of solicitors, where he specialises in asbestos litigation. In his spare time he travels to far-flung destinations like Greenland, Alaska and Chile (as a passenger in airliners), but still glides several times a year at the Ulster Gliding Club's new home at Magilligan.

My first impressions of Newtownards Airfield were not positive: I could see little more than a faded orange windsock flapping in the breeze and a collection of rusting Nissen huts straight out of the 1940s.

It was actually October 1973 and I had just joined the Queen's University Gliding Club at the beginning of my first year as a law student. Looking around the bleak vista of crumbling concrete and weed-infested tarmac, I found it hard to imagine Ards as a dynamic centre of flying activities. One of the dilapidated Nissen huts served as a clubhouse. It came with grubby vinyl armchairs and a one-armed bandit, but apparently no pilots. It was all rather depressing.

But my concerns were a little premature. Within an hour a small army of eager would-be pilots had gathered around the imposing, headmasterly figure of Grenville Hill, chief flying instructor of the Ulster Gliding Club. We dragged open the doors of the airfield hangar, revealing an Aladdin's cave of light aircraft. Some were twin-engined, most were single-engined and one very special machine had no engines at all. The Blanik two-seater trainer was an impressive aluminium glider which would prove to be my passport to the skies.

Two hours later I was strapped into the front seat, ready for my first flight. Behind me sat instructor Gordon

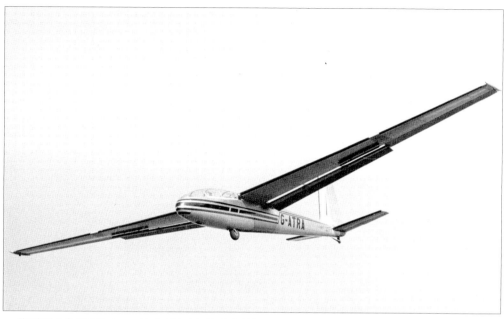

The Blanik on final landing approach to Ards (photo by Martin Smith)

Mackie. Visible ahead of us through the perspex canopy crouched a Piper Supercub, single engine roaring, ready to tow us high above the airfield on the end of a long rope or 'cable'.

Using a series of hand signals, Gordon alerted the pilot of the 'tug' that we were ready for launch, and barely 24 hours after joining the university gliding club I was accelerating down the main Ards runway on my first flight. As the Blanik parted company with terra firma I gazed in awe at the patchwork-quilt landscape of fields, roads and hills which opened up around us. Straight ahead lay the hazy summits of the Mournes. As we banked to the right, Scrabo Tower dropped beneath us and distant Bangor swam into view. Continuing our turn, we flew over the streets and houses of Newtownards, then over the blue-grey waters of Strangford Lough. All of these places were familiar to me, but not from this

Geoffrey in the Blanik after an early solo-flight

heavenly perspective.

We released the cable at 2,000ft. and I stared down at the airfield below, now transformed into a real flying centre. I could see where two shorter runways intersected the 2,600ft. main tarmac strip from which we had launched. It took a few minutes before I came to a crucial realisation: I had absolutely no concerns about circling high above the ground with nothing to support me but the lift created by the flow of air over the wings of this remarkable, engineless metal bird.

Between October 1973 and March 1978 I had 214 official launches from Ards and numerous unrecorded passenger flights. The airfield became a second home and the dozens of regular visitors an extended second family. As with most families, our flying community had its splits and its rivalries, most notably between the Ulster Flying Club and its poor cousin, the Ulster Gliding Club. Many power-pilots had little time for those of us who rode the thermals, flying high without burning petrol.

In fairness to the power-pilots, operating two clubs off one airfield inevitably caused some disruption. A typical example occurred during my first solo flight as I soared 400ft. above the Portaferry Road, preparing to turn onto my landing approach. A single-engined Cessna appeared from the direction of Bangor. We couldn't both land at the same time and I had no engine to allow me to 'go round again' so it was the Cessna pilot who had to veer off and circle around.

Group Captain Douglas Bader shares the Mayor's chain of office with Alderman John Algie at the official opening of the Ulster Flying Club's new premises in April 1975. Looking on are Stanley Woods, a vice-president of the Flying Club, and his wife. 95-19-104

Some power-pilots had feet in both camps: Wally Galloway was a UFC member who also flew gliders and occasionally instructed trainee glider-pilots. Wally was always welcomed by the gliding fraternity, particularly when accompanied by his wife Monica (herself a solo-pilot) and daughter Jane. Eric Vint was another friendly face who occasionally abandoned his aeroplane to sample the delights of pure, unpowered soaring flight.

In 1975 the Ulster Flying Club opened a brand new, purpose-built clubhouse on raised ground behind the hangar. The opening ceremony was performed by Douglas Bader, the legendary Battle of Britain flying ace.

The clubhouse became the centre of social activities for power-pilots and glider-pilots alike, but oil and water tend not to mix well. The Gliding Club occupied the small 'snug bar' on most Saturdays and Sundays after flying, leaving the main bar area for the 'power-shower.'

A colourful cast of characters passed through the 'snug' over the next three years, none more memorable than club secretary and gliding stalwart Bob Rodwell. A freelance journalist from London who had set up home in Belfast, Bob was always loud and opinionated and could be dogmatic, argumentative and exasperating. He was also enormous fun to be around (most of the time) and was the beating heart of the gliding club. Bob occasionally brought his family to the airfield, usually ending up rattling windows in Newtownards by bellowing the names of one son or another who had gone missing at going home time. Bob was once affectionately described by a fellow journalist as "the only man who could slam a revolving door".

Other regulars included father and daughter solo pilots Eric and Caralyn Page and the Lisburn trio of Jim Weston, Jim Wallace and Laurence McKelvie, three dedicated pilots who continue to glide decades later.

Long summer days at Ards brought out an amazing collection of flying machines. In addition to the conventional Pipers and Cessnas, the improbably-named 'Tipsy Nipper' caused jaws to drop by lofting its pilot into the air while looking more like a model aircraft than the real thing.

One Saturday afternoon two Army helicopters landed in a deafening blizzard of swirling grass close to our centre of gliding operations. It emerged that the Army's General Officer Commanding, General Sir David House, had requested a flight in one of our gliders. The second 'chopper' was his escort, a role its pilot continued to exercise even while the General was airborne with our own 'GOC', Grenville Hill. Not many gliders have armed aerial protection!

One of the Tiger Moth biplanes based at Ards in the mid-1970s

Scrabo Tower and Scrabo golf course from the air (c. 1975)

An even more remarkable sight one memorable afternoon was the spectacle of four Tiger Moth biplanes roaring down the runway and taking off one after the other in an evocation of the days when Ards operated as a wartime training base.

Deteriorating relations with the Ulster Flying Club and the need for a dedicated gliding site eventually caused the UGC to decamp to Magilligan on the north coast. My last flight at Ards airfield took place on 18 March 1978, but although the Magilligan field-site was better for gliding, there was one dominant feature of Ards that I will always remember with great fondness. Looming over the airfield like a giant finger pointing skywards, Scrabo Tower on top of its steep-sided little hill was a magnet to glider-pilots. It was enormous fun to buzz very low over the golf course on Scrabo's summit, then bank steeply past the base of the tower before landing back at the airfield. There were no recorded 'hits' from golf balls!

On lazy summer afternoons in 1976 and 1977, sea breezes often wafted up the steep east-facing slope of Scrabo, providing sufficient 'lift' to allow the pilots of single-seat gliders to fly 'figure of eight' manoeuvres level with the base of the tower. The sight of walkers waving across (and sometimes down!) at me will remain a glorious and indelible memory of those far-off days when I flew gliders at Ards.

Gillian Murphy

remembers ... Ards Ladies Hockey

Ards Ladies Hockey Club entered the Seventies with a pedigree in Ulster and Irish hockey to be admired. The new decade would bring little silverware in terms of the major trophies, but enough club development to keep Ards competitive in the top league and boosted by a number of individual successes.

For a number of players the key hockey moment of the Seventies was wearing the colours of Regent House School to win the Schools Cup for the first time in March 1977. North Down, with a long tradition in cricket and men's hockey, added ladies to the equation and witnessed the steady rise of their women from junior through to senior ranks.

In the early Seventies, Ards Ladies' matches continued on the grass pitches at the Comber Road venue but the arrival of gravel pitches in Londonderry Park on the Portaferry Road saw the girls make the move to a new stage and a different era. Moulded studs on canvas boots were changed to trainers, the heads of the sticks shrank considerably and the tunics gave way to skirts. Sweatshirts became a reality for the first time but old traditions continued for Ards with tea and biscuits offered to the opposition at the end of every game.

Marian Mateer recalls that Hazel Emo was the key recruitment agent in those days. She came into the Regent

Having enjoyed all sports from an early age, Gillian was introduced to hockey at Regent House before progressing to Ards Ladies when club officials came looking to drag her mum out of retirement in 1975 and she offered them her elder daughter instead.

Gillian made her debut for the club 1sts a year later, enjoyed cup success with Regent House in 1977 and played for the Ulster and Irish schools teams a year later.

Having studied at Loughborough University she returned home to feature again for Ards 1sts right through until 2002 and she was also selected to represent Ireland in Home Countries and European indoor competition.

Gillian played a key role in the push for an Astroturf pitch in Ards and has spent the last decade working hard to advance the Junior section of the club.

House changing room on a Saturday morning, checked who lived in Ards and told them what time they would get picked up to play for the town side that afternoon!

Julie Menzies featured regularly for the Ulster senior team and Joan McCormack played for the Ulster Schools team, as did Mandy Woodburn and Alison McKelvey. Yours truly became the first Regent girl to feature for the Irish Schools team and shortly after that Joanne Menown entered the Eighties already established as a full senior international.

Umpiring honours were enjoyed at Irish level by Norma Gartside and Lynda Walsh. Club stalwart Nan Dalzell continued to give an array of services to Ulster hockey in her twilight years as did Margaret Hoffmeister, initially as Ulster president and then as president of the Irish Ladies Hockey Union.

Regent House represented the first taste of hockey for most girls in the Borough; canvas bags with double buckles holding the sticks being a regular sight at Ards bus station on Saturday mornings. Many of us came through the hands of the revered Kay MacDonald (Mrs Mac) in junior school with roll-ins and bully-offs still accepted traditions of the game in the Seventies.

Progress was tangible with the School 2nds winning the McDowell Cup in 1975 and the 1sts sharing the Ulster Schools' Plate (with St Dominic's) in 1976. Three of the school team moved up a gear in the 1976-77 team by becoming regulars for Ards 1st XI in the top club league. This, combined with other players offering a variety of strengths, was moulded by ambitious coaches Isobel Mills and Anita Hiles into a special team with growing belief.

The cup run of 1976-77 was character-defining, with 1-0 victories in the quarter and semi-final against St Dominic's and Strathearn respectively. The mood at Regent was akin to an American high school during that middle week of March 1977 as the girls paraded in the curtain raiser at Bladon Drive on the 16th against Rainey Endowed, with the 1st XV there in force to support despite their own Ravenhill final 24 hours later.

With Rainey entrenched in their own half for long periods of the game, it seemed to be destined to a shared 0-0 outcome when young forward Linda Davidson was fouled in the circle and the resulting penalty stroke gave 16-year-old Gillian Murphy – that's me – the chance to grab the victory the team and coaches so richly deserved. My experience as penalty stroke taker for Ards 1sts no doubt made the difference and the celebrations when captain Elaine Smyth received the trophy were memorable.

Featured players included: Carolyn Weir, Caroline Agnew, Elaine Smyth, Pamela Bell, Beverly Heaney, Norma McMullan, Samantha Livingston, Linda Donnan, Marian Mateer, Linda Davidson, Elaine Gibson and myself.

Sadly the twist of fate, with telling injuries, proved to be not so kind to our boys

Regent House 1st XI, Ulster Schools Cup Winners 1977: Back: Mrs Ferguson, Fiona Marsden, Pamela Bell, Wendy Crosby, Carolyn Weir, Caroline Agnew, Linda Davidson, Linda Donnan, Dr. Maguire. Front: Mrs. Hiles, Marian Mateer, Gillian Murphy, Samantha Livingston, Elaine Smyth (Captain), Norma McMullan, Elaine Gibson, Beverley Heaney.

in the St Patrick's Day rugby final a day later. However, hockey ended the decade with the Regent girls a threat in each cup competition they played and another senior trophy lifted on a shared basis in 1979.

The Regent House 1st XI hockey team after they tied 1-1 with Friends School, Lisburn, in the final of the Senior Schoolgirls Cup in March 1979. The two schools shared the trophy. Back (from left): Wendy Nesbitt, June Mawhinney, Janet Shields, Caroline Agnew, Helen Carr, Linda Nesbitt. Middle: Wendy Crosby. Beverley Heaney (vice-captain), Linda Davidson (captain), Joanne Menown, Mandy Crosby. Front: Patricia Henry, Tara McMillan and Sonya Jamison (reserves). 421-12-4

As I was not old enough to feature before the mid-Seventies I asked current club president Norma Gartside for her memories. Norma, who has served the game of hockey at every level, including on the world stage through administration and umpiring, was at the peak of her own playing career in the early Seventies and recalls the following:

This was a fairly uneventful time at the club although some trophies were won, namely: 1969/70 – 1st XI Senior Plate; 1970/71 – 1st XI Senior Plate; 1971/72 – 1st XI Senior Plate; 1974/75 – 2nd XI Intermediate Plate, and 1976/77 – 2nd XI Intermediate Plate.

During this time some older members were be-moaning the fact that grass pitches were becoming defunct with the 'advance' of the new all-weather shale pitches, yet this was probably the most significant event in the decade when the pitch on the Portaferry Road came into being. She remembers this pitch was first used by the club in the season 1973/74.

Another significant move was the appointment of a club coach; following discussions at the AGM in 1974/75 Trevor Allsop was appointed in 1975. He also combined this with the role of umpire. He was a key influence on the up and coming hockey talent at Ards, who contributed so much to the Regent House cup success.

Ards Ladies, winners of hockey's Ulster Senior at the beginning of May 1970. 224-28-3

The third significant change followed some years of discussion regarding the matter of the tunic versus skirt debate, with the skirt lobby finally winning the day. The new skirt was modelled and approved at the AGM in 1976.

At the end of the decade we again had club representation on the UWHU Council through Norma Gartside, whilst Margaret Hoffmeister was to become president of the UWHU and the next year she was elected president of the ILHU.

To close out, the season 1979/80 also saw the start of the distinguished club reign of the late Joan Kennedy who for so long was our own 'President Kennedy'.

Clive O'Neill

remembers ... Newtownards Market

I was born in John Street, Newtownards, on 18 July 1953 and growing up in the town I never knew anything about markets. In truth the closest I ever got to one was the harvest fair day which was held each year on 23 September. Our Cubs' Scout group had a stall to raise funds, as did a lot of local organisations from the town, including the churches and the Boys' Brigade from Greenwell Street.

It was about 1976 when I was working in a local factory that I started selling fruit and veg round the doors. I started on the North Road and after a time I was calling each week with an expanding number of customers and making a few bob extra to help pay the mortgage. It was my father-in-law Bob McMillan who told me about a new market starting in West Street, at the back of the Queen's Hall. I made a few enquiries and was able to get a pitch. It was launched by a Scotsman called David Johnstone who had run markets in Scotland for years. He had looked at other towns but as Newtownards was a market town before the war he was sure it would work here.

Although I didn't start at the market on the first day, and had to borrow a few trestles from my father-in-law, I will have been there 40 years in 2016. Not knowing how much I would sell proved nerve-wracking; even though I'd been selling fruit and veg round the doors this was all

Born in John Street, Newtownards, in 1953, Clive O'Neill attended the Model Primary School and then the Tech in Victoria Avenue.

After leaving school, he worked in the Berkshire factory for three years where he met his wife-to-be, Roberta – "the best thing that ever happened to me".

Following a move to a factory in Bangor, which unfortunately subsequently closed, Clive's father-in-law encouraged him to start working for himself and after 40 years as a market trader here we are today.

Clive has two children, four grandchildren and in his own words "to crown it all my mum will be 90 this year – life is good!"

Harvest Fair day in September 1979. 244-20-6

very new to me. I was very much the new boy on the market because most of the other traders were old hands but they never said 'no' when you needed advice or a helping hand.

In addition to those trestles and some boards, I also had an old set of brass scales to weigh the potatoes. All my vegetables came from my father-in-law's farm and when he was low on supplies he knew where I could get more at the right price. My mother and father came down to help and they were as green as me, but help they did and the stall started making me a few extra pounds each weekend. If it rained we had no cover so I used to stand inside the back of my old van but I was younger then and the rain didn't seem too bad!

When my parents were going on holiday and I needed help my Aunt Hannah from Pound Street was always there, as was my mother-in-law. They were great as they were happy to work for free, which was always good to know. I was also able to call on my cousin Margaret, who ended up working for me for 17 years and never once let me down. I even remember the time she fell through a glass door on a Friday night and arrived the following day for work with her arm in a sling. They don't come any better than that!

The market stayed at West Street for about two years but things were beginning to happen in the town. The opening of the new Ards Shopping Centre, or Woolco as we called it, was having a big impact on trade. At the time the market was still being run from Scotland with two managers coming over every week to look after it. David Johnstone asked me to fly over to discuss plans to move the market to Conway Square. I knew from the past, when the market opened at West Street, that many shopkeepers were opposed to it, so this would clearly be a huge step for everyone in the town centre.

However, agreement was reached and the market moved to the Square, which was no longer open to cars because of the Troubles. I had a new stall made with a new cover, not to mention new weighing scales, and things were really looking up for me.

I'd previously worked in a factory in Bangor but it closed so I made the decision to go self-employed as a full-time market trader with additional stalls in Bangor and at Rathcoole in Belfast. I was also appointed market manager in Newtownards. Not bad for a cub who two years earlier didn't even have a stall!

The market itself was larger with an increased

Newtownards Market – something for everyone!

number of traders, which attracted more shoppers to the town centre. Local folk loved it, arriving from all parts of the Borough. Conway Square was a hive of activity and the town was fighting back. I can remember it as if it were just yesterday. James Mawhinney, who had a butcher's shop in the Square, placed a sign in big letters in his window announcing 'Newtownards Saturday Market Specials' and the customers were queued out onto the street. He knew very well if the market brought people into the town, he could attract customers into his shop.

Of course, not everyone was happy; I could certainly understand that from their point of view we were bringing market traders into the town centre on the busiest day of the week. All the same, after a few months things settled down and the town centre was alive again. There were over 70 stalls, with some traders operating on a single space and others more than that. I think the rent back then was £7.50 per stall and the traders arrived from all parts of Northern Ireland. I can put my hand on my heart and say all were friends. We never let the Troubles bother us.

Over the years a number of the older traders retired or unfortunately passed away. I can recall visiting traders arriving on a Saturday morning to start a new business or to try out Newtownards for the first time. Most of them stayed and are still here today.

Market trading has been my whole life. In truth I couldn't do anything else. I love my job even though it means you are up early in the morning and out in all weather. Some people ask me when I plan to retire and I just tell them I am too young. I don't see why I should as long as I have my health and I enjoy it. I'll gradually slow down although my wife says if I get any slower I will stop!

A lot of things have happened in Newtownards over the past 40 years. The town has grown and the shops have changed but it is still a great place to live and work in. I will always say I am very proud to live and work here and I'm also proud to be called a market trader. You can take the boy out of Ards but you can't take Ards out of the boy!

1978

Making the News in the Chronicle

The worldwide skateboard phenomenon reached Newtownards and district, with a New Year estimate of some 1,000 new skateboard owners in the area in search of places to practice their hobby. Ards Borough Council Recreations Manager Jim Ritchie acknowledged the local authority would need to give serious consideration to the provision of purpose-built skateboard parks in local towns and villages.

A gas explosion in East Street, Donaghadee, late at night on 4 January ripped open pipes the length of the road, shaking houses and in some instances rupturing flooring although, curiously enough, no windows were broken and thankfully no injuries were sustained. One house had its living room door frame buckled by the force of the blast, which many residents feared had been caused by a bomb. It was believed a build-up of gas in a road drain had been ignited.

A committee involving local schools, clubs, churches and youth organisations was formed in Comber in mid-January to formulate plans for a proposed festival week during the summer months. Determining the precise date was complicated by a number of established events, including similar festival weeks in Donaghadee and Newtownards, as well as the 1978 World Cup. Committee members included Brian Laughlin, Jim Middleton, Laurence Rowan and Jim Sandford, who eventually settled on 25 June – 1 July for the festival.

A formal planning application for stock car racing at Ballyskeagh Road, Newtownards, was refused by the Divisional Planning Office in late January. Applicant Andrew Cooke was told it would "give rise to conditions which would prejudice the amenities of neighbouring residential properties and would create a hazard along a narrow and dangerous section of the road, prejudicing the free flow of traffic and general safety."

Councillors were advised that operators of such ventures could still do so on 14 days a year without requiring planning permission. However, the planners later warned them that the concession would not apply if the races were held on a regular basis.

Newtownards man John McFetridge, better known as 'the lone walker,' walked overnight to Coleraine on 21 January to watch Ards play Coleraine in an Irish League fixture. Although the match result was disappointing, with Ards losing 2-0, John was able to raise £15 for handicapped children along the way.

'Lone Walker' John McFetridge presents a cheque for £40 on behalf of the Ards Summer League to John Stewart of Manor FC who had been injured in a recent match. The presentation took place in late July 1978 and also included are: J. McCready, D. Hagen and R. Poole, all from Manor FC. 190-6-3

Former Prime Minister Terence O'Neill, by then Lord O'Neill of the Maine, made his first speech locally since leaving office nine years earlier, when he addressed the annual meeting of the Unionist Party of Northern Ireland (UPNI) in Newtownards Town Hall on 27 January. He described the fall of the power-sharing Executive in 1974 as a great tragedy, adding that "in years to come Ulster people will look back on it as a great chance missed."

Although none of the 12 victims who died in the IRA's firebomb attack on La Mon House on Friday 17 February resided in the Ards area, the impact of the atrocity on the Borough was just as devastating.

Most of the dead would have been known to local people through their membership of the Collie Dog Club and the Northern Ireland Junior Motorcycle Club, the two organisations with members numbering some 500, who had been enjoying annual presentation events in the popular Gransha nightspot. In addition, some of those injured were from the Borough, including Newtownards businessman Trevor Bennett (30) and his wife Lynn (27), who both sustained serious burns.

In a particularly moving main story, the Newtownards Chronicle stated:

"It was to be a night of enjoyment, a night of pleasure, a night of friendship and a night of success for people both young and old who were congregated at La Mon…

"But there was no pleasure and no happy memories. In their place was massacre and the murder with a capital M of 12 innocent people, not to mention the 23 injured, 11 of whom were detained in hospital as a result of the bomb explosion. For those who were there to see this holocaust it was sickening, sickening to see pieces of a human body, limbs and other parts, being lifted.

"Many of them were just pure red flesh so indistinguishable that even the best brains in the world of forensic science found difficulty in sifting out their identification. It was only by getting down to some of the most minute details – teeth, hair, steel items belonging to the victims – that it was possible to arrive at identification.

"Children were left without parents, mothers without daughters, fathers without sons, husbands without wives, wives without husbands, and friends without friends in the most horrific scene witnessed for a long time.

"Words are just not in the English language to do justice to the scene or to condemn it adequately: horrifying, dastardly, massacre and murderous, are just not strong enough."

As a mark of respect many businesses in Newtownards and around the Peninsula closed their doors the following Wednesday, with an impromptu service taking place at St Mark's Parish Church at the suggestion of a number of distressed factory workers. It was conducted by the rector, the Rev. R. J. Chisholm, along with the Revs. J. McCrory (Methodist Church) and C. H. McKeown (Presbyterian Church).

In addition, Ards Borough Council donated £1,000 to the La Mon Disaster Fund established by Castlereagh Borough Council, while Andrews Memorial Primary School in Comber was one of the first to respond to the appeal by collecting £200.

Four workmen who found 14 old coins dating back to the 14th Century while digging a trench at High Street in Newtownards received their due reward following a treasure trove inquest at Newtownards Coroner's Court on 23 February. The coins, consisting of seven Scottish groats, six English groats and an English penny, were valued at around £400 and it was agreed the men would share this sum, namely Ronald Edmonds, Hickory Avenue, Newtownards, Samuel Gilmore, Pamela Way, Comber, John Anderson, Old Shore Road, Newtownards, and Michael Stenning, Ballyminetra Gardens, Bangor.

Star Wars was screened for the first time in the North Down area when it opened at the Comber Cinema on Monday 20 March. The Newtownards Chronicle described it as "a romantic science fiction adventure story in the traditional movie-world mould of good guys vs. bad guys in their somewhat updated though nonetheless recognisable guises."

At an international event in London in early March Comber man Roy Spence – a teacher in Newtownards – was nominated for the third year running as one of the 10 best amateur film-makers in the world.

Ards Borough Council voiced opposition in early April to plans by the South Eastern Education and Library Board to close Dunover Primary School at Ballywalter, with the pupils transferring to other local schools.

A new Junior Chamber of Commerce was launched in Newtownards on 13 April following a meeting in the Wiltshire Inn. The president was Dennis Harrison, vice-president was Leslie Hughes, treasurer was Brian Maxwell and secretary was Mr D. Crozier.

A new church building for Newtownards Congregational Church was opened and dedicated at Victoria Avenue, in the town, by the Rev. William Smylie, chairman of the Congregational Union of Ireland, on 15 April.

Members and friends of Portavogie Presbyterian Church Choir had a frightening experience during a trip to London when their hotel, the Shaftesbury, caught fire as they were enjoying a meal there. The premises were promptly evacuated as the blaze was being dealt with. The party, none the worse for their scare, carried on with their trip, which also included Amsterdam and Brussels.

A resolution calling for the restoration of capital punishment was defeated by a single vote, eight to seven, at a meeting of Ards Borough Council on 22 May. Forwarded to Ards by colleagues on Coleraine Borough Council, where it had been passed, the resolution sought the return of hanging "in view of the deplorable high level of death and destruction in our Province."

European Commissioner Richard Burke, during a visit to Northern Ireland on 7 June, announced that an EEC grant of £1.2m would be provided towards the modernisation of Portavogie Harbour. The work would proceed in four phases and would involve the relocation of industries and services, the excavation of a new harbour basin, the construction of a new access road and the development of a new fish market.

Mrs Elizabeth Quinn (née Gilmore, of Glastry) returned to her native land in early July after spending more than 50 years in California, USA. Predeceased by husband Patrick (of Ardkeen), she was accompanied by one of her sons, Bill, who was paying his first visit to Northern Ireland.

Comber man Sammy Curry, of Darragh Road, marked his 80th birthday in late July by walking the 15 miles from Comber to his son Willie's home in Ballywalter. He left his home at 10.30am and reached his destination by mid-afternoon, where he was the guest of honour at a special birthday party.

Ards Borough Council supported plans, revealed in early September, to transfer Movilla High School to a new site at Ballyharry.

Portaferry and district GP Dr T. F. Duff retired in September, bringing to an end a career that had given the community some 42 years of dedicated service. In recognition of that service, Dr Duff and his wife were honoured guests at a farewell presentation function in St Columba's High School.

A proposal to sell cars in the Ards Shopping Centre car park and the recent opening of a new garden centre at the same location evoked the wrath of local Councillors in September because the two businesses were operating on Sundays. A petition was launched by the town's First Presbyterian Church, while objections were raised by other car dealers in Newtownards and by local residents. In addition, the Free Presbyterian Church staged a protest meeting at the shopping centre on the first Sunday morning after the news was announced.

Comber man David Kinnier, of Dermott Walk, was voted Ulster's Personality Milkman of the Year in October, receiving a prize of £250. The Co-op employee, who was married with two children, had a delivery route that included Carrickfergus. He was nominated by one of his customers from that town.

Despite the temporary removal from service of the Portavogie/ Cloughey lifeboat in late October, during construction work at Portavogie Harbour, the Royal National Lifeboat Institution insisted that no decision had been taken to close the station permanently. The RNLI indicated "the requirement to re-establish a lifeboat will be reviewed when the Institution is advised of the likely date when the Harbour is due to be reopened."

A nine-year-old boy from West Winds in Newtownards was admitted to hospital with a fractured skull after falling from the luggage compartment of a moving Ulsterbus within the estate on 6 November. According to the police a number of young people were dicing with death by forcing open the locked boots of buses with a screwdriver, climbing in and then making a journey free of charge. The "dangerous practice" was particularly prevalent in the West Winds Estate.

A £1m scheme to provide 60 new homes in Donaghadee, announced in late November, was the first outside Belfast to involve a partnership between the Northern Ireland Housing Executive, Equity Sharing and the Masonic Housing Association, with each organisation being responsible for 20 houses. The site in question was at Killaughey Road and was already owned by the Housing Executive. In the case of the Masonic Housing Association the homes were specifically for elderly people. Work was expected to start in late 1979 and would include landscaping of part of the old Comber-Donaghadee railway line as a scenic route.

Heather McDonald, from Hillcrest Avenue in Newtownards, received a bouquet of flowers and a special certificate in late November from the South Eastern Education and Library Board in recognition of her 11 years of unbroken attendance at Victoria Primary School and Regent House. Her sister Norma achieved 10 years' unbroken attendance and brother Trevor 'just' eight.

Newtownards man Samuel Moore, of Saratoga Avenue, who ran a pharmacy business at Main Street, Ballywalter, was elected president of the Northern Ireland Pharmaceutical Society in December. He was a former pupil of Kirkistown Primary School and Regent House.

Ards Borough Council announced plans in early December for a visitor centre in conjunction with the public park at Castle Grounds in Portaferry. The scheme, it was intimated, would include an aquarium, a cinema showing films on matters of interest relating to Strangford Lough and a tourist information centre.

With major roadworks by then almost completed, the new dual carriageway between Newtownards and Dundonald was already open to the public in the final days of 1978. It was viewed as the greatest transport change seen in the district since the opening of the new road between Newtownards and Bangor in the 1960s.

Mrs and Mrs James Magee, of Carrickmannon Road, Ballygowan, reported seeing an unidentified flying object while attending to a frozen water trough in one of their fields at 7pm on 31 December. Travelling towards Killyleagh from the Newtownards direction, it appeared to have a bullet-shaped nose, was very big and bright and had a long trail of white vapour. No sound was heard and the UFO was travelling quite quickly.

Millisle Young Farmers' Club members who took part in a Young Farmers' Clubs of Ulster debating competition at Regent House, Newtownards, in January 1978. 62-11-51

Scrabo High School's pantomime in January 1978 was The Babes in the Wood. Principal cast members included (standing) Sharon Caughers and Sharon O'Neill, along with (seated from left): Gary Johnston, Grace McCoubrey, Mark Lilburn and Walter Doak. 45-10-1

The antlers of a long-extinct Giant Irish Deer – thought to have been between 8,000 and 10,000 years old – were unearthed near Newtownards by John McCann and Robert Presho in January 1978. 8-17-1

The official opening of the Enler Youth Club premises in Comber was performed in February 1978 by management committee chairman Jim Palmer due to the unavoidable absence of Minister of State Lord Melchett who had a bad dose of flu. Picture shows (from left): Sir John Andrews, club president, Jim Palmer, the Rev. Mervyn Kingston, a key figure in the formation of the club, and youth leader Jim Sandford. 68-10a-1

Children from Carrowdore Primary School who took part in a sponsored silence presented cheques for £50 each to Dr Barnardo's Homes and the Northern Ireland Council on Disability in February 1978. The children's fundraising endeavours were boosted by collections in local churches. From left: teacher-in-charge Mrs J. Hunter, Gillian Cox, Susan Kennedy, Rhonda Hewitt and Joan Armstrong. 76-4a-1

Jean Douglas, officer in charge of Ballygowan Girls' Brigade, shows her obvious delight in March 1978 after the Brigaders won the Strangford and Mourne District and Northern Ireland PE competitions. They also gained fourth place in the All Ireland finals in Dublin. Team members were Linda Miskelly, Margaret Wylie, Heather Hunter, Marina Gibson, Hilary McMurray, Elsie Spratt, Diane Scott and Pamela McBride. 148-18-1

Members of Carrowdore and District Jumping and Agricultural Society who attended a reception at the home of Lord and Lady Dunleath in March 1978. 193-4-1

A bottle, thrown into the sea at Portrush the previous year by three Newtownards girls, made it all the way to a beach at Dubbs Point, just outside New York, where it was discovered by a local man. The trio, sisters Liz (16) and Margaret Gourley (18) and friend Gail Mayne (16), were amazed to learn their bottle had travelled some 3,000 miles. 202-10-1

Nine-year-old Gerald McGrattan, from John Thompson Park, Portaferry, won the award for the most promising boy dancer aged under 11 at Bangor's Open Festival in May 1978. 67-7-2

Duke of Edinburgh Award winners from Conlig Girls' Brigade with their parents in April 1978. From left: Mrs Grigg, captain, Mrs Lawrence with daughter Dianne, Mrs Conway with daughter Patricia, Mrs Murphy with daughter Deborah, Mr Lawrence with daughter Caroline, and Mr and Mrs Kearney with daughter Maree. 257-12-1

The newly-formed Greyabbey Junior LOL No. 253 led members of North Down District Junior LOL No 2 to their divine service in Trinity Presbyterian Church in May 1978. During the service a new Union Jack standard, collarettes and cuffs were dedicated. 4-16-2

Mr and Mrs S. J. Leckey, of Quarry Close, Comber, celebrated their golden wedding anniversary in June 1978. They are pictured with seven of their four sons and four daughters – Samuel, George, John, Hugh, Sadie, Marie, Mary and Marty. 181-18-2

Pupils from St Finian's Primary School in Newtownards won the under-12 category of the annual Columba Cup Race in June 1978. From left: Elizabeth McCloskey, Anne Ayre and Harry McCall. 195-11-2

Northern Ireland's lorry driver of the year for 1978 was Des Somerville, from Whinpark Road, Glen Estate, Newtownards. He beat 60 other drivers that June at Nutts Corner, headquarters of the Road Transport Industry Training Board. 7-10a-3

Comber High School principal Harold Cameron retired from the position in June 1978. He is shaking hands with Elsie Spratt of form 5G after being presented with a set of golf clubs, complete with trolley. Mrs Cameron was presented with a bouquet of flowers by Judith Frazer of form 2F. Included are staff members and officials, among them South Eastern Education and Library Board chief executive Michael Gledhill. 32-11-3

Members of Carrowdore Youth Club who took an active role in cleaning up their area through a Summer Opportunities Scheme in August 1978. 332-16-3

Mrs Groves from the Save the Children Fund visited Kirkistown Primary School in November 1978 to receive a cheque for £100, scrap woollen items and used postage stamps from the pupils. Cathy Bailie is handing over the stamps. Included are principal Mrs Lyttle and other teachers. 548-4a-3

Pictured at the ordination of the Rev. Jim Hartin at Portavogie Free Presbyterian Church in November 1978, are (from left): the Rev. Ian McVeigh, who chaired the service, the Rev. Alan Dunlop, the Rev. Jim Hartin, the Rev. Cecil Menary and the Rev. William Beattie. 80-6-4

Children from Ballyeasboro Church Sunday School planted poppy crosses in November 1978 on the graves of five RAF members who were stationed at Ballyhalbert and were killed during the Second World War. Included is the Rev. F. W. A. Bell. 10-18-4

Popular Newtownards man Billy Graham, accompanied by his wife May, is pictured with members of one of the many ladies' keep-fit classes he ran in the town during the 1970s and beyond.

Violet Brown (right), from Ballywalter Presbyterian Church, received a Sunday School Special Award from the Sabbath School Society for Ireland in December 1978 for eight years of unbroken attendance at Sunday School. Making the presentation on behalf of the Sabbath School Society is Mrs McIlveen, with the Rev. S. J. McIlveen, minister of the church, looking on. 102-12-4

Children from the Ards Nursery School who enjoyed their Christmas party in December 1978. 192-14-4

1978

Sport in the Chronicle

Danny Ferris, a 13-year-old member of Ards Amateur Swimming Club, won gold in the front crawl at the Ulster Branch Minor Schools Championships at Ballymena on 14 January. He was runner-up in the backstroke. Three of the club's young members, Lucia Doherty, David Scott and Michael Davidson, were narrowly beaten in their events.

Billy Humphries agreed to give up his position as player-manager of Ards FC, instead taking on the full-time role of secretary-manager of Ards FC and Ards Football Sports and Social Club with effect from 1 April. It was seen as an indication by the directors that the task of running the business side of the club was beyond someone undertaking the duties in an honorary capacity.

Regent House, despite the disappointment of a Schools Cup exit at the hands of local rivals Bangor Grammar School, won the Ulster Schools Sevens title on 15 March, defeating Coleraine Inst. 20-0 in the final. They went on to win the Rosslyn Park National Schools title in London, gaining the unofficial title of British Schools champions.

The Regent House Sevens squad Back (from left): Brian Iveston, Rodney Jess, David Duke, Tim Johnston, Lee Mackie. Front: David Baird, Alastair Moles (captain), Gary Scott and Phillip Matthews.

Gillian Murphy from Regent House became the first girl from her school to be selected for the Irish Schools hockey team (having previously represented Ulster), playing in early April in a British Isles tournament. She completed a sporting double, also representing Ulster and Ireland in table tennis.

Described as "the greatest day of the greatest year in the history of Ards Rugby Club", the 1st XV defeated old rivals Ballymena IIs in a play-off for the Section 2 title and thus earned promotion to Section 1 (the old Senior League). For the first time ever there was the prospect of the top players in Ulster rugby in League action at Hamilton Park, all the more important as it was the club's 50th anniversary year. The 2nd XV also won their league and gained promotion.

Having already won their league title, Ards Vs brought a very successful 1977-78 season to a close by defeating Lurgan 25-0 and securing the Ravenhill Cup for the first time in the club's history. Scorers included Trevor Breen, Raymond McCabe, Ken McKinnan, Bobby Bishop and Martin Davidson. The team's captain was Derrick Nash.

North Down 3rd XI beat their Annadale counterparts 2-1 on 18 May to bring hockey's Ulster Junior Shield back to Comber for the first time in 57 years. Dennis Artt and Alan Cave scored the goals while 'keeper Derek Wishart saved his third penalty in the competition to secure the victory. Team captain was Robert Johnston.

Ards Cycling Club members Lennie Kirk and Archie Cunningham were part of the six-strong cycling team selected to represent Northern Ireland at the forthcoming Commonwealth Games in Canada.

Ards FC entertained visiting North American side the Tulsa Roughnecks, which listed several well known former stars in its ranks, including captain Colin Waldron (ex-Burnley and Manchester United) and goalkeeper Colin Boulton (ex-Derby County). The head coach was Bill Foulkes, a former Busby Babe and a member of Manchester United's 1968 European Cup-winning team. The match, played on 12 September, finished in a 1-1 draw, with Billy Kennedy scoring for the home side. Neither of the named former stars featured in the game.

Former Regent House player Nigel Carr was selected to play for Ulster against Yorkshire at Ravenhill on 7 October. He thus became the first Ards player to represent his province at senior level. Other local players, notably Blair Mayne, went on to represent Ulster, but not while playing for Ards at the time.

Donaghadee Golf Club won the inaugural Irish Club Mixed Foursomes competition, defeating Ennis 4-1 at Royal Portrush. The final was held in early October and sponsored by P. J. Carroll and Co. Team members were Jack Stout (captain) and Mrs Joan Beatty, along with G. Bunting and Mrs E. McKibbin, V. Stephens and Mrs E. Collette, J. Nelson and Miss J. Campbell, P. Cummings and Mrs M. Devlin.

Former Bangor and Cardiff City goalkeeper Billy Irwin, just married and home on a break from America where he played for the Washington Diplomats, signed for Ards for six weeks in early December. He made his debut for the club in a 2-1 victory over Linfield at Windsor Park. This was followed by a 3-0 win over Portadown and a place at the top of the Irish League.

Stars Dennis Taylor (left) and Graham Miles took part in an exhibition match at the Queen's Hall Billiards Club in January 1978, with the Englishman defeating his Ulster counterpart by five games to four. 69-15a-51

The final of the West Winds Youth Club under-13 five-a-side football tournament was held in the Ards Arena in January 1978. Special guest Warren Feeney of Glentoran presented the medals to the winners and runners-up (West Winds Youth Club and Holywood Star respectively). 52-8-51

Members of Ballywalter Indoor Bowling Club were beaten finalists in the North Down Rinks competition in March 1978. From left: William Warnock, James Warnock, William Angus and David Cavan. 94-12-1

By March 1978 the Castle Gardens Bar Darts A team had remained unbeaten in the Newtownards Vintners League for two years, securing the League Cup, the McKinley and McGinley Cup and other trophies along the way. 98-14-1

Pupils of Ballywalter and Portavogie Primary Schools who played a friendly badminton match at Ballywalter Parochial Hall in May 1978. Back (from left): Mark Wilcock (captain), Tommy Cromie, Allison Blair, Nicola Bennett, Alan Brown, Iain Patton, all Ballywalter PS. Front: Janet Kelly, Ruth Ennis, Leona Adair, Margaret Moore (captain), Shirley Kelnan and Edwina Mawhinney, all Portavogie PS. 298-13a-1

Members of the Strean Presbyterian Church badminton club who recorded a number of successes in May 1978. The 'A' team won the Hume Cup and were runners-up in the North Down Shield, while the 'B' team were runners-up in Division 9. 67-9-2

Ards Mayor Alderman John Scott presents Nario Cafolla with the trophy for winning the Northern Ireland Pool Championship at the Strangford Arms Hotel in June 1978. 150-14-2

Members of the Regent House Minor Girls athletics team who won the Ulster Schools Cup in June 1978. From left: Helen Cathcart (long jump and 100m finals), Debbie Orr (100m winner in 13.5 secs), Adele Bailie (fourth in the 800m in 2 mins 35.35 secs), and Heather Preston. All the girls won the 4 x 100m relay race in an Ulster Schools record time of 54.6 secs. 195-13-2

Ballywalter Primary School won a mini rugby tournament organised for local schools by Donaghadee Rugby Club at the end of June 1978. Recipients of the Donaldson Cup were (back, from left): Victor Boyd, Barry Atkinson, Mark Wilcock, David McCullough. Front: Norman Carlisle, Alex Johnston, Tommy Cromie (captain), Iain Patton and Victor Chrimes. 282-3a-2

Twelve-year-old William Burgess, from Comber, on his Yamaha 100cc motorcycle after winning the intermediate class of the British Schoolboy Championships in England. William finished first out of 81 riders in August 1978. 250-7-3

Junior competitors who won Captain's Day prizes at Kirkistown Golf Club in August 1978. Included are other contestants and prizewinners. 300-4a-3

Noel Johnston

remembers ... Donaghadee Sailing Club

The 1970s proved a significant decade for sailing in the 'Dee. For a few years after the demise of the former Yacht Club – based on Dorman's Isle – little happened other than a few characters careering about in an old ship's lifeboat trying to reach the harbour mouth while going nowhere sideways.

Some improvement was occasioned when *Imp*, a 16-footer, was recovered from Groomsport and restored. With a Flying Fifteen mast and sails she went like smoke in any sort of a breeze.

Not to be outdone by our near neighbours, this group also decided that Donaghadee should again have its own club for sailing and so on 2 December 1970 some 17 people crammed into the front room of 25 The Parade and voted unanimously to form a club to be known as Donaghadee Sailing Club.

This title was considered to be suitably egalitarian in the emerging age of the plywood dinghy. Also it echoed Donaghadee's little-known sailing history as the previous club of the same name existed from the latter part of the 19th Century until well into the 20th and had just two honorary secretaries!

A modest little article in the next Newtownards Spectator reported that a caretaker committee had been formed. It was said the Club would be able to start sailing the follow-

A Donaghadee man all his life, Noel has always had a passion for all things nautical.

After leaving school he took over his father's hardware shop in Moat Street in the town, which he ran until 1972 when he made a career change and joined the N. I. Civil Service where he worked until retirement.

He was bought his first boat, a two-seater skiff named *Swallow*, at age 12 and has maintained a small fleet ever since but it was his experience on Aubrey Quiery's Glen class yacht the *Glenreagh* which got him firmly hooked on sailing.

For the last forty years Noel has played a central role in all aspects of Donaghadee Sailing Club and in that time has held every Honorary position in the club.

Mirror dinghies at the slipway 244-64-2

ing year with at least five Mirror dinghies – the wee ones with the red sails – with potentially a further four under construction. Following ratification of the Club's formation at a public meeting on 20 January 1971, all effort was focused on finding a clubhouse.

Meetings and gatherings often happened courtesy of Andy Baldie at the Old Griddle Bakery, but more often than not the members gravitated to the Ensign Bar, which had been acquired by famous Northern Ireland footballer Sam McCrory. "Are ye for Sam's?" was an oft-heard refrain. Indeed most of the serious planning and organising took place there but early of an evening and a good attendance was always a certainty!

But others too were working assiduously in the search for a more permanent home and at a meeting in May 1971 chairman Kenneth Apps confirmed he had secured the tenancy of Hills Hall in Bridge Street – latterly the Wells tyre store – as a temporary home. But this was to be short-lived as his ongoing negotiations secured the tenancy, at the beginning of 1972, of the two-storey property at 20 Shore Street and the adjacent derelict cottages. Further good news was the local Council's agreement to permit the use of the former Baths Hotel site as a dinghy park.

Club funds were boosted by the £22 proceeds from a coffee morning. I will leave it to others to calculate the present day value but I know every penny counted in those formative years. A sailing programme was devised and the first race was held on Sunday 16 May. DSC was a trailblazer in that it was the first sailing club, certainly in this part of Ireland, to race on Sundays.

Racing continued during the summer with two classes (Mirrors and everything else under handicap). Numbers of starters increased as the season progressed and tea after racing became a tradition – at least for a while. There was also the first appearance of 'Snips' under the pseudonym of 'Emm Tee', beginning a club tradition of the irreverent teasing of members.

The Club's steady expansion continued throughout the year with new members with dinghies from near and far participating. Courses were enlarged under the management of Race Officer Jimmy Muirhead and competition remained hottest in the Mirror Class. No one was spared the caustic and cryptic comments of Jaunty Angle, author of the weekly sailing notes.

It was reported that three DSC boats had entered the Royal Ulster Yacht Club's annual regatta in Bangor, managing to finish well up the fleet. At that early stage race protests were few and far between because not many were familiar with the Racing Rules. That didn't last!

Competitors preparing for the start of the Club Regatta 35/12-8

Then crews travelled to East Antrim Boat Club in Larne to race in the Northern Ireland Mirror Class Championships, with all five finishing between third and tenth. It was another impressive performance by our rookie sailors in their first competitive season. Festival Week prizes were awarded during a buffet dance in the Croagh Patrick Hotel.

Under the headline 'All work and no sail' in the Breezes, it was reported that 'a mini army of members' had attempted to clear stones from around the slipway. An urgent request was made to the local Council to pump out stagnant water from the former swimming pond at the Baths Hotel. Grateful thanks was subsequently extended to Willie Harper and his crew from the local Fire Station who removed the water and the Council was approached to fill the pool with hardcore.

Later in the first season DSC combined with the Belfast School of Lifesaving for a life-saving demonstration. A highly realistic capsize in the harbour drew a large crowd of onlookers who initially believed it was for real!

The Club took part in the Irish National Mirror Championships at Dunmore East while, at home, class racing continued throughout the summer with boat numbers steadily increasing until the end of activities in September.

The first annual dinner dance and prize distribution was held in December in the Imperial Hotel, with over 100 members and guests attending. Mr James McVeigh presented the McVeigh Cup for the Mirror Class and distributed prizes to class winners as follows: Scorpions – 1, Brian Bowles; 2, Sammy Ferguson. Handicap – 1, David Thompson; 2, Ian Baldie; 3, Richard Tomalin. Mirrors – 1, John Turtle; 2, Wallace McVeigh; 3, Jennifer Baxter. Along with his first prize John Turtle also received the Berkshire Cup, held in trust by Aubrey Quiery following the demise of the former Yacht Club.

It is strange looking back now to remember our large functions were held in either the Imperial or Dunallen Hotels, both now long gone.

Presentation of the Club's first rescue boat in spring 1971. From left: J Muirhead and colleague (Northern Bank), K Apps, (DSC chairman), J B Handyside (Guinness), N Johnston, W McVeigh and M Taylor

The next year (1972) dawned with early good news that we had acquired our first purpose-built rescue boat – an Avon Searider RIB, co-funded by Guinness and the Northern Bank, which was presented in May. The list of 'firsts' continued with a picnic race to the Big Isle, while the tradition was established of "a loaf of sandwiches and a dozen buns" from each family for the first summer regatta in the 'Dee for well over a decade. It was a limited class event on 11 August and perhaps no surprise that three of the five classes were won by local sailors!

A record 21 boats crossed the start line during July and later that month across in Bangor Bay, 19 Club boats raced under the burgee of the Royal Ulster Yacht Club. This arose from a generous invitation to our fledging Club from the Flag Officers and members of RUYC. After racing, welcome tea and hot food was served up by the good ladies of Royal Ulster. Mind you, I don't know what the members there made of the rag, tag and bobtail outfit that turned up on their doorstep. Lifejackets yes but most of us had only heard about wet suits!

Our silverware collection expanded further with the presentation of the Motor Boat Cup by Mr and Mrs J. Donnan – again this was a survivor from the town's sailing history. Subsequently, the Coronation Cup – presented to DYC by Sir Walter Smiles MP – was handed over to the Club by custodian Bill Oliver.

All the while improvements were being made to our 'new' clubhouse, which quickly became our cherished home. Although water from the single bath with shower leaked through the kitchen ceiling, members put up with many privations in those early years as ac-

Mr K Apps, chairman of the club, was presented with the McVeigh Cup (to be awarded to the winner of the Mirror 14 class) by Mr J McVeigh at the first Annual Dinner. From left: Mr N. Johnston (treasurer), Mrs J. McVeigh, Mr K Apps, Mr J McVeigh, Mrs K Apps and Mr M Taylor (secretary)

tivity on the water and socially too steadily increased. The old building creaked and bulged during the frequent fundraisers and assorted other events. Fancy dress parties were in vogue but no one needed to visit Elliott's for a costume. Much-needed income for the development fund was the result.

At year's end, as Hon. Secretary, I was able to report the purchase of the Club's first training boat – a Mirror dinghy – to encourage sailing by the younger members and was able to quote from the RYA Chief Coach's comments on the junior advanced training course as follows: "The instructors feel many excellent helmsmen can come from this Club, given the proper drive from officials." And the old chestnut of ownership and improvements to the harbour got the annual airing when I opined the hope that I would live long enough to see this long overdue work carried out even if age and infirmity prevent me from participating afloat.

The purchase of an Avon Searider rescue boat was the welcome news that reflected the need for more safety for the increasing fleet of boats. Lectures on the Racing Rules were organised – not before time some would say – and improvements to the comfort and amenity of the Clubhouse were implemented.

Some of the less energetic sailors were looking for an alternative to hiking out and so the Flying Fifteen keelboat class emerged. It grew to nine moored in the harbour, thus adding a further dimension on the water and becoming a mainstay of racing for many years. Miracle and Marauder Classes represented the latest in dinghy development. Romance was in the air too with a raft of knot tying amongst the membership.

Cannons announcing the start of the regatta: Back from left: W McNeice, J Hamilton, F Quiery, R Simms and F Humphries. Front: Mark McPeake and Gordon Miskimmin

Cannon fire was heard again over the town as one annual regatta followed another, echoing the sounds of yesteryear and prompting successful negotiations for the return to the town of the cannons used previously by the Yacht Club. A couple of championship events were staged for the Marauder and GP 14 Classes with great success, while behind-the-scenes efforts continued to secure the Club's survival.

Now and again there were spells of optimism but mostly it was gloom and doom with many disheartening reverses during the decade. However, headlines such as 'Club's existence under threat' served only to stiffen the resolve of successive committees to pursue the dream. From a position where the Council felt unable to grant a lease for the Baths Hotel and the threat of being outbid for the site by commercial interests to planning refusal for a new-build clubhouse, the tide eventually turned in our favour.

The site was purchased outright and after a review of the situation the Club management opted for a renovation of the existing building and, as they say, the rest is history.

Glen McGivern

remembers ... Stock Car Racing

I met and married my wife Rosaline 48 years ago, back in 1967, and we went on to live in a worker's cottage on the Mountstewart Road, Carrowdore.

Reading the Belfast Telegraph one night I saw an advert from a stock car promotions company in England, asking if anyone was interested in helping to start up the sport here and indicating they were looking for a track.

I replied that I was interested and, in due course, Joe Black of Barracuda Promotions contacted me to say he wanted to meet me. Lo and behold the wheels were then set in motion.

Joe and his manager Dave arrived and, looking for somewhere to stay, I said they could move in with us until they found a permanent base. My wife was not best amused as they stayed with us for six months!

Joe and I travelled to several venues but none proved suitable. Eventually we met with the directors of Bangor Football Club who were persuaded by Joe's offer and in due course Clandeboye Park became the recognised home of local stock car racing.

Spring 1968 witnessed the first

Glen McGivern has lived at Cardy Road, Carrowdore, all his life. After finishing his education at Newtownards Tech, he started working for Russell Bros. as an estate agent, moving to Osborne King and Megran before converting his hobby of commentating at stock car racing into a full-time job.

Following the birth of his son, Craig, he expanded a part-time business he had set up into the well known Cardy Timber Yard.

However, his interest in speed did not wane and he took up powerboat racing, becoming NI offshore powerboat champion in the early Eighties.

Now retired from active participation, Glen still takes a keen interest in all forms of motorsport, particularly motorbike racing.

Stock Car Racing

Saturday 7.30 p.m.

Ballyskeagh Raceway
Newtownards

SALOONS   HOT RODS   FIGURE 8

Large field of stock cars at Clandeboye Park

meeting, after we'd erected safety fencing that comprised steel girders and wire rope to prevent the cars leaving the football pitch, along with the addition of a tarmac track.

Drivers had been sought through advertising and local companies were asked to sponsor them. Firths' Meat Wagon, the Six Road Ends Service Station, Marshall's Cycles and Flood's Garage were all among some of the businesses that responded to the appeal.

Large crowds attended and 50 cars became a common sight every Saturday. I took on the role of commentator and disc jockey, playing Swinging Safari – our theme tune – during the weekly parade lap, plus golden oldies during the breaks.

One particular meeting had the crowds cheering to the heavens as a car left the track and demolished the goal posts. Within six days they had been fixed for the next match.

Car No.	DRIVER	TOWN	Roof Colour
1	JIM MINNIS	Tandragee	Red
4	DEREK SANDERSON	Lisburn	White
6	DAVID IRWIN	Newtownards	White
7	MICHAEL CARR	Banbridge	Blue
15	ROBERT ACKERMAN	Bangor	White
19	ELLISON STRAIN	Donaghadee	White
20	MERVYN McCOMB	Ballyclare	White
21	ERIC McKINSTRY	Crumlin	Red
24	RICHARD LONG	Belfast	Yellow
25	JOHN GOWDY	Newtownards	White
26	GEORGE QUINN	Bangor	White
30	JIM CARSON	Newtownards	White
34	HUGH ANDREWS	Bangor	White
39	JOE BRADSHAW	Comber	White
41	DAVID MUCKLE	Carrowdore	White
42	WALTER THOMPSON	Bangor	White
45	ADRAIN LIGHTBODY	Bangor	Blue
51	ALEX. GRAY	Millisle	Yellow
62	TERRY FERGUSON	Bangor	White
64	DAVID HANLON	Banbridge	White
68	TOM ADAMS	Millisle	Red
70	BRIAN TAYLOR	Groomsport	Yellow
76	ROBERT GYLE	Holywood	White
77	ERIC SCOTT	Bangor	Yellow
79	JOHN DUNCAN	Comber	White
80	RICHARD BROWN	Bangor	White
82	CROSBY WEIR	Bangor	White
86	LIAM McGRATTAN	Groomsport	White
90	JOHN BLACK	Newtownards	White
93	ALAN FRENCH	Groomsport	White
94	ERIC FERGUSON	Newtownards	Blue
101	DAVID SPIERS	Newtownards	Blue
102	JIM NESBITT	Lisburn	White
105	ALBERT McCUCKIN	Nutt's Corner	Red
111	RICHARD GRIMSHAW	Glengormley	White
114	RONNIE FRANCIS	Bangor	Blue
115	IVAN McKINSTRY	Crumlin	Red
121	NELSON WAIDE	Donaghadee	White
123	JOHN ORCHARD	Bangor	Yellow
127	ALAN SUITOR	Holywood	White
134	RONNIE WALKER	Lisburn	White
135	WILL WALKER	Lisburn	White
137	FRED LONG	Belfast	White
150	GEORGE ADAMS	Millisle	Blue
007	JIM McCLOSKEY	Bangor	White
008	SAM McKIBBIN	Comber	White
032	SAMMY MELLON	Bangor	White
300	"HACKER" GRAHAM	Bangor	Red

DRIVERS ENGAGED FOR THIS MEETING

Around this time other promoters, seeing the popularity of the sport, decided to open their own tracks. Hence Dunmore Greyhound Stadium, Ballymena Raceway and Portadown Stadium, to name a few, were born and stock car racing really took off in a big way.

I moved with the times and became involved as commentator, disc jockey and start marshall, amongst other duties, at most of these venues, as well as the Newry Showgrounds, St. Angelo in Enniskillen, etc.

In the 1970s I was employed by an estate agency in Belfast and drove a firm's Jaguar. However, one night at Dunmore, upon leaving the commentary box, I somewhat foolishly entered the spectator race and by the following Monday I was unemployed. Yes, I'd had a run-in with Geordie Stows' red van; he won as I ended up in the safety fence in a big way.

The promoter was so impressed with (or sorry for) me that he asked me to go to the Isle of Man with him and my wife. I moved there and we found Onchan Stadium, which was how stock car racing was born on the island.

I very well remember going out every week and seeing how many Ford Populars I could buy and we then converted them into the popular 'stockies'.

We lived there for a year during which time my wife and I ran the Glen Helen Hotel. One job in particular was unheard of in those years – as well as being a commentator I was also the resident stunt driver at Onchan! My brother George also went to live there for 10 years and became Isle of Man champion in his favourite No. 13 car.

Returning home, Cooke Brothers of Newtownards approached me about starting up a track at

The figure 8 track at Ballyskeagh

Ballyskeagh. That's how the Ballyskeagh Figure 8 track became the local attraction for a new breed of racers with ordinary production cars, stock cars, spectator cars and even pram races. Yes, I have the photographs to prove it!

Large crowds attended the Saturday night meetings and with me doing the com-

DRIVERS ENGAGED FOR THIS MEETING			
1	CECIL PEARSON		Newtownards
10	W. ADAIR		Portavogie
11	T. G. FLEMING		Dundonald
12	HENRY LEMON		Carrowdore
14	JACKIIE McCORMICK		Newtownards
15	PRILIP O'HANLON		Holywood
16	JOE FUSCO		Holywood
17	ALLAN SUITOR		Holywood
18	JIM FERGUSON		Newtownards
19	ROBIN KERR		Carrowdore
20	JOHN BLACK		Newtownards
21	DREW COOKE		Newtownards
22	D. McCRACKEN		Dundonald
23	D. YEOM		Hillsborough
24	B. PEARSON		Ballyskeagh
25	JOHN GOUDY		Newtownards
28	W. STEVENSON		Newtownards
29	W. WILSON		Millisle
33	L. GRAHAM		Belfast
41	DAVID MUCKLE		Carrowdore
68	D. REID		Newtownards
77	ERIC SCOTT		Bangor
94	ERIC FERGUSON		Newtownards
100	DES JESS		Bangor
200	FLEET COOKE		Newtownards
201	ARTHUR LOCKHART		Newtownards
202	DREW COOKE		Newtownards
203	DAVID STRICKLAND		Comber
204	JOHN ANGUS		Kircubbin
205	ROBIN KERR		Carrowdore
206	DAVID LEDGERWOOD		Newtownards
207	FERGUS GRIFFITH		Bangor
208	JAMES LAWSON		Kircubbin
209	ALAN PEARSON		Newtownards
210	D. McGAFFIN		Aldergrove
211	REGGIE McCULLOUGH		Newtownards
212	STUART GILKISTON		Clandeboye
214	NORMAN PEARSON		Newtownards
215	ALAN GRAHAM		Clandeboye
216	ROBERT GORMAN		Newtownards
217	DAVID GREER		Bangor
218	CARSON LINDSAY		Helen's Bay
219	B. HARROL		Helen's Bay
220	W. STRICKLAND		Comber
221	IVAN BAILIE		Newtownards
224	W. McKEE		Bangor
226	S. DONNAN		Groomsport
227	L. BLACK		Bangor
228	R. KERR		Newtownards
229	M. McALORUM		Belfast
230	B. MILLIGAN		Newtownards
231	I. HOUSTON		Comber
232	R. ROBINSON		Belfast
233	L. GRAHAM		Belfast
234	B. KELLY		Comber
244	M. SEMPLE		Comber
245	R. SHAW		Portavogie
273	RONALD CRANGLE		Bangor
275	ROBERT CRANGLE		Bangor
276	J. BATES		Carrowdore
301	CECIL PEARSON		Newtownards
308	R. MACK		Comber
600	PAUL REA		Bangor
601	J. McMILLAN		Newtownards
000	KELVIN ROBERTSON		Donaghadee

mentary and my wife the lap scoring, it very quickly became the place to be, especially for the big race of the night, the Figure 8 final. I still believe they deliberately hit each other in the middle and did not try to avoid each other as they were supposed to do. That is what the crowds came to see and the drivers did not want to let them down!

Among the highlights at the big summer meeting was the appearance by the Dublin Hell Drivers from Santry Stadium and the large crowd was not disappointed. For our return match at Santry, our boys were not so lucky and it was more of a demolition derby than a race but that was the 1970s.

A dispute amongst drivers and the promoters led to a split in the ranks and although Ballyskeagh continued for a while, Carrowdore quarry was the next and final local track to once again promote stock car/ production car racing.

Lining up for a race at Carrowdore

With a 'figure 8' track on offer, the local population was once again treated to some fine Saturday night racing, with local roads and Carrowdore's Main Street packed to capacity.

Stock car racing has always been a family sport. Men, women and children came here as families and I still meet people who attended 40 years ago with their dads and mums, even their grandparents. The enjoyment they had reflects very favourably on this particular sporting event, which sadly no longer exists locally.

1979

Making the News in the Chronicle

The early days of the New Year witnessed particularly wintry conditions, with one of the heaviest snowfalls in years, coupled with ice-bound roads following a further hard frost. Ards Hospital reported the admission of 177 new patients during the period of severe weather, with 56 of that number having sustained fractures.

With petrol in short supply several filling stations imposed a £3 limit on motorists, while the Army was called in to help deliver a consignment of heating oil to the local hospital.

Ards Borough Council, which had decided some years earlier to convert Conway Square into a pedestrianised area, produced two models for consideration in late January. It was agreed to consult with the Roads Service and local traders to determine the future of the Square. Both models featured trees, shrubs and flowers prominently.

The Council agreed, on the proposal of Alderman Eddie Gaw and seconded by Alderman Jim McBriar, to promote a public meeting as the first step in a process to establish a Citizens' Advice Bureau in Newtownards.

Comber father-of-10 Jim Coey won £4,804.80 from a £1.60 four-dog accumulator at the end of January. He had intended to back four horses but the bad weather intervened and all races were cancelled. Instead, he opted for dogs – backing, in each case, the one running from trap five. It was the biggest pay-out ever by L. Stanley Ltd. in Comber and they hosted a champagne reception in Jim's honour.

Seven-year-old Maurice Cairns, son of Mr and Mrs M. W. Cairns of Brantwood Way, made his debut in the world of male modelling by appearing in an advertisement for camping equipment in the special walking, back-packing and camping magazine The Great Outdoors. He was a pupil at Victoria Primary School and a member of the Ulster Boys Rally Club in Newtownards.

Vandals targeted the stained-glass windows of St Patrick's Parish Church, Millisle, in mid-March, causing damage that ran into hundreds of pounds. The attack was described by the Newtownards Chronicle as "one of the lowest and most disgusting acts of wanton destruction for some time."

The Department of the Environment demolished Primitive Methodist Church in Portaferry at the end of March. Also used as a schoolhouse, it dated back to 1818. There had been considerable controversy over previous months about whether or not the building should be preserved and it was twice granted a stay of execution while consultation was under way. The building, behind Meetinghouse Lane, was on land vested by the Department for a new car park.

Portavogie widow Mrs Margaret Wallace got the surprise of her life in April when she received an official White House greetings card signed by US President Jimmy Carter and Mrs Rosalyn Carter, wishing her a happy birthday. She was a regular visitor to the USA and indeed had lived there for 48 years with her late husband James, who was buried in the States, but it was a complete mystery to her as to how the President had known about her birthday.

Police raided the notorious 'mushroom' shelter at Park Way, Comber, on 23 April and recovered a considerable quantity of alcohol. The RUC had received numerous complaints about young people using the shelter as an illegal drinking den. A number of youths were interviewed by officers; those questioned were said to have been "drinking and smoking."

A 17-year-old Newtownards youth, who was disorderly at a soccer match between Ards and Portadown at Castlereagh Park the previous February, was jailed for three months at the local court in early May. Police, who were trying to keep rival fans apart, were subjected to a torrent of abuse from the teenager, who also taunted Portadown supporters after Ards scored an equalising goal.

The defendant, who was already serving a six-month sentence for another offence of disorderly behaviour, was told by Magistrate Wishart Mills that "anyone who goes to a football match intent on spoiling the enjoyment of others can expect to be sent to prison."

There were angry scenes at Castle Street in Comber on 6 June when Department of the Environment workmen attempted to cut down an historic Irish Oak, said to be one of only two still existing in Northern Ireland, to make way for an entrance to the town's new car park. Local Councillor Hamilton McKeag, the newly-elected Mayor of the Borough, subsequently announced that an agreement had been reached to allow the tree to remain where it was. However, the tree had sustained considerable damage and there were fears it would still have to come down.

A new £25,000 hall for Scrabo Presbyterian Church was officially opened and dedicated as the Eagleson Hall on 2 June. The Moderator of the Presbyterian Church, the Rt. Rev. Dr David Burke, attended – it was his final engagement after serving his year-long term of office. The building was named after the Rev. G. McK. Eagleson, minister of both the Scrabo and Strean Presbyterian congregations.

There was a British Empire Medal for Kircubbin man Samuel Brown, of Rubane Road, in the Queen's Birthday Honours List in June. He had worked as a heavy goods vehicle driver for 42 years, being employed by the Northern Ireland Road Transport Board (later renamed Northern Ireland Carriers). Newtownards car park attendant Samuel Wylie, of Halifax Walk, was another BEM recipient.

The Northern Ireland Housing Executive ended considerable speculation at the beginning of July when it announced that Frederick Street, Newtownards, would be the location for its new South East Regional Office. The Executive had originally planned to open the office in Downpatrick, but it faced considerable pressure from Ards Borough Council and other neighbouring authorities. Newly-appointed regional controller Colin James was responsible for housing matters relating to the Ards, North Down, Down, Castlereagh and Lisburn Council areas.

Belfast Ropework Ltd. announced 200 redundancies over the next 13 weeks, commencing in July, at its factory in Ballygowan after ending the manufacture of rope and twine products, as well as carpet fibre, at the plant. The company was a subsidiary of the McCleery L'Amie Group, which said it had sustained heavy losses over recent years despite investing in new equipment and machinery.

Ards Borough Council announced in late July the closure of Tullynakill graveyard outside Comber and Whitechurch graveyard near Ballywalter as both were virtually full. Those with plots that were not as yet filled were advised they could still seek permission for burials through the Council.

Portavo Point, former home of North Down MP Sir Walter Smiles, who lost his life in the Princess Victoria tragedy of 1953, was placed on the market in early August by current owners Sir Nigel and Lady Fisher. Offering a commanding view of the coast between Donaghadee and Groomsport, opposite the Copeland Islands, the six-bedroom house was built by Sir Walter in 1931.

Donaghadee RNLI took delivery of a new high-speed Waveney class lifeboat, the Arthur and Blanche Harris, in mid-August. A crew of five volunteers, including coxswain Jim Bunting, travelled to Poole in Dorset to bring the vessel back to Donaghadee and their six-day journey, in exceptionally rough conditions, was not without incident as they had to respond to a distress call from a yacht off the Cornish coast.

The Divisional Planning Department granted permission in late August for the reinstatement of the Copelands Hotel at Warren Road, Donaghadee. Six objections had been submitted by local residents and objections on their behalf were articulated at a meeting of Ards Borough Council by local representative Lord Dunleath.

The IRA murder of Lord Mountbatten at the Sligo village of Mullaghmore on 27 August was felt particularly keenly in Newtownards, where another of the victims, 15-year-old Paul Maxwell, had a number of relatives. The boy, a regular visitor to the town, was mourned by uncle Billy Jamison, aunt Sally and cousins Sonia (19), Scott (12) and Anne (5), of Edith Helen Road. Paul's mother Mary was a native of the town and attended Regent House.

One of the standard bearers at Lord Mountbatten's funeral was Newtownards man Jack McDade, of Robert Street, who had been nominated to represent the Northern Ireland Royal British Legion.

Comber traders were up in arms at the beginning of October after the Department of the Environment announced plans for double yellow (no parking) lines along the main streets in the town. They enlisted the support of local MP Jim Kilfedder in a call to have the proposal shelved. A special meeting of Comber Traders Association had one notable absentee – a representative from the DoE. However, the Department did agree to temporarily suspend the parking restrictions pending discussions with the traders.

An extension of the Northern Ireland Housing Executive's house sales policy, announced by chief executive Charles Brett on 11 October, saw no fewer than 6,780 houses in the Newtownards area being offered to their tenants. The policy did not include flats, maisonettes and sheltered dwellings.

Dr W. A Maguire, headmaster of Regent House for the previous decade, left the post in the middle of October to become Keeper of Local History at the Ulster Museum in Belfast.

Although a considerable amount of money had been spent over a number of years on the Donaghadee outdoor swimming pool, it was decided in October that it should be closed permanently. Numbers using the Warren Road facility had fallen considerable with the income during 1979 from users falling to just £39. To reinstate the pool, including resurfacing its floor, would have cost the Borough Council almost £23,000.

In a double blow to the town Ards Borough Council was notified by the Department of Commence later in the year that "as the economic climate is in a depressed state" there would be no funding available for an indoor swimming pool in Donaghadee.

The death occurred on 26 October of former Newtownards Chronicle editor Robert McNinch, who held the position between 1951 and 1974. He had succeeded his own grandfather, having previously served on the editorial staff. He also worked for the News Letter and Hansard at Stormont during a long career in journalism.

The Strangford Arms Hotel was included in the newly-published 1980 Egon Ronay Guide. Only 10 Northern Ireland hotels were mentioned in the publication, which appeared in late November, and it was a first-ever appearance for the popular Newtownards establishment.

Four incendiary devices were discovered and made safe in Woolworth's at Conway Square, Newtownards, on 1 December. Another two firebombs, which were not found in an extensive search, exploded but the resulting blazes were extinguished by the manager who had remained on the premises overnight. No substantial damage was caused.

The Ballywalter seafront development scheme undertaken by Ards Borough Council was the sole recipient of a Certificate of Merit in the 1979 British Airways Tourism Endeavour Awards. The scheme involved a clean-up of the seafront, the provision of a toilet block and improvements to the area's recreation facilities.

The new £400,000 Andrews Memorial Primary School in Comber was officially opened on 10 December by Sir John Andrews. The vision of the long defunct Down County Education Committee, it was finally realised by the South Eastern Education and Library Board and provided schooling for around 350 pupils.

In an emotional final message of the 1970s, Mayor Hamilton McKeag said the past decade had "brought with it some of the most terrible atrocities imaginable, but the courage and indomitable spirit of the people of Northern Ireland has never wavered and I feel we can march into 1980 with renewed hope for a better and brighter future.

"In the end law and order must prevail and I would express the hope that the 1980s will bring a resurgence of faith and belief in the battle against those who would seek to destroy our heritage. May Faith, Hope and Charity be always uppermost in our thoughts, words and deeds as we battle into 1980."

Mr McGowan, of Pound Street, Newtownards, and son Samuel, who won an Italjet motorcycle in a competition run by local company Court Motors in January 1979. Hugh McCartney, of Court Motors, made the presentation at a 'Speed Show' in the Queen's Hall. 220-2a-4

Cast members from the Sam Cree comedy Stop It Nurse, which was presented by the Moneyreagh Amateur Dramatic Society in the local Lyttle Memorial Hall in January 1979. Included are Robert Connolly, Gwen Kinnear, Wilma McFarland, Margaret Kerr, Hugh Hogg, Joseph Kelly, Betty Magill, Margaret Hogg, Doreen Dornan, Margaret Dearden and James Lappin. 229-12a-4

Portavogie man William Mahood, of Springfield Road, celebrated his 100th birthday on 24 January 1979, joined by relatives from Portavogie, Newtownards, Scotland and the United States of America. 250-8-4

William McClements presents a cheque on behalf of the Ards Hospital maintenance staff and boilermen to retiring colleague Charlie Wilson in January 1979.
1-51-1

Portaferry members who attended a St Vincent de Paul Society dinner at the New Mount Royal Hotel, Donaghadee, in February 1979.
269-21-4

2nd Comber Presbyterian Church Robins pictured in March 1979 with the mountains of silver paper they collected in aid of Cancer Research. Included are leaders Betty McBriar, Doris Collum, Willa Henry, Helena Magowan and Eileen Gibb.
392-4-4

Officials from the Donaghadee branch of the Ulster Farmers' Union with prizewinners at the annual distribution in March 1979. Included are Frank Armstrong (chairman), Lynn Semple (president), Hugh Irvine, Ian Logan, Alan Semple, James Caughey (who presented the trophies), Harry Humphreys and Robert Gamble. 264-8-4

Teams from Carrowdore, Ballywalter, Kircubbin and Ballyeasboro Youth Clubs who took part in the Blue Lamp area quiz final at the McVeigh Hall, Ballyeasboro, in March 1979. Seated are the winners from Ballyeasboro YC with leaders Anne Nevin and Iris Keag. 439-15a-4

The cast from Mischief in Ballinderry which was presented by the pupils of Londonderry Primary School, Newtownards, in March 1979. 443-2a-4

Mrs Martha McMillan, formerly of Pound Street, Newtownards, and then living at New Road, Donaghadee, celebrated her 100th birthday on 27 March 1979. Family and friends joined her for a party at the Newtownards home of granddaughter Edna Hurley. 471-16-4

Members of Newtownards and District Ladies Circle held their charter dinner at The George, Clandeboye, in March 1979. Back (from left): Mrs J. Hughes, Mrs K. Ferguson, treasurer, Mrs J. Crawford, Mrs J. Michael. Front: Mrs R. Savage, Mrs M. Copeland, vice-chairman, Mrs J. McBriar, chairman, and Mrs C. Morrison, press officer. 462-19-4

Mr and Mrs George Smart, of Myola Place, Newtownards, with family and friends who attended their golden wedding anniversary at the Wiltshire Inn, Newtownards, in April 1979. 504-6-4

Officers and members of Sister S. Baird Memorial WLOL No 164 at their annual dinner in the Regency Restaurant, Newtownards, in April 1979.
511-13-4

Cast members from the Comber High School production of Pinocchio in April 1979.
523-9a-4

Members of Portavogie Accordion Band on parade on Easter Monday (16 April) 1979.
13-4-5

Pupils from Ardmillan and Ballymacashon Primary Schools with principals Gary McCreery and Mrs J. Turley before leaving on an educational visit to France, Belgium and Holland in April 1979. 7-7a-5

David and Frances Caughey, from Ballyeasboro, Portavogie, are pictured at a surprise party organised by family members at the Portaferry Hotel in April 1979 to mark their 40th wedding anniversary. The couple were married at Ballygalget in April 1939 and had six sons and three daughters. 59-4-5

Presentations were made to Canon and Mrs Hamilton Leckey and family prior to their departure from St Mary's Parish Church, Comber, to Bangor Abbey, in May 1979. Canon Leckey had been rector of St Mary's for more than 16 years. From left: Mr R. M. Frazer, Rector's Glebe Warden, Mr Gordon Orr, People's Church Warden, Michael Leckey, the Rev. Canon H. Leckey, Jennifer Leckey, Mrs Leckey, Stephen Leckey, Mr David Galbraith, Rector's Church Warden, and the Rev. R. Lee, curate. 117-8-5

P6 and P7 pupils from Alexander Dickson Primary School, Ballygowan, were preparing for a four-day trip to the Isle of Man in May 1979 – only to find their flight had been cancelled because the airport near Douglas was fog-bound. A 'cavalry' of parents ensured the disappointed children made it back safely to Ballygowan. Included are headmaster Mr M. Coulter and teachers Mr K. Stewart and Miss S McKee. 155-4-5

Kirkistown Primary School pupils with the banner they prepared for their educational trip to the Isle of Man in May 1979. It won them first prize in a competition held during their visit. Included are teachers Mrs L. S. Kennedy, Miss E. Palmer and Mrs E. J. C. Lyttle. 148-2-5

Mr and Mrs Joseph Cafolla, of Frances Street, Newtownards, celebrated their 60th wedding anniversary in June 1979. The couple, who were married at Mortale in Italy in 1919, had two sons and two daughters, 13 grandchildren and five great grandchildren. 162-7-5

Mr and Mrs Thomas Gourley, of Comber Road, Ballygowan, celebrated their golden wedding anniversary at their own home in May 1979 with members of their wide family circle, which included one son, four daughters, 19 grandchildren and five great grandchildren. 189-10-5

Above: Belfast Lord Mayor Alderman David Cook was among the dignitaries who visited Portaferry on 27 May 1979 to bid 'bon voyage' to adopted local son Declan Mackell before he set sail on a two-year trip around the world in his Contessa 32 racer-cruiser Sean-ois. Belfast-born Declan had put The Ards in the headlines two years earlier when he became the first Ulsterman to sail single-handed across the Atlantic, receiving a hero's welcome when his journey from Toronto ended at Portaferry. He chose there because he wanted to visit his sister, Mrs Moira Bannon, who lived at nearby Cloughey. Declan's round-the-world trip finally ended in 1983 when he returned to Toronto. 213-18-5

Outgoing Mayor Alderman John Scott presented 'Lone Walker' John McFetridge and his wife Sarah with a letter of greetings for the Mayor of Coleraine prior to the couple's fundraising walk from Newtownards to Portrush in June 1979. They hoped to collect £500 for Guide Dogs for the Blind. 278-13-5

Mr and Mrs William Johnston pictured in July 1979 with the gifts they received from residents of Millisle and district following Mr Johnston's retirement after 40 years as Postmaster in Millisle. Included with the couple are Doris Johnston and members of the organising committee, namely Mr and Mrs J. White, Miss J. McKee, Mrs J. McKee, Mrs W. Jackson, Mrs J. Davidson and Mr T. Waugh. 408-7-5

Four Newtownards brothers were reunited after 53 years in July 1979. Tom Eagleson, a former Post Office telegraph messenger in the town, emigrated in the mid-1920s to Australia, where he became a farmer, as well as marrying and having four children. This was his first home visit in all that time and he quickly caught up with brothers Jim (Market Street), Robert (North Street) and Lexie (Scrabo Estate). Back: Jim and Lexie. Front: Tom and Robert. 389-14a-5

Members of the newly-formed Kircubbin Boxing Club in July 1979. 434-13-5

Award recipients from Comber Primary School following a prize distribution at the end of June 1979. Included is principal Mr W. J. I. Johnston. 383-15a-5

Dr Wright Memorial Pipe Band from Newtownards travelled to France in August 1979 to take part in 12 days of piping and drumming under the auspices of the Irish Tourist Board. Audiences at some of the performances were expected to reach up to 80,000. 30-2-6

Mr and Mrs W. Burns, from Broadway in Ballywalter, celebrated their 60th wedding anniversary on 23 August 1979 with family members at the Dunover Road home of granddaughter Mrs Joan Markey. The couple received many cards congratulating them on reaching their diamond anniversary, including one from Buckingham Palace. 126-6-6

Stephen Robinson, from Greenwell Place in Newtownards, had a tenth birthday to remember in September 1979. In addition to attending Manchester United's 1-0 victory over Derby County at Old Trafford, he also met star player Jimmy Greenhoff who presented him with the shirt he had worn in a friendly match against Benfica. 247-14-6

Portaferry members of the St John Ambulance Brigade's Nursing Division at their annual inspection in the Market House in October 1979. 334-12a-6

Pupils from Victoria Primary School, Newtownards, presented fruit and vegetables from the school's harvest service to senior citizens in the East Street area in October 1979. From left: Lesley Johnston, Mrs McConnell, Clare Parsons, Mrs Hamilton, Sharon Coey, Mrs Armour, Mr Armour, Ashley Armour, Zelda Auld and Mrs Spence. 363-16a-6

Ards Choral and Orchestral Society honoured retiring conductor Ernest Browne at a social evening in the Queen's Hall, Newtownards, in October 1979. A programme of musical items was followed by presentations to Mr Browne, who had served as conductor for 32 years. From left: Robert Morrison (chairman), Mr Browne, Mrs Muriel Browne and Miss G. Lyttle, secretary. 432-11-6

The institution of the Rev. Jonathan Barry (centre) as rector of the Parishes of Ballyphilip and Ardquin (Portaferry) took place in December 1979. Taking part in the service were (from left): The Ven. Gordon McMullan, Archdeacon of Down, the Rev. Canon J. H. R. Good, Registrar, the Rt. Rev. G. A. Quin, Bishop of Down and Dromore, the Rev. J. E. Moore and the Rev. Canon C. Jackson. 100-10-7

Ballywalter Youth Club members who helped erect the village's Christmas decorations in December 1979. 55-5a-7

Children from the Debretta factory nursery school presented a Christmas play in December 1979. 84-3-7

1979

Sport in the Chronicle

A rds FC manager Joe Kinkead won his first Fiat 'Manager of the Month' award in January, with the team also honoured for scoring the most goals – 22 in seven games during December 1978.

Bangor beat Ards 6-3 in the final of the Bass Boston Floodlit Cup on 23 January, with all local supporters in agreement that the home side had rarely taken such a beating and still turned out as victors. Wes Campbell scored a penalty for Ards.

Former Donaghadee 4th XV player Ronnie Elliott was selected to play for Ireland. He had turned out for the team just the once back in 1970, while still a pupil at Regent House, in a fixture against CIYMS 4As. Donaghadee won 25-6, Elliott scoring two tries and converting five. The referee was the Rev. Neil Cameron, who in 1979 was minister of Millisle Presbyterian Church.

Jonathan Galloway (11), from Mountain Road, Newtownards, was named County Antrim Minor Chess Champion in March, following his success in a series of competitions in Ballymena. He was a first year pupil at Regent House.

Comber girl Liz Cash, of Graffan Gardens, was awarded a bronze medal at the fifth Commonwealth Table Tennis Championships, which were held in April in Edinburgh. She was a member of the Northern Ireland team, which also secured a silver medal.

Second Donaghadee Cubs, attached to High Street Presbyterian Church, won the five-a-side Cub Scout Tournament, the most coveted award in Cub football, following a 4-1 victory over the Strabane Cub Group at Crawfordsburn in April.

A 3-3 draw with bottom-of-the-table Ballymena United cost Ards FC second place in the Irish League and qualification for European football during the 1979-80 season, not to mention a £2,000 runners-up cheque. As a result of the draw, second place (behind champions Linfield) went to Glenavon.

Fourteen-year-old Anthony Mitchell, from Edith Helen Road in Newtownards, was selected to ride for Northern Ireland in the English Schoolboy Cycling Association Championships at Filey towards the end of May. He was a member of the Toyota North Down Cycling Club.

Beverley Heaney, a pupil at Regent House, was selected in May to play for both the Ulster and Irish Schools hockey teams. She was a member of the North Down club.

Newtownards man Tommy Murphy became All Ireland youth billiards champion on 2 June after defeating Dubliner John Carney by three frames to one in a best of five frames final at the Teachers' Centre in Dublin.

Seventeen-year-old Comber cricketer Robin Haire was selected in July to represent Ulster at both senior and junior levels and also to play for an All Ireland team in Canada. The North Down club member was described as a 'left-arm spinner who is also useful with a bat.'

Donaghadee golfer Paul Brunton (16), from Beechfield Avenue, won the Ulster Boys' Golf Championship at the end of July. It was the third time in six years that the trophy had been won by a Donaghadee player. In fact, Paul had former champions Ken Campbell (1974) and Colin Glasgow (1976) as his caddies at Holywood. He won the title 4 and 3 over 1977 champion Neil Anderson of Shandon Park.

Comber's William Burgess (13), from Ballystockart Road, won the intermediate class of the British Schoolboy Scrambling Championship on his 100cc Yahama for the second year in a row. His victory came in early August at Donington Park near Bristol.

Colin Ritchie, from the Ivy in Newtownards, won the £300 Smithwicks Individual Pool Championship at the Coachman in Bangor on 30 August. His opponent was Davy Manderson from the host venue.

North Down Cricket Club's 1st XI secured Section 2 of the Senior League at the beginning of September.

Following a bad run with just three wins out of 12 matches, Ards FC dispensed with the services of manager Joe Kinkead on 21 October, with second team coach Billy Nixon taking over in a caretaker capacity. He commenced his managerial career with a 4-1 victory over Distillery. The appointment was made permanent on 26 November.

North Down Cricket Club announced the appointment in late November of Ireland and Waringstown cricketer Michael Reith as official club coach. The appointment was made possible thanks to sponsorship from local garage Kane of Comber.

Eleven-year-old Edwina Mawhinney from Portavogie Primary School won the Champion of Champions title at the Ulster Schools' Badminton Championship which was held in the McCallum Hall, Belfast, on 1 December. It was the school's sixth success in eight years.

Officials of Star of the Sea Indoor Bowling Club with prizewinners from their triples tournament at Nunsquarter Hall, Kircubbin, in January 1979. 230-5a-4

Members of the football team from Alexander Dickson Primary School, Ballygowan, wear the new skip purchased by the PTA in January 1979. Back (from left): Richard Jones, David Fletcher, David Gibson, Robert McMurray, Lee Drake, Raymond Anderson, Alan McKeag. Front: Alvin Cairnduff, Mark Douglas, John Collins, Graham McConnell, Robert Gourley and Peter Coulter. 1-49-1

Members of the Greenwell Street Presbyterian Church junior badminton team who won the Presbyterian Junior League and Knock-Out Cup in April 1979. Back (from left): Colin Heron, Alan Carnduff, Alison Brown, Alan Jackson, Philip Murray. Front: Joy Carser, Mandy Cowan, Julie Wright, Pamela Haughan. 35-16-5

North Down Ladies 1st XI, winners of the McConnell Shield in June 1979. Back (from left): C. Mitchell, N. McMullan, B. Heaney, G. Dickson, J. Ferguson, H. T. Thompson. Front: E. Gibson, W. Crosby, D. Barr (captain), M. West and H. Hiles.
323-6a-5

Members of the Newtownards Chronicle Golfing Society before setting out for their annual Editor's Day competition at Clandeboye Golf Club in October 1979.
389-11-6

Members of the Newtownards Baptist Campaigners football team pictured in October 1979 wearing the new skip they had purchased at the start of the season. Back (from left): Trevor Scott, Nigel Berry (captain), Rodney Scott, Charlie Davidson (manager), Graham Moore, Philip Moore, Philip McCullough. Front: Paul Davidson, David Irvine, Johnathan Berry, Samuel Roberts, Mark Heasley and Raymond Robinson.
401-8a-6

Dear Reader,

I hope you have enjoyed this publication from Ballyhay Books, an imprint of Laurel Cottage Ltd. We publish an eclectic mix of books ranging from personal memoirs to authoritative books on local history, from sport to poultry, from photographs to fiction and from music to marine interests – but all with a distinctly local flavour.

To see details of these books, as well as the beautifully illustrated books of our sister imprint Cottage Publications, why not visit our website **www.cottage-publications.com** or contact us on +44 (0)28 9188 8033.

Timothy S Johnston

BALLYHAY BOOKS